# Smart Cities and Tourism:
## Co-creating experiences, challenges and opportunities

# Smart Cities and Tourism:

## Co-creating experiences, challenges and opportunities

**Editors:**

**Dimitrios Buhalis, Babak Taheri and Roya Rahimi**

(G) **Goodfellow Publishers Ltd**

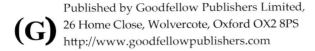
Published by Goodfellow Publishers Limited,
26 Home Close, Wolvercote, Oxford OX2 8PS
http://www.goodfellowpublishers.com

British Library Cataloguing in Publication Data: a catalogue record for this title is available from the British Library.

Library of Congress Catalog Card Number: on file.

ISBN: 978-1-915097-08-8

DOI: 10.23912/9781915097088-4973

Copyright © Dimitrios Buhalis, Babak Taheri, Roya Rahimi, 2023

All rights reserved. The text of this publication, or any part thereof, may not be reproduced or transmitted in any form or by any means, electronic or mechanical, including photocopying, recording, storage in an information retrieval system, or otherwise, without prior permission of the publisher or under licence from the Copyright Licensing Agency Limited. Further details of such licences (for reprographic reproduction) may be obtained from the Copyright Licensing Agency Limited, of Saffron House, 6–10 Kirby Street, London EC1N 8TS.

Design and typesetting by P.K. McBride, www.macbride.org.uk

Cover design by Cylinder

Printed by Printforce, Biggleswade

Distributed by UK Marston Book Services, www.marston.co.uk

# Contents

| | |
|---|---|
| Introduction<br>*Dimitrios Buhalis, Babak Taheri and Roya Rahimi* | vii |
| Author biographies | xiv |

## Part 1: Smart Cities: Concepts and Issues

**1**  Smart cities' digital transformation  1
*Ekaterina Glebova and Wojciech Lewicki*

**2**  Smart technology trends in the tourism and hospitality industry  14
*Evrim Çeltek*

**3**  From Smart City 1.0 to Smart City 3.0: Deep understanding of the smart cities concept and evolution  43
*Diogo Correia and Leonor Teixeira*

**4**  Smart sports in smart cities  60
*Ekaterina Glebova and Michel Desbordes*

## Part II: Smart Tourism and Smart Tourists

**5**  Advances in smart destination management and public governance: Tourism innovation ecosystems for digital transformation  74
*Carlos Romero-Dexeus, Aurkene Alzua-Sorzabal, Diana Gómez-Bruna, Francisco Femenia-Serra and Edurne Vidal López-Tormos*

**6**  Smart tourists in smart cities  90
*Tomáš Gajdošík*

**7**  Co-creating and co-destructing personalised experiences through smart tourism  106
*Katerina Volchek, Dimitrios Buhalis and Rob Law*

## Part III: Smart Cities and Smart Tourism Destinations

**8**  Smart city or smart tourism destination? The formation of smart Ljubljana in Slovenia  124
*Abbie-Gayle Johnson and Jillian M. Rickly*

**vi** Smart Cities and Tourism

**9** Tourism destination metagovernance and smart governance
in Milan, Italy 142
*Alberto Amore, Pavlos Arvanitis, Francesca d'Angella and Manuela De Carlo*

**10** Smart model of sustainable tourism development: Lessons from
Madeira Island, Portugal 159
*Luiz Pinto Machado and António Manuel Martins de Almeida*

**11** Smart City strategy as a means to improve residents' quality of life:
The Case of Barranco, Lima, Peru 179
*Otto Regalado-Pezúa, Luis Felipe Galarza Cerf and Leonardo Toro*

**12** Smart tourism destinations: Europe's smartest and most
visited cities 195
*Kadir Çakar*

Conclusion 215
*Dimitrios Buhalis, Babak Taheri and Roya Rahimi*

Index 217

# Introduction

The urbanisation, growth and associated challenges of modern cities, coupled with the rapid development of new Information Communication Technologies (ICTs), propelled the development of the 'smart cities' concept (Yin et al., 2015). The term 'smart city' appeared first in the early 1990s with emphasis on technology, innovation and globalization in the process of urbanization (Gibson et al., 1992). It was regarded initially as the possibility of providing citizens with information and services via the integration of ICTs into a city's infrastructure (Ahvenniemi et al., 2017). Smart cities aimed to support and encourage economic growth and human development, leading to improvements in the quality of life for the residents, visitors, companies and institutions that coexist in cities (Silvia et al., 2018).

The smart cities concept has attracted great attention since 2008, with the launch of IBM's Smarter Planet project (Palmisano, 2008). Since then it has continued to grow through research and evolution. The term has been defined differently by different scholars, and new definitions and conceptualisations of smart cities are still emerging. Harrison et al. (2010) defined a smart city as an instrumented, interconnected and intelligent city. A common definition for a smart city is using ICT to make a city (e.g., administration, education, transportation) more intelligent and efficient (Washburn et al., 2009). Smart cities drive the next generation of urban and tourism marketing management evolution. The smart cities of tomorrow engage locals, visitors, governments and businesses in an intelligent, collaborative and connected ecosystem (Yin et al., 2015).

Global urbanisation is progressing rapidly, resulting in human concentration in urban economic centres which offer a wide range of services. In 2015, there were 29 megacities – cities with more than 10 million inhabitants – and the forecast is that there will be over 40 megacities by 2030 (Allianz, 2015). The so-called *gigacities*, with more than 50 million inhabitants are emerging, mainly in overpopulated countries such as India, Brazil and China. Cities increasingly use integrated technologies to centralise resource management, improve efficiency, sustainability and mobility in order to address the effects of urbanisation.

By becoming smart, cities can generate urban economic development and change systems to benefit from greater convenience, growth in revenues and reductions in costs, reduced bureaucracy and increased transparency (Vinod Kumar, 2017). The IoT (Internet of Things) network can create a smart city infrastructure which supports every aspect of urban management, including transportation, health care, agriculture and entrepreneurship (Yasuura et al., 2018). Governments globally invest in smart city initiatives to better manage resources by integrating human and technological capital (Angelidou, 2015; Calzada & Cobo, 2015).

Smart city infrastructure includes strategic health care and intelligent transportation systems (Caragliu et al., 2011). Several frameworks for strategic smart sustainable development have emerged, primarily for urban regions with the potential to transfer these set-ups to different regional contexts (Bibri & Krogstie, 2017).

There is growing interest in the convergence of ICT and IoT in tourism and smart cities (Buhalis, 2020; Boes et al., 2016; Thompson et al., 2022; Buhalis & Amaranggana, 2014; Um & Chung, 2019; Gretzel et al., 2016; Kromidha et al., 2021; Huang et al., 2017). Global tourism has been evolving with technology through the integration of ICT towards an eTourism system (Buhalis, 2003). Advances in ICT have enabled the development of products and services on a variety of levels, from assembly lines to multi-stakeholder complex and interconnected systems. The proliferation of Internet connectivity through distributed networks, *Big Data* and the *Internet of Everything* have revolutionised the production and consumption of tourism experiences, ultimately reengineering economies at both micro and macro levels (Buhalis, 2020).

Smart tourism destinations take advantage of the smartness and smart city developments by applying data science to decision-making in destination management and marketing, urban planning and policy making (Shafiee, et al., 2021; Xiang et al., 2015). Gretzel et al. (2015) suggest that the key aspect of smart destinations is the integration of ICTs into physical infrastructure. Stemming from the conceptualisation of smart city, smart tourism destinations emerge to take advantage of interoperability and interconnectivity of networked organisations and co-create innovative products and services to maximise value for all stakeholders (Buhalis, 2020; Boes et al., 2016; Buhalis & Amaranggana, 2015; Buhalis & Foerste, 2015).

Smartness is effectively the glue of interconnected and mutually beneficial systems and stakeholders that provide the infostructure for the value creation for all (Buhalis, 2020). It is primarily about technology-empowered agile management and marketing that performs dynamic big-data mining, appreciates internal and external contextual factors and maximises benefits brought to all stakeholders in real time (Buhalis & Sinarta, 2019). Smart cities also empower digital accessibility and tourism for all, reducing inequalities (Fernández-Díaz et al., 2022). Buhalis et al. (2022) demonstrate how cruise ships emerge as smart destinations through smart cruising and technology diffusion throughout their ecosystem. Smart tourism destinations also address deconstruction of value in the system through the sharing economy (Buhalis et al., 2020) or other forces.

This book, with its three parts and 12 chapters, provides a comprehensive insight into the current issues and opportunities on smart cities and smart tourism in the next generation of urban evolution. It provides a better understanding of city services, but also enhances and evaluates the local and visitor experience as well as city decision making processes by examining how smartness creates liveable environments and business solutions.

## Part 1: Smart Cities: Concepts and Issues

This part explores the smart cities concepts and issues offering a comprehensive analysis. It starts with smart cities' digital transformation. Ekaterina Glebova and Wojciech Lewicki in their chapter provide the theoretical basis for analysing the concept of a smart city. The chapter explores digital transformation phenomena in the urban area, as well as the main drivers of change, various impacts, and the contributions of stakeholders of smart cities to development projects in any context. It further focuses on the main challenges for smart cities, related to technological progress, and explains what makes modern cities smart. It proposes a conceptual framework for the implementation of digital technologies within the concept of a smart city. In Chapter 2, *Smart technology trends,* Evrim Çeltek focuses on using artificial intelligence, big data and robotic technologies in processes and organizations. In Chapter 3, Diogo Correia and Leonor Teixeira focus on a deep understanding of the smart cities concept and evolution. The chapter provides a comprehensive examination on the evolution of the concept, highlights the associated comprehensions and terms, and proposes a common understanding of the smart city concept.

In Chapter 4, Ekaterina Glebova and Michel Desbordes focus on the development of strategies that connect sports and cities. The chapter explores the three main categories of smart sports related actors: (1) the sports environment user, a citizen practicing physical activity and using sports facilities, (2) the team player or athlete, who practices as part of a club, amateur or professional (3) the sports fan, spectator or/and follower, a person who is interested in sports content consumption (live or mediatory watching). It provides a theoretical basis to learn and analyse the interrelation of sports and the concept of smart cities, followed by real examples. By distinguishing different types of sports, urban infrastructure, and their nature and purposes, it provides a comprehensive review of the nature, features, and dimensions of sports in the smart city framework.

## Part 2: Smart Tourism and Smart Tourists

This starts with Chapter 5 by Carlos Romero-Dexeus, Aurkene Alzua-Sorzabal, Diana Gómez-Bruna, Francisco Femenia-Serra and Edurne Vidal López-Tormo. The chapter tackles the research problem of how city governments can take ownership of smart city/smart destination projects to ensure that they create value for residents and local organizations. Therefore, it focuses on the value smart services create and how local governments can ensure that value is created and delivered. In Chapter 6, Tomáš Gajdošík focuses on smart tourists in smart cities and the ways smart cities contribute to citizen value co-creation and sustainability and improve the quality of life. Chapter 7 by Katerina Volchek, Dimitrios Buhalis and Rob Law is on co-creating and co-destructing personalised experiences through smart tourism. This chapter conceptualizes the potential of a smart tourism city to co-create and co-destruct tourist experiences through personalization. It defines personalization as a service offering in tourism and explains the reason why this is acknowledged as one of the determinants of the advanced tourist experience. The chapter applies Service-Dominant Logic (SDL) to conceptualize the potential of not only co-creating but also co-destructing tourist experiences through the process of personalization.

## Part III - Smart Cities and Smart Tourism Destinations

The last part starts with Chapter 8 by Abbie-Gayle Johnson and Jillian M. Rickly. In this chapter Ljubljana in Slovenia is selected as a case study to focus on the formulation of smart tourism destination. This chapter explains the role of collaboration in bringing together diverse stakeholders and roles. Chapter 9, by Alberto Amore, Pavlos Arvanitis, Francesca d'Angella and Manuela De Carlo, provides empirical evidence from Milan, Italy, through a longitudinal analysis of destination meta governance and smart governance processes between 2004 and 2019. From a destination meta governance perspective, the genesis of Milan as a tourist destination saw a shift from a networked hierarchy to a more collaborative and adaptive mode of smart meta governance. The insights from Milan provide a timely reflection on the nexus between new technologies, governance archetypes, and meta governance responses and how these contribute to the development of a city into a culturally vibrant and smart destination.

Chapter 10, by Luiz Pinto Machado and António Manuel Martins de Almeida, explains the practical difficulties involved in building up the required infrastructure of a smart island/destination. These include implementation complexities as well as transformative and disruptive concepts in traditional tourism ecosystems that have been operating for years relatively smoothly. This chapter bridges the theoretical foundations of smart tourism with empirical research focused on less studied insular geographical settings. Hence it interprets operators' attitudes regarding several key factors affecting the development of smart tourism in Madeira, Portugal. The chapter includes policy-making aspects, supply-side elements, and in-house technical competencies. Valuable insights regarding strengths, weaknesses, and challenges are discussed to analyse the current state of affairs and devise a coherent and comprehensive methodology to adopt a progressive agenda focused on smart tourism on islands.

Chapter 11, by Otto Regalado-Pezúa, Luis Felipe Galarza Cerf and Leonardo Toro, is based on the case of Barranco, Lima, Peru. It focuses on technological management of a smart city which is followed by the case of the district of Barranco, Lima in Peru. Chapter 12 by Kadir Çakar examines the competitiveness of four European smart cities that are classified as smart destinations from a comparative analysis perspective. The chapter aims to examine to what extent the four selected cities offer innovative services and smart facilities, based on the smart city initiatives, for both residents and visitors. Thus, the research contributes to the literature by offering valuable insights and key implications for destination managers.

The book, with its comprehensive approach, serves as a main reference point for smart cities researchers, scholars, students and practitioners. It provides definitions and conceptualisations of smart city and smart tourism through exploring the implications of technological developments, stakeholder engagement and sustainability. This book uses a multi-disciplinary approach to explore different cities from around the world whilst exploring smart user behaviour, information system design, and service management.

## References

Ahvenniemi, H., Huovila, A., Pinto-Seppä, I., & Airaksinen, M. (2017). What are the differences between sustainable and smart cities?. *Cities*, 60, 234-245.

Allianz, (2015), The megacity state: The world's biggest cities shaping our future, Allianz Munich. https://www.allianz.com/content/dam/onemarketing/azcom/Allianz_com/migration/media/press/document/Allianz_Risk_Pulse_Megacities_20151130-EN.pdf

Angelidou, M. (2015) Smart cities: A conjuncture of four forces, *Cities*, 47, 95-106.

Bibri, S.E. & Krogstie, J. (2017), Smart sustainable cities of the future: An extensive interdisciplinary literature review, *Sustainable Cities and Society*, 31, 83-212.

Boes, K., Buhalis, D. & Inversini, A. (2016). Smart tourism destinations: ecosystems for tourism destination competitiveness. *International Journal of Tourism Cities*, 2(2), 108-124.

Buhalis, D., (2003), *eTourism: Information technology for strategic tourism management*. Pearson Education.

Buhalis, D., (2020), Technology in tourism-from information communication technologies to eTourism and smart tourism towards ambient intelligence tourism: a perspective article, *Tourism Review*, 75(1), 267-272 https://doi.org/10.1108/TR-06-2019-0258

Buhalis, D. & Amaranggana, A. (2014). Smart Tourism Destinations in Xiang, Z. and Tussyadiah,I. (Eds.). *Information and Communication Technologies in Tourism 2014*, pp. 553-564. Dublin: IFITT

Buhalis, D. & Foerste, M., (2015). SoCoMo Marketing for Travel and Tourism: Empowering Co-Creation of value, *Journal of Destination Marketing and Management*, 4(3), 151-161.

Buhalis, D., and Sinarta, Y., (2019), Real-time co-creation and nowness service: lessons from tourism and hospitality, *Journal of Travel and Tourism Marketing*, 36(5), pp.563-582 https://doi.org/10.1080/10548408.2019.1592059

Buhalis, D., Andreu, L. & Gnoth, J., (2020), The dark side of the sharing economy: Balancing value co-creation and value co-destruction. *Psychology and Marketing*. 37(5), 689–704. https://doi.org/10.1002/mar.21344

Buhalis, D., Papathanassis, A. & Vafeidou M., (2022), Smart Cruising: smart technology applications and their diffusion in cruise tourism *Journal of Hospitality and Tourism Technology* https://doi.org/10.1108/JHTT-05-2021-0155

Calzada, I. & Cobo, C., (2015). Unplugging: Deconstructing the smart city. *Journal of Urban Technology*, 22(1), 23-43.

Caragliu, A., Del Bo, C., Nijkamp, P. (2011). Smart Cities in Europe, *Journal of Urban Technology*, 18(2), 65 – 82.

Fernández-Díaz, E., Jambrino-Maldonado, C., Iglesias-Sánchez, P.P. & de las Heras-Pedrosa, C. (2022), Digital accessibility of smart cities - tourism for all and reducing inequalities: tourism agenda 2030, *Tourism Review*, 77. https://doi.org/10.1108/TR-02-2022-0091

Gibson, D.V., Kozmetsky, G. & Smilor, R.W. eds., (1992). *The Technopolis Phenomenon: Smart cities, fast systems, global networks*. Rowman & Littlefield.

Gretzel, U., Sigala, M., Xiang, Z. & Koo, C., 2015, Smart Tourism: Foundations and Developments. *Electronic Markets*, 25(3), 179–188

Gretzel, U., Zhong, L., & Koo, C., 2016. Application of Smart Tourism to Cities *International Journal of Tourism Cities*, 2(2), 101-107

Kromidha, E., Gannon, M., & Taheri, B. (2021). A profile-based approach to understanding social exchange: authentic tour-guiding in the sharing economy. *Journal of Travel Research*, 00472875211062616.

Harrison, C., Eckman, B., Hamilton, R., Hartswick, P., Kalagnanam, J., Paraszczak, J. & Williams, P., (2010). Foundations for smarter cities. *IBM Journal of Research and Development*, 54(4), 1-16.

Huang, C. D., Goo, J., Nam, K., & Yoo, C. W. (2017). Smart tourism technologies in travel planning: The role of exploration and exploitation. *Information & Management*, 54(6), 757–770

Palmisano, S.J., (2008). A smarter planet: the next leadership agenda. *IBM*. November, 6, pp.1-8.

Shafiee, S., Rajabzadeh Ghatari, A., Hasanzadeh, A. & Jahanyan, S. (2021), Smart tourism destinations: a systematic review, *Tourism Review*, 76(3), 505-528. https://doi.org/10.1108/TR-06-2019-0235

Silva, B.N., Khan, M. & Han, K., (2018). Towards sustainable smart cities: A review of trends, architectures, components, and open challenges in smart cities. *Sustainable Cities and Society*, 38, .697-713.

Thompson, J., Taheri, B., & Scheuring, F. (2022). Developing esport tourism through fandom experience at in-person events. *Tourism Management*, 91, 104531.

Um, T. & Chung, N., (2019). Does smart tourism technology matter? Lessons from three smart tourism cities in South Korea. *Asia Pacific Journal of Tourism Research*, pp.1-19.

Vinod Kumar, T.M. (Ed.), (2017) *Smart Economy in Smart Cities*, Springer, Berlin.

Washburn, D., Sindhu, U., Balaouras, S., Dines, R.A., Hayes, N. & Nelson, L.E., (2009). Helping CIOs understand "smart city" initiatives. *Growth*, 17(2), 1-17.

Yasuura, H., Kyung, C., Liu, Y. & Lin, Y.L., (2018). *Smart Sensors at the IoT Frontier*, Springer, Berlin.

Yin, C., Xiong, Z., Chen, H., Wang, J., Cooper, D. & David, B.,(2015). A literature survey on smart cities. *Science China Information Sciences*, 58(10), 1-18.

# Author biographies

### Editors

**Professor Dimitrios Buhalis** is a Strategic Management and Marketing expert with specialisation in Information Communication Technology applications in the Tourism, Travel, Hospitality and Leisure industries. He is Director of the eTourism Lab and Deputy Director of the International Centre for Tourism and Hospitality Research, at Bournemouth University Business School in England. He was Visiting Professor at the School of Hospitality and Tourism Management, Hong Kong Polytechnic University during the academic year 2021-2022. He is the Editor in Chief of the most established journal in tourism, *Tourism Review*, and the Editor in Chief of the *Encyclopedia of Tourism Management and Marketing*. His research pioneers smart and ambient intelligence tourism with a particular focus on innovation, entrepreneurship and destination ecosystems management. Professor Buhalis has written and co-edited more than 25 books and 300 scientific articles. He is a world expert in strategy, marketing, technology, tourism and hospitality. His research is referenced widely, and Professor Dimitrios Buhalis was recognised as a Highly Cited Researcher 2020, 2021 and 2022 by Clarivate™. He is the 3rd most cited for tourism, 2nd most cited for hospitality, 10th on strategy, and 29th in Marketing on Google Scholar with more than 55000 citations and h-index 101. For more information, books, articles and presentations see www.buhalis.com.

**Prof Babak Taheri** is a Professor of Marketing in Nottingham Business School at Nottingham Trent University, UK. He has an established reputation in the marketing field with emphasis on marketing management, consumer behaviour and tourism, leisure and cultural consumption. The innovative nature of his research is underpinned by multi-disciplinary work and methodologically robust measurement of key concepts. Babak has over 120 academic publications, and currently serves as Senior Editor of *Tourism Management Perspectives* and Associate Editor for *The Service Industries Journal* and *International Journal of Contemporary Hospitality Management*.

**Dr Roya Rahimi** is a reader in Marketing and Leisure Management. She is the REF coordinator of UoA 17 at the University of Wolverhampton, Business School. She has more than 50 academic publications including 3* and 4* journals with high impact factors. Her work has been published in top-tier journals such as *Annals of Tourism Research, Journal of Tourism and Hospitality Research, Journal of Travel & Tourism Marketing, International Journal of Contemporary Hospitality Management* and *Anatolia*. Her work has also been presented at various international conferences and appears in book chapters released by Routledge, CABI, Emerald and IGI. She has been published in a variety of languages. Roya is the Associate

Editor for *Journal of Tourism Management Perspectives*, and book reviews editor for *Journal of Hospitality and Tourism Technology*. She sits on the editorial board of leading journals including the *Journal of Hospitality and Tourism Technology, European Management Review, European Journal of Tourism Research, Journal of Hospitality & Tourism Management* and the *International Journal of Tourism Sciences*. Roya co-edited a special issue on sustainability for the *International Journal of Contemporary Hospitality Management*. She received the Valene L. Smith Prize for the best-presented paper at the International Conference of Service Quality in Hospitality & Tourism in Isfahan in 2016. She was shortlisted for her outstanding contribution to research in the University of Wolverhampton's Vice-Chancellor awards for staff excellence in 2017 and 2018. In 2018 two of her papers were selected as Outstanding Papers of the year in the 2018 Emerald Literati Awards. Roya has been invited as a keynote speaker and panellist to several academic and non-academic conferences and workshops in the Middle East and the UK.

## Authors

**António Manuel Martins de Almeida** holds a PhD from the University of Newcastle upon Tyne. He is currently an associate professor at the Faculty of Social Sciences and the coordinator of the Tourism Observatory at the University of Madeira, and a member of the research group Center of Applied Economics Studies of the Atlantic. His research interests lie in the areas of tourism economics, island economies and regional development. António Almeida has participated in consultancy projects for public and private organizations and has been involved in a number of competitive projects.

**Aurkene Alzua-Sorzabal** received a Ph.D. in International Tourism from Purdue University. She currently holds a dual affiliation, Nebrija University and Deusto University, and is co-founder of Lurmetrika Labs, a data-driven company. She has led competitive research projects and collaborated with national and international administrations. Now, she leads the research group on Smart Tourism and Innovation at Nebrija University. Her research focuses on tourism, advanced analytics, and smart solutions. Her latest work has been focused on smart tourism destinations and the identification of emerging metrics for advanced modelling in travel and tourism. She is the author of several articles on tourism and information technology.

**Alberto Amore** is a lecturer in Tourism and Air Travel Management at Solent University, UK. He holds a PhD in Management (University of Canterbury, New Zealand) and an MA in Tourism, Territory and Local Development from the Università degli Studi di Milano-Bicocca in Italy. His research interests include urban planning, urban tourism and urban regeneration, with a focus on post-disaster urban governance and destination resilience.

**Pavlos Arvanitis** is Senior Lecturer in Aviation Management at the Department of International Business, Marketing and Tourism, University of Bedfordshire. He has over 20 years' research experience in the fields of air transport and tourism and over 10 years' teaching in tourism and air transport related areas. He taught in further education for a number of years prior to moving to higher education. He started his career as a country sales executive in Greece, for a small regional Italian carrier based in Venice, Italy.

**Francesca d'Angella** is assistant professor in Management in the Faculty of Communication, Public Relations and Advertising in IULM University, Italy where she is the member of the teaching staff of the PhD program in "Communication, Markets and Society". She is also a member of the quality committee of the two-year master degree in Strategic Communication and an Erasmus examiner for the Faculty of Communication, Public Relations and Advertising.

**Kadir Çakar** is an associate professor at the Faculty of Tourism at Mardin Artuklu University in Turkey. His PhD examined the motivations and experiences of travellers visiting the Gallipoli Peninsula within the context of dark tourism. His main research areas include qualitative research, dark tourism, tourist destination governance, information communication technologies, crisis management, sustainable tourism and sharing economy.

**Manuela de Carlo** is full professor of Tourism Management, Director of the graduate programs in Tourism and Hospitality and member of Academic Board of PhD in Communication Markets and Society at IULM University Milano, Italy. In 2004 she launched the Master in Tourism Management, the first masters programme in tourism taught in English in Italy, and in 2016 she launched the M.Sc. in Hospitality and Tourism Management, in partnership with the Rosen College of Hospitality Management of the University of Central Florida. Manuela currently teaches tourism management; destination management; managing hospitality and guest service organizations.

**Evrim Çeltek** Ph.D. is an associate professor at Gaziosmanpaşa University, Zile Dinçerler Tourism Business and Hotel Management College, Turkey. Evrim obtained her MSc in tourism business administration from Sakarya University (Turkey) and her PhD in tourism and hotel management from Anadolu University (Turkey). Her research focuses on tourism marketing. She has several articles, books and chapters about mobile and digital marketing, e-commerce, mobile commerce, advergame, augmented and virtual reality, gamification and electronic customer relationship management.

**Diogo Correia** is an invited professor at the Department of Economy, Management, Industrial Engineering and Tourism at the University of Aveiro and at the School of Design, Management and Production Technologies,

North Aveiro School in Portugal. He holds a Ph.D. in Management and Industrial Engineering and his research interests and scientific publications cover the areas of smart cities and urban logistics. He has worked as Smart Cities Manager in Ubiwhere Software company in Aveiro, Portugal and is the Co-founder, Board Member and Chief Operating Officer of LUGGit.

**Michel Desbordes** is an affiliate professor of Sports Marketing at Emlyon Business School in Lyon, France, and a marketing professor at the University of Paris-Sud, France, and previously taught in the University of Ottawa, Canada, and the Shanghai University of Sports, China. Dr. Desbordes has published 32 reference books in the field of sports marketing, as well as numerous academic articles. As a media consultant, he is regularly consulted by BFM, France Télévisions, Europe 1, Le Monde and L'Équipe to discuss matters of sports business. Since 2009, he has also been the chief editor of the *International Journal of Sports Marketing and Sponsorship*.

**Carlos Romero Dexeus** holds a degree in Economics from the Complutense University, an Executive Master in Tourism Management from Instituto Empresa and he is currently a PhD student at Deusto University. At the moment, he is Director of Research, Development and Innovation at SEGITTUR, a public agency. He has been the Executive Director of the Affiliate Members of the World Tourism Organization (UNWTO), and General Manager of the UNWTO Themis Foundation. He has extensive experience in the tourism sector internationally, particularly in the fields of smart tourism destinations, entrepreneurship, tourism innovation, travel technology, tourism statistics and public policy instruments, and has participated in projects for the European Commission, UNWTO, EUROSTAT and the Inter-American Development Bank (IDB).

**Francisco Femenia-Serra** holds a PhD from the University of Alicante. He is currently a lecturer at the Department of Tourism, Nebrija University (Madrid, Spain) and a member of the research group Smarttour-INN. His work focuses on smart tourism and destinations planning, management and marketing, as well as on the intersection between technologies, human behavior and experiences in the travel context. Dr Femenia-Serra has been involved in several competitive research projects and has been a visiting researcher at the University of Surrey and the Salzburg University of Applied Sciences. He frequently collaborates with public innovation, research and development organizations and destinations in Spain.

**Tomás Gajdosík** is an associate professor at the Department of Tourism, Faculty of Economics, Matej Bel University in Banská Bystrica, Slovakia. His research focuses on smart tourism and tourism information technologies, and deals with the issues of destination management, governance and leadership. He has contributed to several monographs, textbooks and journals.

**Luis Felipe Galarza-Cerf** is an independent researcher with an MBA in Advanced Project Management from the ESAN Graduate School of Business, in Lima Peru. His thesis was about Smart City Model approaches for the district of Barranco in Lima city. He graduated in Architecture and Urbanism from the Ricardo Palma University in Peru and in Industrial Engineering from the University of Lima in Peru. He has more than ten years of experience in design and coordination of housing, educational and cultural infrastructure projects.

**Abbie-Gayle Johnson** is an assistant professor of Tourism at The Hong Kong Polytechnic University. She graduated from the University of Technology in Jamaica and earned her MSc in Tourism at Bournemouth University, UK before completing her PhD in Management and Marketing at the University of Nottingham in the UK. Dr Johnson is a past Commonwealth Scholar as well as a Caribbean Hotel and Tourism Association education foundation scholar. Her research interests are in smart tourism, destination management, sharing economy and value co-creation.

**Ekaterina Glebova** has over 10 years of international experience in marketing, consultancy and business development. She is pursuing her academic interests in research at an intersection of sports and technological transformation at the University Paris Saclay in France. She has published numerous book chapters and articles in peer-reviewed journals (e.g. *Journal of Sport Management and Marketing, Frontiers in Psychology, Physical Culture and Sport Studies and Research*). Ekaterina holds a few visiting faculty positions, including at the Hungarian University of Sports Science in Hungary and the EDHEC Business School in Nice in France.

**Diana Gómez-Bruna** holds a Ph.D. in tourism from Nebrija University, a Master in Sustainability and Corporate Social Responsibility, and a Master in Tourism. She currently is the Department Head of Tourism at Nebrija University and a member of the research group on Smart Tourism and Innovation, Smarttour-INN. Her work focuses on governance, smart tourism, destination planning and CSR in tourism. She has participated as a researcher in competitive projects of the national R&D framework: Tourism Intelligence and Innovation Network and the generation of virtual tourism scenarios, among other. She has worked and co-operated with various private companies and international institutions such as the World Tourism Organization.

**Rob Law** is University of Macau Development Foundation Chair Professor of Smart Tourism and Deputy Director of Asia-Pacific Academy of Economics and Management. He is also Honorary Professor of several other reputable universities. Prior to joining the University of Macau in July 2021, Prof. Law worked in industry organizations and academic institutes, and is an active researcher. He has received 90+ research related awards and accolades (e.g. recognized as the most prolific tourism/hospitality researcher in the world over two decades from 2000 to 2019 – *International Journal of Contemporary Hospitality Management*, 2021). Prof. Law has edited four books and published 1,000+ research papers (including hundreds of articles in first-tier academic journals). His publications have received more than 55,000 citations, with h-index/i 10-index = 108/489. In addition, Prof. Law serves different roles for 200+ research journals, and is a chair/committee member of more than 180 international conferences.

**Wojciech Lewicki** currently works at the Department of Economics, West Pomeranian University of Technology, Szczecin in Poland. Wojciech does research in transport economics, EU regulations, automotive market, electromobility, smart-city, vehicle cost based on research related to supply chain management, energy economics, manufacturing automotive systems and transportation engineering. His expertise include transport economics, automotive industry, telematics and logistics.

**Edurne Vidal Lopez Tormos** holds degrees in tourism and multilateral project management, specialising in tourism destination development and tourism policy. She is currently Director of the Palacio de la Magdalena Municipal Company in Santander City. She was responsible for SEGITTUR's Smart Tourist Destinations programme, which promotes digital transformation in the sector, coordinating the design of the diagnostic and planning methodology for the development of smart tourist destinations, setting requirements and metrics. She has directed development projects in local tourist destinations, in Spain and abroad and coordinated the Network of Smart Tourist Destinations of the Ministry of Industry, Trade and Tourism of Spain.

**Luiz Pinto Machado** holds a PhD in Economics from the Universidade Técnica de Lisboa. He is currently an assistant professor at the Faculty of Social Sciences, University of Madeira, with affiliation in the research group CEFAGE, Center for Advanced Studies in Management and Economics (Universidade de Évora). His research interests lie in the areas of tourism economics, island economies and regional development. Luiz has participated in consultancy projects for public and private organizations and has been involved in a number of competitive projects. He is currently executive member of the Tourism Observatory of the University of Madeira, Portugal

**Otto Regalado-Pezúa** is a full professor of Marketing at ESAN Graduate School of Business in Lima, Peru. He holds a PhD in Management Sciences and a masters degrees in Management Sciences from the IAE at Côte d'Azur University in France, Quantitative Marketing from the IAE at Pierre Mendès-France University, and Business Administration from the ESAN Graduate School of Business, Lima, Peru. He has published chapters in books as well as articles in many prestigious scholarly journals in the following research lines: digital competencies, tourism management, and higher education.

**Jillian Rickly** is Professor of Tourism at the Nottingham University Business School in the UK. She is a tourism geographer and has spent much of her career examining the role of authenticity/alienation in tourism motivation and experience. This research has been situated in a variety of tourism contexts: heritage, nature, adventure, dark, among others. She has developed a research agenda related to accessibility and travel behaviour, focused on people with disabilities who have assistance dogs. She examines the role of this human-animal relationship to travel behaviour across the transport, travel and tourism sectors. This has inspired collaborations with Guide Dogs for the Blind and Assistance Dogs UK. She serves an Associate Editor for the *Annals of Tourism Research* and is on the editorial boards of *Mobilities*, *Tourist Studies*, and *Journal of Qualitative Research in Tourism*.

**Leonor Teixeira** is an assistant professor of the Department of Economics, Management, Industrial Engineering and Tourism at the University of Aveiro. She is also a researcher at the Institute of Electronics and Telematics Engineering and collaborator at research unit on Competitiveness, Governance and Public Policies of University of Aveiro in Portugal. She has a M.Sc. in Information Management, and a PhD in Industrial Management (Information Systems) from the University of Aveiro, Portugal. She has over 100 publications in peer-reviewed journals, book chapters and proceedings.

**Leonardo Toro** is a part-time professor in marketing, business and entrepreneurship at ESAN Graduate School of Business, in Lima, Peru. He has a Master in Marketing Science from ESIC and an MBA specialized in Marketing from ESAN. He is a professional in finance and foreign trade, trained at the University of the Chamber of Commerce of Bogotá Uniempresarial, Colombia. He has served as director of the virtual modality in a specialised educational institution in Colombia. He has extensive experience as a consultant in commercial marketing, strategic planning and innovation in the higher education, automotive, services and oil sectors in Colombia and Peru

**Katerina Volchek** is a professor and a manager of the DigiHealth & Smart Tourism lab at Deggendorf Institute of Technology. She is an expert in customer experience, information and communication technologies and marketing strategy for tourism, including design of personalised services and optimisation ROI through marketing attribution. Her research interest lies in the capabilities of neuromarketing and smart environments for the service industries. Katerina serves as a Director for Marketing at the International Federation for Information Technologies and Travel & Tourism.

# Part 1:
# Smart Cities: Concepts and Issues

# 1 Smart cities' digital transformation

*Ekaterina Glebova and Wojciech Lewicki*

The functioning of modern cities is inextricably linked with the dissemination, implementation, and use of modern technologies and digital tools. Dameri (2013) defined technology as the main factor in their development, whilst Ostrom et al. (2015) identified technology as the most dramatic change and a "Game Changer" in the field of services. Strengthened and accelerated by the development of Artificial Intelligence (AI), robotics, cloud computing, big data, the Internet of Things (IoT), and mobile computing technologies, digital transformation is becoming an important topic for academic and practical reflection (Buhalis et al., 2019). While the concept of "smart city" continues to evolve, the development of smart cities is supported, powered, and integrated by digital technologies, propelling urbanization. In the era of ubiquitous globalization, digital solutions are becoming the most powerful and effective additions to life in cities. The integration and application of these solutions inevitably lead to digital transformation.

Many researchers emphasize that IoT, big data, AI, and immersive technologies (virtual and augmented reality – VR / AR) are the main elements of digital transformation (Buhalis et al., 2019; Albino et al., 2015; Ostrom et al., 2015; Ivanov, 2020; Mohanty, 2016; Glebova, 2020). Ivanov (2020) identifies automatic technologies, such as industrial and social robots, self-service kiosks, AI, chatbots, face recognition technology, voice-controlled technologies, worn and implanted technologies, additive manufacturing (3D printing), IoT, and other technologies that are used to produce and deliver goods and services. They create products and services based on technology, such as: digital assistants, smart homes, service robots, mobile applications, HVAC, intelligent transport devices, face recognition tracking systems, etc. Observation of the market realities shows that IoT products and services are gradually becoming available to every consumer. City digital twin technology is emerging, and it is a useful tool to create, develop and maintain smart cities (Grübel et al., 2022). Earlier, urban planners used the predecessors of digital twins, technology through CAD (Computer-Aided Design) and smart maps powered by geospatial analytics. Digital twins provide an opportunity to manage an area (for example, city, district, street) cost-effectively and efficiently (Glebova et al., 2022). Digital twins make a virtual simulation of architectural and technological plans before implementing them in a reality (Ramu et al., 2022). These modern digital-based products and services are designed to increase automation, safety, and comfort. Smart urban environments are usually consolidated into several smartphone applications. Internet connectivity combined with large data sets, display devices, and personalized delivery options makes it possible to access products and services instantly. New buildings use more digital tools, as they become more connected and accessible, facilitating day-to-day operations.

This chapter provides the theoretical basis for learning and analyzing the concept of a smart city. It explores digital transformation phenomena in the urban area, the main drivers of change, various impacts, and the contributions of stakeholders of smart city development projects in any context. The chapter focuses on the main challenges for smart cities, related to technological progress, and explains what makes modern cities smart. It proposes a conceptual framework for the implementation of digital technologies within the concept of a smart city. Albino et al. (2015) developed different and overlapping systems for the dimensions of smart cities, namely: (1) security, quality of life, lifestyle, (2) infrastructure and services, (3) connectivity, ICT and communication, (4) people and society, (5) environment and sustainable development, (6) management and administration, (7) economy and finance and 8) mobility and transport. They define a smart city as a multidimensional structure and analyze it in the context of digital transformation.

One of the indicators of intelligence is the Cities in Motion Index (CIMI). This parameter assesses urban areas based on 10 key criteria, namely: management, town planning, public management, technology, environment, international popularization, cohesion policy, mobility and transport, human capital, and economy (Berrone et al., 2015). As illustrated in Figure 1.1, London, as an example of a smart city, takes the lead in the overall ranking for its results in terms of international reach (1st place), human capital (1st place), mobility and transport (3rd), and the economy (12th). However, London does not have such a strong position in terms of social cohesion (position 45) and environment (position 34). Ongoing initiatives and processes aim to transform this metropolis into a smart city across all factors (Berrone et al., 2015).

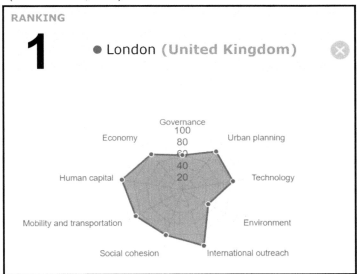

**Figure 1.1:** CIMI ranking of London. Source : screenshot from https://citiesinmotion.iese.edu/indicecim

Considering the main dimensions, the challenges in cities and the effects of digital transformation should address:

- Digital infrastructure structure
- Automation and robotization
- Personalization
- Connectivity, internet coverage, connected future
- Information availability
- Safety and security
- Variety of intelligent transport and mobility options
- Wellness, healthcare, and sport culture
- Mobile applications: consolidation all needs
- Evolving customer experience.

The evolution of smart cities and the digitization process need more than just technology. Smartness is a system and culture that includes the awareness and involvement of all stakeholders (Boes, Buhalis, and Inversini, 2016; Buhalis & Park, 2021). The city's "smartness" is not only about fashionable digital interfaces in the existing infrastructure or improving the city's functioning. It is about "intelligent" implementation and use of smart tools, processes and technical data across the entire network, especially for the problem-solving and ensuring the improvement of the quality of life. The development of digital technology itself is the main driver of the digital transformation of smart cities and shaping a culture of intelligent consumption, as well as citizen awareness (Bethune et al., 2022). Hence smart cities need to understand how and why cities are changing; appreciate the importance of emerging technologies for modern life and anticipate future lines of research in the field of smart cities. They should develop comprehensive strategies to address:

- Digital transformation in smart cities;
- Digital technologies and their impact on the daily life of city dwellers;
- Different types of digital technologies and their nature and purposes;
- Awareness of emerging problems and trends that affect the current and future implementation of technologies in smart cities;
- Factors that contribute to changing and improving the experience of city dwellers;
- The importance of the wide dissemination of technology and its impact on urban areas;
- Research needs, data analysis; and
- Responsibility in planning implementing, and managing technologies in the life of the city.

## Connectivity, digital infrastructure and management

Based on traditional infrastructure, smart cities build digital infrastructure by automating and digitizing infrastructure functions, resulting from the development of information and communication technologies (ICT) (Law et al., 2014). Smart cities are based on models that use the latest ICTs and digital management to strengthen their infrastructure. Intelligent management introduces positive results in regions as Web portals, mobile applications, online forums, and other online services help citizens to share their inquiries, experiences, and suggestions with government authorities (Osman et al., 2022). Digital infrastructure requires professional digital management. Government organizations focus on the needs of citizens and need to explore digital transformation towards citizen services. ICT-based e-government has been implemented in many countries to transform several services into one comprehensive system that supports effective and efficient governance.

## Case study: Dubai as a smart city

The government of Dubai, United Arab Emirates launched in 2001, the eGovernment Portal (www.dubai.ae, www.u.ae) as part of the eGovernment Information Framework. It is widely recognized as an innovative gateway to all government departments and services. It was designed following the guidelines of the Content Advisory Committee, which included representatives from all government departments (Sethi and Sethi, 2008). Dubai, for example, applied the five-step e-government model defined by the United Nations, namely:

☐ Official appearance of the government on the Internet.

☐ Dynamic information to improve the number of government sites;

☐ Interactivity: Users can download forms, send e-mails to officials and interact via the web.

☐ Transactional: Users can pay for services and other online transactions.

☐ Hassle-free: full integration of e-services across administrative boundaries.

The promotion of e-government requires a tripartite approach to awareness, help, and reassurance (Lykidis et al., 2021; Khan et al., 2022). The Dubai e-government has carried out several social activities to raise awareness and adopt e-services such as shows, competitions, promotions, online marketing, marketing with government departments, market awareness research, and rewarding e-service users. For example, Dubai Municipality has awarded the most frequent user of electronic transactions, the most frequent user of ePay, as well as other user groups from various fields. In addition, promotions of the newly launched e-services also took place through Dubai's e-government monthly *e4all* magazine, which featured a series of informative articles on e-services. Covering various aspects of e-governance, the authors intend to familiarize readers with the basic concepts of e-services, used hardware and software, e-learning, and the participation of the private sector in e-services. "Building awareness" about government e-services was the first step.

Table 1.1 illustrates how "Improving computer literacy indicators" was central in the the second phase of Dubai's eGovernment assisting e4all.

Overall, e4all involved several other smaller programs, eCitizen, eEmployee, eLearn, and eManager. The Dubai e-government provides a variety of online services to both individuals and businesses. The lessons learned from the implementation of the Dubai e-government can serve as a guide in managing similar complex initiatives: (1) strong leadership, commitment, and vision (2) flexible and reliable infrastructure (3) central flexible model (4) vision and mission, (5) human resources development, (5) public-private partnerships.

**Table 1.1:** Dubai's eGovernment initiatives

| eCitizen |
| --- |
| eCitizen was founded by the e-government in Dubai in partnership with seven local training centers to provide 16 hours of classroom instruction for Dubai citizens and residents. Consisting of 4 modules, citizens are trained in basic computer and Internet literacy, as well as training in individual and business government services provided by various government departments. Participants will receive eCitizen certification from Dubai e-government if they complete the training. |
| **eEmployee** |
| eEmployee was launched specifically to raise the level of IT competence of government employees and provided a 40-hour training program using both online and classroom training in collaboration with several training institutes. It included training in basic computer skills in English and Arabic languages to receive an eEmployee certificate from Dubai e-government and ICDL START jurisprudence. |
| **eLearn** |
| eLearn to further enhance the IT competencies of individuals and government employees, the Dubai government has developed more than 3,000 bilingual online courses in a variety of fields including e-business, e-commerce, and information technology. Developed in a multimedia format, these courses can be taken at a pace that is adapted to individual needs. |
| **eManager** |
| eManager was launched back in 2007, an initiative aimed at managers and supervisors to improve project management and leadership skills through three online modules and certification levels. |
| **e4all Magazine** |
| This monthly Dubai e-government publication aimed to raise public awareness of the availability of e-services. It covers various aspects of e-governance, and introduces readers to basic concepts of e-services, private sector participation in e-services, hardware and software systems, and e-learning. |

Sources: Sethi & Sethi, 2008; Lykidis et al., 2021.

Fast internet access is at the core of the Smart City concept, through implementation, maintenance, and management. Smart cities must have three key features: intelligence, interconnections, and the instruments provided by IoT; thanks to these demands the concept of smart cities can function (Mohanty, 2016). According to Mohanty, as part of IoT, it can perform the following activities: (1) identify and store information, (2) collect information, (3) identify commands, (4) send and receive messages, (5) recognize and (6) boot the system. IoT can be used to build intelligent transport, smart healthcare, and energy management in smart cities (Mohanty, 2016). Experts point out that 5G technology is the key to building smart cities in the area of connectivity. The many advantages of this technology will be shown, but most of all, it is the ability to support many thousands of simultaneous connections of wireless sensors. Such a function makes it possible not only to build smart homes but also smart cities. Thanks to the high bandwidth and 5G network, it will be possible to build systems communicating with each other with smaller databases, so that the management process covers not only one intersection, but the entire district or city.

## Smart buildings, intelligent transport, security, automation and robotization

Fast Internet provides comprehensive solutions for buildings and homes that can collect and analyze large amounts of data (Big Data), maximizing the operational and energy efficiency of intelligent buildings, and optimizing maintenance and operation. The benefits of an intelligent building may include: (1) data-driven decision-making for high-performance, low-cost operations, (2) greater use of resources, (3) reduced capital structure and operating costs, (4) risk identification and proper management, (5) sustainable development (Mohanty, 2016).

Intelligent transport systems are based on a combination of advanced digital technologies with the existing transport infrastructure (Tyagi et al., 2012). Moving around smart cities is facilitated by six digital transport services: travel planning, car sharing, intelligent parking, carpooling, and micro-mobility. Thanks to various digital solutions in the field of intelligent mobility, moving around the city becomes smoother, which leads to improved safety, environmental protection, and increased efficiency of transport processes (Buhalis et al., 2022). Multi-mobility means that citizens can choose and combine different types of transport. Change from one mode of transport to another is efficient and trouble-free based on "intermodal" coordination and communication for the entire networked. Citizens choose the fastest or the most convenient variant of travel with one or more available means of transport. Buses, trams, and the metro are relatively cheap, but only serve certain routes and have fixed timetables. Taxis work but are expensive. New companies with so-called 'ride-hailing' offer to bridge the gap between them. As with a taxi, you can get on and off at almost any point in the city. However, for the vehicle to be fully used, other passengers traveling in a similar direction must have information about the destination.

Shortly, autonomous electric vehicles will become an integral part of urban mobility and complement the available means of communication in smart cities as part of the fleet. Using a special application, ciitizens will reserve a car left at the charging station or somewhere in densely built-up areas. The search for a parking space in modern cities is a significant problem. One solution is to share parking spaces. Tenants or owners of private parking spaces and garages can make them available for a specified period. Thanks to the appropriate applications, you can pay for a parking space from the car without having to look for a parking meter and conveniently settle fees once a month via the Internet (Lewicki et al., 2020). Carpooling turns a private car into a means of public transport in a smart city. Thanks to smart platforms and apps, finding the right companions in a given direction becomes easier. When developing future concepts for intelligent mobility in urban areas, the gap between the door of the house and the nearest stop or between the workplace and the stop should be bridged. This stretch is also known as the "last mile". Instead of walking, citizens can use the smallest electric vehicles.

Automation plays a key role in the security of a modern city: speed cameras, facial recognition, and other identification feature, QR codes, tracking systems, and many more. The Safe City concept is a necessary condition for Smart City's life. The role of mobile applications in the security of citizens is growing. For example, the Noonlight app (noonlight.com) allows residents to report online to the police just by holding down a button on their mobile phones. This is the solution involving a link to a mobile phone with a geolocation function, the police can find the citizen and help him quickly. According to Finka et al. (2016), the intelligent concept of urban security covers "a wide range of aspects and activities related to public space, from crime prevention to physical environmental protection, accessibility, to institutional and organizational aspects."

One of the examples of the use of smart technology is drones. They are already used to monitor traffic, search for missing persons and carry out reconnaissance activities in geodesy and cartography, urban planning, and spatial management. They are also used to secure mass events, trace air pollution sources, and monitor the state of the environment. Furthermore, drones help in achieving situational awareness and manage resources in crises. In a smart city, drones are increasingly used for transport and logistics purposes, when speed and flexibility is required, such as blood transport. They can monitor city forests and parks, the condition of rivers and dikes, and road infrastructure. they can also inspect municipal buildings, infrastructure, and line facilities and to control public utility facilities. Researchers predict that over time, the operation of drones will be automated and integrated with other smart city systems.

## Data, personalisation and the evolution of the customer experience

Mobile applications (tools) in all their forms can be considered as the material embodiment of the idea of IoT. Overall, the applications available have become the quintessence of new technologies and perhaps an extension of human body. They offer an integrated interface and connectivity to the benefit of all market participants. Over time, the development of their functions allows them not only to satisfy specific needs and desires (Glebova & Desbordes, 2020; Schut & Glebova, 2022) but also to create one general information-sharing system. Technological progress is the most important force in business development and modern consumption. At the same time, ICTs lead to changes in the way of concluding transactions and making purchases. Providing a convenient and personalized customer experience is the present and future of smart cities. In particular, smart technologies are a major engine for improving citizens' lives and experiences. Thanks to these solutions, users have become intelligent customers who thoughtfully makes their purchasing decisions based on the analysis of many factors. The development of rapidly evolving digital technologies has fundamentally changed the way customers communicate and interact in the following areas (Glebova et al., 2020):

- Comfort
- Interactive and engaging ways of delivering experiences
- Personalization
- Ease of access to information, anytime, anywhere
- Product / content quality / services
- Possibilities of reaching people and objects virtually at a physical distance
- Increased experience in the development of services and products.

Personalization aims to support the provision of services for individuals. Data addresses a range of functions including (1) complexity, (2) volume, (3) diversity, (4) variability, and (5) truthfulness (Mohanty, 2016). Google searches have been recognized as a methodology for collecting data about users similar to social networking sites (Davidowitz, 2017). Using big data in real time context can supports processes that fulfil individual needs (Stylos, Zwiegelaar and Buhalis, 2021, Buhalis and Sinarta, 2019, Buhalis & Foerste, 2015).

Crises such as COVID-19 have identified increasing greater demand in terms of health needs and the development of intelligent health care. Mohanty (2016) noted that healthcare can be understood as a combination of different methods, including traditional healthcare and intelligent systems. Individual elements of intelligent health care and intelligent medical infrastructures (hospital, medical points) take advantage of smart technologies for health care. In smart medical institutions and hospitals, various mechanisms exist, including ICTs, applications, and advanced data that can be used for customer service, diagnostics, and even treatment. Patient data can be shared in real-time with each specialist without having to move them. Medical technicians, nurses, and doctors can access data online at multiple information points. Online medical consultation (telemedicine) provides a particular example of the digitization of healthcare, especially in customer service. Telemedicine can also be considered a subgroup of smart healthcare (Mohanty, 2016). The development of immersive technology will create a new level of opportunities for online medical services (Glebova, 2020). Telemedicine can reach any location by using information and communication technologies (ICT) to deliver healthcare. This approach is useful in remote locations where healthcare services are not readily available. Hence, telemedicine partially eliminates distance barriers and broadens access to medical consultations (Vaishya et al., 2020).

Privacy is one of the most controversial issues in smart cities. The use of digital technologies and big data facilitates monitoring people's behavior by creating multiple digital touch points that leave digital traces. These include cashless payment and digital identity systems, as well as passports of smart city residents. The introduction of the so-called chipping humans and the creation of systems based on the idea of the "Social Credit System" is already the key to building the "supervisory infrastructure" in the social management process (Meissner, 2017). Despite this, this technology also has many supporters who point to the benefits of its implementation as in extreme cases, this technology can save lives in the event of an accident or loss. However, the phenomenon of tracking people leads to their objectification, depriving the individual of basic human rights. Chip technology also creates a new basis for the activities of cybercriminals who can efficiently use the data on the medium. This creates new threats and challenges for the cybersecurity of a smart city. The evaluation of the usefulness and functionality of such solutions must be supported by a thorough analysis of possible benefits and social and ethical risks as well.

## Conclusions

The Smart City concept is a term that is constantly evolving to reflect technological developments that drive new best practices across stakeholders. Smart cities represent a systemic approach to the ongoing urbanization processes and require effective infrastructure management. Smart Cities take advantage of available digital technologies, e.g. the digital cloud to support networking and towards the development of every city in the world. Smart Cities adapt to changing conditions by exploring a range of digital technologies such as drones, citizen recognition systems, electronic payments, alert notifications. The idea of a Smart City is a flexible city that adapts to the changing lifestyle of its inhabitants, technology, and environmental conditions.

The future the Smart City concept will consist in increasing the awareness of residents about the available services and functions resulting from digital technology solutions. The main challenges for smart cities relate to emerging technologies, and the willingness of stakeholders to implement the Smart City innovations. Nevertheless, the impact of emerging digital technologies on the development of Smart Cities is evident globally and will determine the competitiveness of regions.

## References

Albino, V., Berardi, U. & Dangelico, R.M.: (2015) Smart cities: definitions, dimensions, performance, and initiatives. *Journal of Urban Technology*, 22(1), 3–21

Berrone, P., Ricart, J.E. & Carrasco, C. (2015) *IESE Cities in Motion Index*, IESE Business School.

Bethune, E., Buhalis, D., & Miles, L. (2022). Real time response (RTR): Conceptualizing a smart systems approach to destination resilience. *Journal of Destination Marketing & Management*, 23, 100687.

Boes, K., Buhalis, D. & Inversini, A. (2016), Smart tourism destinations: ecosystems for tourism destination competitiveness, *International Journal of Tourism Cities*, 2(2), 108-124. https://doi.org/10.1108/IJTC-12-2015-0032

Buhalis, D., Harwood, T., Bogicevic, V., Viglia, G., Beldona, S. & Hofacker, C. (2019). Technological disruptions in Services: lessons from Tourism and Hospitality, *Journal of Service Management*, 30(4), 484-506 https://doi.org/10.1108/JOSM-12-2018-0398

Buhalis, D. & Sinarta, Y., 2019, Real-time co-creation and nowness service: lessons from tourism and hospitality, Journal of Travel & Tourism Marketing, 36(5), 563-582 https://doi.org/10.1080/10548408.2019.1592059

Buhalis, D. & Foerste, M. (2015). SoCoMo marketing for travel and tourism: Empowering co-creation of value. *Journal of Destination Marketing & Management*, 4(3), 151-161. https://doi.org/10.1016/j.jdmm.2015.04.001

Buhalis, D. & Park, S. (2021). Brand management and cocreation lessons from tourism and hospitality: introduction to the special issue. *Journal of Product & Brand Management*, 30(1), 1-11.

Buhalis, D., Papathanassis, A. & Vafeidou, M. (2022). Smart cruising: smart technology applications and their diffusion in cruise tourism. *Journal of Hospitality and Tourism Technology*, (ahead-of-print).

Dameri, R. (2013). Searching for smart city definition: a comprehensive proposal, *International Journal of Computers & Technology*, 11(5), 2544-2551.

Davidowitz, S.S. (2017). *Everybody Lies: Big data, new data, and what the internet can tell us about who we really are*, Dey Street Books

Finka M., Ondrejička V. & Jamečný Ľ. (2016). *Urban safety as spatial quality in smart cities*. Smart City 360° Bratislava. https://doi.org/10.1007/978-3-319-33681-7_73

Glebova E. (2020). Définir la réalité étendue dans les sports : limitations, facteurs et opportunités. In M. Desbordes & C. Hautbois (Eds), *Management du sport 3.0, Spectacle, fan experience et digital*, Economica.

Glebova, E., Desbordes M. (2020). Technology enhanced sports spectators customer experiences: Measuring and identifying impact of mobile apps on sports spectators customer experiences, *Athens Journal of Sports,* 7(1), 26.

Glebova, E., Gerke, A. & Book, R. (2022). The transformational role of technology in sports events, In: Basu, Desbordes, Sarkar, *Sports Management in an Uncertain Environment*, Springer.

Grübel, J., Thrash, T., Aguilar, L., Gath-Morad, M., Chatain, J., Sumner, R. W., & Schinazi, V. R. (2022). The hitchhiker's guide to fused twins: a review of access to digital twins in situ in smart cities. *Remote Sensing*, 14(13), 3095.

Ivanov, S. (2020). The impact of automation on tourism and hospitality jobs. *Information Technology & Tourism* (in press). https://doi.org/10.1007/s40558-020-00175-1

Khan, S., Shael, M., Majdalawieh, M., Nizamuddin, N. & Nicho, M. (2022). Blockchain for governments: The case of the Dubai Government. *Sustainability*, 14, 6576. https://doi.org/10.3390/su14116576

Law, R., Buhalis, D., & Cobanoglu, C. (2014). Progress on information and communication technologies in hospitality and tourism. *International Journal of Contemporary Hospitality Management*, 26(5), 727-750.

Lewicki W., Stankiewicz B., Olejarz-Wahba A.A. (2020) The role of intelligent transport systems in the development of the idea of smart city. In: Sierpiński G. (ed.) *Smart and Green Solutions for Transport Systems*. TSTP 2019. Advances in Intelligent Systems and Computing, vol 1091. Springer, Cham. https://doi.org/10.1007/978-3-030-35543-2_3

Lykidis, I., Drosatos, G., & Rantos, K. (2021). The use of blockchain technology in e-government services. *Computers*, 10(12), 168. https://doi.org/10.3390/computers10120168

Meissner, M (2017) China's social credit system: a big data-enabled approach to market regulation with broad implications for doing business in China. *Metrics China Monitor* 39, 1-13

Mohanty, S.P. (2016). Everything you wanted to know about smart cities: The Internet of things is the backbone. *IEEE Consumer Electronics Magazine*, 5, 60-70. DOI: 10.1109/MCE.2016.2556879.

Ostrom, A. L., Parasuraman, A., Bowen, D. E., Patrício, L., & Voss, C. A. (2015). Service research priorities in a rapidly changing context. *Journal of Service Research*, 18(2)

Ramu, S. P., Boopalan, P., Pham, Q. V., Maddikunta, P. K. R., Huynh-The, T., Alazab, M., & Gadekallu, T. R. (2022). Federated learning enabled digital twins for smart cities: Concepts, recent advances, and future directions. *Sustainable Cities and Society*, 79, 103663.

Sethi, N., & Sethi, V. (2008). E-government implementation: A case study of Dubai e-Government. https://csi-sigegov.org.in/egovernance_pdf/22_185-195.pdf

Schut, P-O. & Glebova, E. (2022). Sports spectating in connected stadiums: Mobile application Roland Garros 2018. Frontiers in Psychology, 4:802852. doi: 10.3389/fspor.2022.802852

Stylos, N., Zwiegelaar, J. & Buhalis, D. (2021), Big data empowered agility for dynamic, volatile, and time-sensitive service industries: the case of tourism sector, *International Journal of Contemporary Hospitality Management*, 33(3), 1015-1036. https://doi.org/10.1108/IJCHM-07-2020-0644

Tyagi, V., Kalyanaraman, S., Krishnapuram, R. (2012). Vehicular traffic density state estimation based on cumulative road acoustics. *IEEE Transactions on Intelligent Transportation Systems.* **13** (3): 1156–1166. doi:10.1109/TITS.2012.2190509

Vaishya, R., Javaid, M., Khan, I. H., & Haleem, A. (2020). Artificial Intelligence (AI) applications for COVID-19 pandemic. *Diabetes & Metabolic Syndrome*, 14(4), 337–339. https://doi.org/10.1016/j.dsx.2020.04.012

# 2 Smart technology trends in the tourism and hospitality industry

*Evrim Çeltek*

## Introduction

The Internet of Things (IoT) offers tourism businesses the opportunity to observe real-time customer experiences and expand their customer base (Buhalis et al., 2019). Using artificial intelligence and robotic technologies in processes, such as sales and customer relations, makes customers feel more special. Tourism companies are differentiating their interactions with the customer with applications such as travel planning and booking with chatbots and artificial intelligence-based destination suggestions (Buhalis et al., 2019). In addition, the use of these technologies in all operational processes that directly or indirectly touch the customer, reduces employee effort, and provides cost optimization. Virtual and augmented reality technologies, which are an imitation of the real world, change the way of promotion and marketing of the service in the tourism sector by making it possible to experience destinations, hotels, restaurants, and similar places to travel without going. Blockchain, which is an advanced record keeping technology at the global level, provides instant access to the data produced in the tourism industry, is used to gather tourist information or to monitor supply and demand in real time. Being aware of these technological trends, which have changed the way of doing in the tourism sector, is important in order not to fall behind (Buhalis & Sinarta, 2019).

## IoT applications in tourism industries

The technological infrastructure that connects via Internet-connected sensors, chips, and communication modules, which allows objects to exchange information among themselves, is called the IoT (Chaouchi, 2013; Schönberger

& Cukier, 2013). IoT connects the devices via the internet or cloud service in order to collect and distribute data. This makes the analysis easier, accurate, and in real time, and ensures the management of visitor flows, road traffic, and reduction of traffic accidents. Tourism companies use IoT technologies to reduce operational risks and costs, offer personalized services and continuous communication (e.g., mobile, kiosk, and sensors) with tourists, create new ways of earning, improve staff productivity and customer experience (Buhalis, 2020). IoT technology is used to remotely connect to lights, heaters, and air conditioners in the hotel room, making it possible to control these vehicles from one place.

Virgin Atlantic airline equips its Boeing 787 aircraft and cargo equipment fleet with IoT. This system enables everything from motors to landing gear to be interconnected, to recognize and solve a mechanical problem that may occur, resulting in safer flights and fewer delays. AirAsia uses IoT to reduces fuel consumption by establishing a partnership with General Electric to minimize both its ecological footprint and cost. Flight efficiency service provides very precise navigation data, preventing approximately 20% route loss in the industry and thus optimizing aircraft and fuel use. Delta and Lufthansa airlines use baggage tracking technology enabling passengers to check the location of their luggage at any time (onboard and at the baggage claim until the time of boarding). With the Lufthansa mobile application, passengers can track their baggage through a link on their mobile boarding pass (Drummond, 2016).

In addition to the examples from airline companies, IoT is widely used in the hotels and lodging sector. In City Hub Amsterdam, which is a smart hotel with capsule rooms, the customer can adjust the light of the room to any color with the phone application; it can even receive a light-based wake up. City Hub Amsterdam also uses wearable device technology and smart wristbands. Thanks to the smart wristbands, room entrance is made, and drink glasses can be taken from the self-service bar in the hotel (Skyscanner, 2017). Carnival Cruises and MSC Cruises use IoT and wearable technology. Smart bracelets are used instead of keys or smartphones to enter the rooms. These are called *Ocean Medallion* on the Carnival cruise ships and *MSC for Me* smart bracelet on MSC cruise ships. Payments are made through this wristband connected with a credit card and the route taken can be followed simultaneously. The wristbands record every activity of the customers, transferring the information to the database, enabling family members to locate each other, and accessing the information they want from the television or their smartphones in their rooms. In addition, a typical MSC cruise ship, the *MSC Meraviglia*, has more than 130 smart features, 144 interactive screens,

# 16  Smart Cities and Tourism

244 information displays, 31 virtual screens for private ferry cameras, 81 video wall monitors, 2,244 near field communication (NFC) cabin, 3,050 Bluetooth signals, and 1200 closed circuit (CCTV) cameras (Leppert, 2017; Buhalis et al., 2022).

## Recognition technology in tourism

Recognition technologies include fingerprint recognition, hand recognition, face recognition, eye retina recognition, voice recognition, body, and motion recognition. Recognition technologies use biometrics, AI technologies, internet connectivity, and IoT. *Biometrics* refers to technologies that measure and analyze individual physical or behavioral features to automate users' authentication process. Physical features include facial patterns, fingerprints, voice, and ocular retinas, while behavioral aspects include writing patterns and body movements. In the tourism sector, fingerprint recognition is used instead of room keys or opening room safes. For instance, Waldorf Towers Hotel in New York is utilizing fingerprint recognition for in-room safes for their presidential suite customers. Disney World theme parks in Orlando have been using two-finger recognition technology since 2005 to increase entry speed and membership passes for individuals over the age of ten (Mills et al., 2010).

Face recognition utilizing video or thermal imaging captures facial features, and analyzes their shapes and patterns (Ryu & Lee, 2016). Facial recognition reduces the lines for check-in, ticket purchase or passport control or even to detect criminals and terrorists at airports (Saulat, 2018). In the hospitality industry, Borgata Hotel Casino and Spa in Atlantic City uses face recognition with cameras to identify card fraud customers. Nine Zero, a hotel in Boston, uses iris pattern recognition technology to identify guests (to provide additional guest security) for upscale suites (Bergstein, 2004).

Voice recognition uses various characteristics of the human voice, such as cadence, pitch, and tone (Levine, 2000). This enables people to interact with computers through voice recognition software. Voice recognition technology is used in the translation of different languages in tourism (to interact with people who speak different languages), in communicating with robots and giving voice commands to machines and robots (e.g., Amazon Echo, which includes the Alexa assistant, Google Home, equipped with Google Assistant, and Apple HomePod, complete with Siri) (Mills et al., 2010). Amazon Alexa, developed for the travel agency Expedia, enables users to easily manage their upcoming journeys with voice interaction technology. With Amazon Alexa, users can perform travel operations from flight information to hotel reservations and car rentals with voice control (revfine.com, 2020).

Moreover, body and motion recognition technologies are used in interactive digital art museums such as Ars Electronica Museum and MORI Building Digital Art Museum (the world's first digital art museum) where visual arts are displayed. In these museums interactive art events can be organized with body and motion recognition technologies. Chinese Marriott uses facial recognition technology for quick and easy check-in at its facilities (Hristova, 2020). Recognition technologies speed up rows at checkpoints such as passport control or boarding gates by up to 40%. Customers' satisfaction can also be measured with emotional recognition technology by analyzing facial expressions related to customer satisfaction or dissatisfaction. Another example is *Seeker*, the program developed by Accor Hotels. Using the smartphone camera and webcam, the travel experiences that tourists will find most attractive can be determined by the responses to stimuli such as pictures and sound. The app uses six different metrics to create a psychological profile and match them with the types of holidays. Headband kiosks to monitor brain waves and wrist bands to monitor heart rate or skin response are being tested at several hotels. (World Travel and Tourism Council, 2018a) Moreover, Abu Dhabi International Airport has launched an application called *Smart Travel* to reduce queues at the airport and improve passenger travel. With Smart Travel, passengers by themselves check in from the kiosks, get boarding passes, and even leave their luggage in the automatic baggage release system. Then, with the e-border gate service (face recognition, etc.), passengers quickly pass the passport control and get their boarding passes approved. This reduces the check-in time of passengers by 70% (Yalçınkaya et al., 2018). In the future, recognition technologies will be able to use biometric indicators such as heart rate, breathing rate, and blink rate for health and marketing purposes.

## Virtual reality in tourism

Technically, virtual reality (VR) is a computer-generated 3D environment where individuals experience the feeling of being there. Users dive into the virtual environment through various technologies (e.g., Head-Mounted Display/HMD). From the moment users enter the environment, they are disconnected from reality and experience the feeling of being completely in the environment where VR is created (Pan & Hamilton, 2018; Tussyadiah et al., 2018). In the tourism industry, VR is used to show the touristic features of the tourism destinations, the museums, historical sites, package tours, or the hotel rooms in the virtual world, and for gamification (e.g., climbing a glacier or underwater diving in the virtual world). In the future, payment will also be made through VR. With VR, tourists can visit Rome or the Roman archaeological museum interactively in the virtual world. VR environments are divided into four categories according to the intensity (level) of the feeling of reality created by the user. These are (1) non-immersive environments; (2) semi-immersive environments (such as flight simulators); (3) full-immersive environments, in which HMD and input devices: joystick, gloves etc. are used (Çeltek, 2020), and (4) collaborative environments, in which users can interact with each other. Buhalis and Karatay (2022) illustrated how mixed reality (MR) can support cultural heritage tourism towards metaverse for for Generation Z.

Thomas Cook travel agency uses the *Try Before You Fly* VR application to allow its customers to experience the holiday spirit and to feel themselves on a virtual holiday island, in a crowded city center, or by the sea. In-agency VR application provides customers with a realistic experience for their future travel by taking them to a hotel or destination before making a reservation. After beginning to use the VR application, Thomas Cook's sales increased by 80%. Marriot Hotels markets their hotels with VR and customers can even rent virtual reality glasses at the Marriot hotels. Virgin Holidays has developed a VR application that enables customers to experience their tours before purchasing. Virgin Holidays recorded the ambient sound to create a real and sensory experience of what the holiday would look and sound like, then turned it into a customer experience using VR glasses (EY, 2019). The Dali Museum in Florida immerses its visitors in a picture of Dali with 360° VR. Ocean Rift is the world's first aquatic safari park VR game. The player can explore a vivid underwater world full of life including dolphins, sharks, turtles, orcas, sea snakes, rays, whales, manatees, sea lions, and even dinosaurs. In the game, the player can swim around, explore, and interact with sea creatures across twelve unique habitats. With the *National Archaeological Museum: Live the Past* VR application the player lives the experience of visiting several towns in the history of Spain and learn how people lived different times in the history of Spain (Oculus.com, 2020).

## Augmented reality in tourism

Using the recognition feature of devices such as smart glasses, tablets, smartphones, and overlaying virtual objects on real images is called augmented reality (AR) (Çeltek, 2020; Çeltek, 2015; tom Dieck & Yung, 2017). While VR takes the person into the virtual world, AR increases or enhances reality by activating virtual objects (i.e., voice, text, image, video) in the real world of the person. To use it, the AR application must be installed on the device. In the tourism industry, AR is used in museums, hotels, tourism destinations, cities, historical areas to give information, to promote, to advertise, to navigate, to guide and for gamification.

The *Paris Then and Now City Guide* application aims to enrich the experience of tourists with AR applications while visiting historical places. With the application, tourists can see the status of more than 2000 different historical places 100 years ago through the cameras of their tablets or smartphones. The National Museum of Singapore uses AR application to tell the history of the building (EY, 2019). *Tripventure* is a location-based AR game and guide which can be played in many cities in Europe. It allows tourists to experience virtual stories in real life via AR. While exploring the actual city, tourists interact with virtual people, solve mysteries, and find hidden items to reach the answers to the questions given (tripventure, 2020). Pizza-maker Domino's has put up 6,000 posters across Britain those look like a normal promotion poster but also serve as an AR marker, and when viewed through the *Blippar* application the user has the option to download deals for their nearest Domino's store, get the Domino's mobile ordering app or view their local menu (Çeltek, 2015).

## Robotics applications in tourism

A robot is a machine designed to execute one or more tasks automatically with speed and precision. There are as many different types of robots in tourism, such as delivery robots, social robots, and service robots. (Karabegovic & Dolecek, 2017). Robots in the tourism industry are used to perform certain jobs, provide services, welcome guests, take orders, prepare food and beverages, provide room service, do check-in/check-out operations, give information about the business or city, clean rooms, places, and pools, mow, carry luggage, and bring materials to the rooms and entertainment (Ivanov et al., 2017). The most important benefit of robots is that they provide service automation, hence reduced costs. Service robots, chatbots and self-service kiosks can work 24/7, which is more than people's working hours. For example, robots can provide room service to hotel customers. Likewise, they can also welcome guests at the hotel check-in and provide information about the services offered at the hotel. Unlike employees who see these tasks as boring and repetitive, they can do it thousands of times without complaining and forgetting to do so (Ivanov & Webster, 2017). Several factors affect hotel managers' intentions to adopt robotic technologies (Pizam, et al, 2022).

Hotels are ideal environments for social robots. Social robots are effective as hotel receptionists. They are an efficient, novel and fun way of providing information to customers, and can add an extra dimension to customer experience (Ivanov & Webster, 2017). Several examples around the world showcase their contribution. Situated in Nagasaki, Japan, Henn-na Hotel was the first hotel in the world to be entirely staffed by robots. Throughout the hotel, robots are deployed to provide information, front desk services, storage services, as well as check-in and check-out services, with technology including voice and facial recognition. Since its opening in Japan in the summer of 2015, the hotel had used 243 robots to manage every element of customer stay at the hotel, including check-in, luggage carriers, a concierge service and a robot assistant that appeared in every guest's room (Mccarthy, 2019; Alexis, 2017). *Connie* is a robot used by Hilton in its McLean Virginia branch. Connie makes use of an artificial intelligence platform developed by IBM and is able to interact with guests and respond to their questions, by its speech recognition capabilities (Ivanov et al., 2017). Connie can inform guests about nearby places of interest, give dining recommendations and information about the hotel. Starwood used two robotic *Botlrs* named A.L.O. in their Cupertino Aloft Hotel. The robotic butlers, built by Savioke, are able to perform tasks in the front of the house and the back of the house, as well as navigate around guests and use elevators (Love, 2014; Crook, 2014). Yotel Hotel used the world's first robotic luggage concierge, which called *YOBOT*.

In addition, the use of robots and avatar robots for the disabled is thought to facilitate their daily lives and travel in tourism (Cheung et al., 2017). Robots used in hotels are mostly included in the group of social robots and service robots. They serve people by providing information and helping in hotel settings (Tung & Law, 2017). A good example of this is the robot named Junko Chihira, the ultra-realistic android robot manufactured by Toshiba. Chihira works full-time in a tourist information center in Tokyo, can greet customers, and inform visitors about current events. The robot can speak Japanese, Chinese, English, German, and even sign language. Unlike humanoid robot applications, ProPILOT Park Ryokan hotel has items such as slippers, cushions and tables equipped with a self-parking feature, which will return to their designated places at the touch of a button (Kayıkçı, & Bozkurt, 2018).

## Artificial intelligence in tourism

Artificial intelligence (AI) is an area of software engineering that emphasizes the creation of intelligent machines that work and respond like humans (Buhalis et al., 2019). AI is the reproduction of human insight forms with machines, particularly computer systems (Keleş et al., 2017). AI is a science that tries to give intelligence to machines by transforming people's decision-making and problem-solving skills into algorithms to enable the computer to display intelligent behaviors. AI is the science of creating machines that are designed by humans and exhibit intelligent behaviors. AI is behind many technologies and innovations developing in the travel and tourism industry. The fields where AI utilized in the industry can be classified into three main categories: machine learning, chatbots or travelbots, and robots. Thanks to AI, operations that often require human intervention and skills that take a lot of time to learn can be automated, so processes can speed up, while quality and performance increase, and costs can be reduced. Gathering customer information implies that AI can be utilized from fundamental customer service to personalized tasks, for further problem solving, direct messaging and even a wide range of functions in sales processes.

The benefits of AI for businesses are voice recognition, synthetic speech, image processing, autonomous learning, and reasoning skills. Tourism enterprises use AI in applications such as communicating with new customers, analyzing the increasing data volume, attracting the target audience, speeding information processing, making synthesis, speeding up the decision-making process, increasing the permanence of customer relations, and reducing costs and human errors (Balkan, 2019). AI can be used to quickly process large amounts of data and draw important analysis and conclusions about customers or potential customers. One example of this is the *Metis AI* platform used by the Dorchester Collection hotel chain. The hotel collects information about customers using AI, via surveys and online reviews, voice or video calls and analyzes this information with AI to draw conclusions about overall performance (Revfine.com, 2019). EasyJet has also invested in an AI algorithm that optionally determines seat pricing automatically, depending on demand. The system can analyze historical data to predict demand patterns up to a year ahead (Feliu, 2019). Southwest Airlines has partnered with NASA to continuously improve airline safety. Using smart algorithms, Southwest and NASA have created an automated system that can break a huge amount of data to mark anomalies and prevent accidents (Feliu, 2019).

Booking.com uses AI in a chat tool that automates online travel searches. By using AI, Expedia can remind customers how many people are calling to change reservations. Customers can operate through the chatbot to change or cancel the reservation without speaking to any staff (i.e without a call center) or logging into the website. By processing big data with AI, it is possible to make smart predictions (such as seat in flight or accommodation preferences) preferred by every passenger and to transform this information into reservations that meet expectations quickly (Saulat, 2018). Hipmunk, Expedia, Skyscanner and Cheapflights use AI in customer service. The smart travel platform WayBlazer created an application for the tourism industry by working with IBM's Watson AI software to make travel suggestions according to the data of the people (Kayıkçı & Bozkurt, 2018). Virtual concierge applications make the hotel room more comfortable for tourists by adjusting the room temperature and providing pillows according to the guests' preferences (Buhalis and Moldavska, 2022).

## Big data in tourism

Big data empowers agility for the dynamic, volatile, and time-sensitive tourism industry (Stylos et al., 2021). A large amount of data sets that cannot be analyzed and managed with traditional data processing tools is called big data (Xu et al., 2019; Manyika et al., 2016). Big data use data such as user generated content data (UGC data: social media shares, online reviews, photos, blogs, videos, texts and recorded files), IoT data (machine-generated data: NFC, RFID, beacon, GPS, street camera, bluetooth and sensors data), traditional business systems data (process-mediated data: customer cards data, reservation data, webpage visiting and selling data). These all are are high volume and variety, and can be processed and defined with big data technologies (Kudyba, 2014; Cackett, 2016). Monino and Sedkaoui (2016) defined big data as the term used when the volume of data used for businesses reached a critical level and new technological storage, processing, and usage methods and approaches are required. Big data is described as 5V: volume, velocity, variety, verification, and value (Atalay & Çelik, 2017).

Tourism businesses and tourism destinations can use big data technologies to gain valuable information, such as better understanding of the behavior of tourists, determining changing preferences and needs, tracking the geographical location of tourists, personalizing services, offering new and competitive products and services, revenue management, and improving pricing strategy (Stylos et al., 2021). For example, it is possible to recommend hotels, restaurants, and events to tourists based on their preferences, geographic location, and online behavior (Brar, 2019; Elisabeth et al., 2013; Davenport, 2013). The effectiveness of policies and regulations in tourism can be monitored with some big data applications. Big data is used to reduce traffic problems in cities or to facilitate access to crowded places such as airports. With big data, drivers can determine the route, depending on their location, destination, preferences and other changing parameters (e.g., weather or accident) (Yazıcı et al., 2013). With big data from a wide variety of sources, tourism destinations can collect information about the country where visitors come from, how long they stay, in which regions they prefer to stay, where they prefer to go and how much they spend.

Hilton uses big data architecture to gain insight from data and provide better service to customers. For getting a 360° view of each customer, Hilton uses data analytics on reservation data, customer profile data, and details how customers use the hotel's facilities. This information allows Hilton to better recognize its customers and generate more value for them (Brar, 2019). One of the tourism businesses that successfully applied big data analysis to develop their personalization strategy is MGM Resorts International. It successfully used Facebook's big data tools and achieved a 300% increase in revenue over a three-year period. The success of MGM's personalized services is based on customers' enrollment in the business' *M Life program*. After customers' data is recorded in the program's database, MGM Resorts can track the customer's movements at all 19 resorts. If tourists start looking at room rates on MGM.com and then start comparing prices with a competitor site, MGM can take them to MGM.com with a relevant Facebook offer (Karampatsou, 2018).

British Airways (BA) uses a smart *Know Me* feature to provide customers with personalized search results. In this impressive big data case study, BA identified that their customer base largely consists of busy, time-pressed professionals who require fast, concise results. Therefore, Know Me uses in-depth data analysis to provide relevant and targeted proposals to consider. BA received a huge amount of positive feedback from customers who were satisfied that the company understood their travel needs (Feliu, 2019). In Amsterdam, tourist behaviors were analyzed, and congestion in the city has been eased by using the data collected with the *City Card of Amsterdam*, which is used for free public transportation and provides access to various touristic areas. In addition, the Visit Amsterdam team sends warning notifications to users when a touristic attraction is crowded with the application called *Discover the City* and even suggests alternative places (World Travel & Tourism Council, 2018b).

In the tourism industry, a variety of big data technologies are used (Stylos et al., 2021). These technologies are IoT, machine learning, cloud computing, data mining, text mining, natural language processing (NLP), Google MapReduce, hadoop and NoSQL. NLP is one of the most important steps in analyzing the texts obtained for institutions and organizations investing in big data technologies (Oğuzlar, 2011). Google MapReduce is a programming model, as well as the application associated with the processing and creation of large data sets. Hadoop can be defined as a large data infrastructure that includes a storage system and distributed processing tools, which is designed to process large amounts of data, from structural and non-structural terabytes to petabytes (Monino & Sedkaoui, 2016). NoSQL (not only SQL) accepts data of different types and sizes and allows searching through these data (Schönberger & Cukier, 2013). Big data is needed to use AI. Without the necessary big data, AI cannot work, and prediction statistics and analysis cannot be made. Therefore, it is necessary to collect big data with the help of software in the tourism industry to facilitate forecasting.

## Blockchain technology in tourism

Although blockchain is famous with virtual currencies such as bitcoin, it offers a distributed communication infrastructure that allows parties involved in the system to trade with confidence, without the need for a central authority. Blockchain applications create new business models that will shape the future as they can eliminate intermediaries to reengineer the supply chain process. (Boucher, 2017; Özcan, 2020). Blockchain applications in tourism are used for secure and efficient communication in passport control at airports, real-time baggage tracking, loyalty reward programs, identity management, smart contracts, and secure/traceable payments. Blockchain technology constitutes a distributed, replicated, and immutable digital ledger that allows the different parties to conduct business in a more trustful and transparent manner without the need for a central node of control (Iansiti & Lakhani, 2017; Fes, 2018). It is simply a new method of orchestrating, structuring, recording, and handling data in blocks which are verifiable, trustworthy and permanent (Kumar et al., 2019).

Blockchain is a technology that publicly stores all transactions produced by a particular network. Each record is encrypted and grouped into blocks that form a chain. After a block or record has been added, all members of the block chain must approve the insertion into the copy stored by each part of the block chain. This process ensures that the data stored on the blockchain is safe, traceable, unchangeable, and transparent (Özcan, 2020). The decentralized (distributed) nature of blockchain technology ensures that all kinds of information or data can never be transferred from the online environment to offline. Data cannot be accidentally or deliberately deleted, stolen, copied, or lost. Transactions can only be followed by authorized persons (Boucher, 2017). For example, *Winding Tree* is the application of a smart contract that runs on the Ethereum platform. It aims to make the hotels', airlines' services (passenger transport and ticketing) more efficient and faster. Winding Tree creates a decentralized market that connects customers of hotels, airlines, or tour operators directly with blockchain-based applications (Özcan, 2020; Nam et al., 2019). In 2018, KLM Royal Dutch's hub company, Air France-KLM, partnered with Winding Tree to eliminate intermediaries with blockchain to reduce large costs. Winding Tree has become a partner of many major global airline companies such as Etihad Airways, Air Canada, KLM Royal Dutch Airlines and Lufthansa (Dinçer, 2020).

Etihad Airways aims to sell its products and services to its passengers on a platform to be developed with the blockchain technique "without intermediaries". Etihad aimed to reduce dependence on global distribution systems (GDS) such as Amadeus and Sabre. Airlines must enter their inventory (such as flight schedule, number of seats) and ticket prices primarily through GDS, whether they are selling tickets through their own sales channel or agency channel. Airlines must pay substantial payments to each GDS company that mediates this transaction. This is the same for other players in the travel industry. Therefore, airlines such as Etihad Airways, Air Canada, Air France-KLM and Lufthansa, as well as ground handling companies Swissport and Nordic Choice, and hotels such as citizenM Hotel and Airport Hotel Basel, collaborate with Winding Tree. In the future, airlines, hotels, and other travel services providers will serve on the Winding Tree platform. Companies interested in the content will be connected to a B2B blockchain-based digital platform to offer special offers according to the needs of their customers (Nergiz, 2019). With blockchain-based e-identity and e-passport, personal information can be stored securely and displayed on the network anywhere in the world when necessary. Thus, counterfeiting is reduced and delays and long queues are prevented at the airport and other identity checkpoints (e.g., hotel check-in) (Özcan, 2020; Nam et al., 2019). Blockchain infrastructure identification system makes it possible to track where the data is used. Thus, if anyone uses identity information negatively, a reaction can be given. All data is stored in a decentralized location that provides a clear transaction history to help identify unauthorized use (Ham, 2018). A blockchain-based travel platform can ensure that customer reviews are real and reliable. Blockchain infrastructure prevents bad comments from being deleted or fake comments made. Thus, a real scoring system can be created between the hotels and the customer without allowing fake comments. Customers can select the service with confidence, by looking at the real comments and ratings on blockchain (Rejeb & Rejeb, 2019; Willie, 2019).

Other blockchain applications used in tourism industry include *Cool Cousin* (travel planning and suggestion platform), *Webjet* (hotel distribution platform), *Sandblock* and *Trippki* (customer loyalty platform for tourism), *Accenture* (digital identity platform) and *Travelchain* (travel planning platform) (Gupta, 2019), *Locktrip* (travel real estate rental platform), *Globaltourist* (online review platform), *Travala* (online booking platform), and *Explore* (travel review platform) (Nam et al., 2019). According to Bova (2018), with Travelchain, tourists can earn money by sharing their experiences directly and securely with travel businesses. For example, thanks to TravelChain, a vegetarian restaurant owner can find out that how many vegetarians live in the neighbourhood in seconds and those who provide this information earn money (cryptocurrency) in return. Another example is Bermuda's Newstead Belmont Hills Golf Resort & Spa, one of the first resorts in the world that allow payment by bitcoin. With the Dubai Token application, tourists can shop in different places and earn Dubai Token via the mobile application. Tourists can spend these tokens they earn at contracted companies. Lastly, travel companies can implement customer loyalty programs with blockchain to gain more customers and satisfy existing customers. Blockchain simplifies the process, allowing customers to easily access information about loyalty points, check their scores, and replace their points with cryptocurrency (Pilkington, 2017).

## QR codes, NFC, and Beacon technology in tourism

The QR code is defined as "pictorial bridges that can be basically embedded in the physical environment" (Coleman, 2011) and is an innovative and fast extension of the standard barcode (Bi et al., 2008). A QR code is the pixel square of the website URL extension created with the QR code converter (free apps) (Brisena et al., 2012). The generated QR codes can be used for giving information and promotion by adding them to product labels or packaging, flyers, brochures, catalogues, billboards, posters, advertisements in newspapers/magazines, tickets, event invitations, greeting cards, business cards and clothing (Rouillard, 2008). In the tourism industry, tourists can obtain information (audio, text, photo, video, web page, etc.) by scanning the codes placed in museums, destinations, hotels, hotel room keys, tourism brochures, books, advertisement brochures, billboards, menus, archaeological areas, plane, train or bus tickets, with the QR code scanner they download to their smartphones or tablets. They can also make reservations and payments (Lai et al., 2015). Tourism businesses can provide information to tourists on all kinds of subjects with QR codes (Marakos, 2015). With QR codes, businesses can make advertisements and surveys, learn about the geographic location of customers, measure the effectiveness of advertising (with tools such as Google Analytics or TrackQR); and tours can be gamified with treasure hunt games.

British hotel chain Radisson Edwardian has presented videos of food preparation using QR codes in restaurant menus. Mirage Hotel and Casino in Las Vegas used QR Codes to advertise on taxis, buses, and signs. In the city of Rio de Janeiro, QR codes created with mosaic stones are placed on the sidewalks for tourists to learn about the city and reach their destination more easily. Cleveland Museum of Art and Bologna's Archeology Museum used QR codes to promote their collections with audio tours. Turkish Airlines, during the Olympic games in 2012, translated the flags of countries into QR codes and placed them in more than 100 bus stops in London. The users that found the most and at the greatest number of locations, and scanned the QR codes in these places, had the chance to win round-trip tickets from Turkish Airlines. Through the mobile site of the campaign, it was possible to follow all the locations, the score status of the competitors, and the number of times the country flags were scanned. Fountainebleau Hotel in Miami Beach has used QR codes that direct customers to their website to market the hotel restaurant, bar, and spa. Long Beach City (Washington) provided information to tourists about the city using QR codes on informative signs in the city (Çeltek, 2017). Thailand has placed QR codes in more than 300 points in the country with the project *Scan Me in Thailand* to give information to local and foreign tourists about tourist destinations.

Technically, Near Field Communication (NFC) is a short-range and wireless communication technology for data transfer without physical touch (Çeltek, 2019; Pesonen & Horster, 2012). NFC provides short-distance, low-bandwidth, high-frequency two-way interaction, such as data exchange between NFC-enabled electronic devices (phone, tablet, and computer) and between electronic devices and the NFC tag. There is no need to download apps to enable NFC apps by smartphones (Pesonen & Horster, 2012). Since NFC technology consists of an interface and protocol developed on RFID (Radio Frequency Identification), it is compatible with RFID technology (Bilginer & Ljunggren, 2011; Dragović et al., 2018). NFC in tourism is used for mutual data exchange between customer and business, ticket sales, smart poster, and map creation, e-wallet, transportation cards, customer loyalty cards, identity and passport checks, check-in/checkout transactions; giving information about destinations, museums and businesses, advertising, and even accessing hotel rooms using smartphones as keys. With NFC, location-based information about customers can be collected. When a smartphone is brought closer to an NFC tag or device, information such as text, image, or sound, a payment screen appears automatically.

Scandinavian Airlines has produced NFC tags that can be used by loyal passengers at the airport, from check-in and check-out to simple baggage checks. In the city of Rio de Janeiro, 5,000 NFC and QR code labels are placed on bus stops to provide information to local people and tourists about bus routes and times, tourist attractions, and destinations (Clark, 2014). India's Madhya Pradesh Tourism Development Company uses NFC and QR codes to provide information about historical sites. With this application, visitors can get detailed information about popular attractions in Hindi, English, Japanese, French (Boden, 2013a). More than 8,000 places (bus stops, subway entrances and exits, hotels, hostels, tourist offices, and tourist sites) are equipped with NFC contact points in Barcelona to provide information to tourists and the local community. Thanks to an NFC-labeled panel placed in the reception area of Aimia Hotel in Port de Sóller, Mallorca, customers can learn about public transportation, places to visit and weather forecasts, the hotel's Wi-Fi password and restaurant menu (Boden, 2013b). In the French city of Grenoble, a local NFC payment system is used for tram tickets and ski cards for citizens and tourists (Clark, 2012). At the Museum of London, visitors can learn about objects on display in the museum, purchase tickets for future exhibitions, and "like" or "follow" the museum on various social media platforms through NFC-enabled devices (Clark, 2011).

Beacon is the common name for small wireless devices that broadcast small radio signals around themselves, which include BLE (Bluetooth Low Energy) technology. To send a signal or message to the user, that person must download the relevant app, activate Bluetooth, and sign up to receive notifications (Yamaguchi et al., 2017). In the tourism industry beacons are used in geo-fencing (i.e., a kind of location-based marketing application) applications such as giving personalized information, promotions, discount coupons to customers passing near to the business. Beacons are used to attract customers to the business, to provide information about historical artifacts in museums, even to create personal guidance services, e-wallets, to greet customers at the hotel, customer loyalty programs, check-in and navigation at hotels and airports, and to collect geo-based information about customers.

When a beacon is placed in a business building, the exact location of nearby customers can be detected, and messages can also be sent to customers' smartphones or tablets at the same time. For example, when a person passes near a museum, they receive a notification to their mobile telephone that there is a museum near here. When the visitor enters the museum, the relevant information (such as the history of the scene) can be sent to the visitor with the beacon. When a smart glass like Google Glass is integrated with beacon technology, the history of the scene can come directly to the ear of the visitor. For example, Miami International Airport helps passengers go to the right gate at the airport with the beacon, and also provides information about nearby shops and restaurants. At Mumbai Chhatrapati Shivaji International Airport, passengers can choose to receive push notifications about flights with beacons. With the beacon technology, a receptionist can see the guest profile on a smart device when the guest enters the hotel and greet him by his name. Beacon can send different types of push notifications to the customer about the facilities from the moment customers check in to the check-out (BLE Mobile Apps, 2018). Marriott has integrated beacon technology into its customer loyalty program at its 14 hotels in the USA. Marriott Rewards members receive location-based mobile offers at hotels with the loyalty program (Poilabs, 2015). In Disney's amusement parks visitors can open the room doors with the wristband provided and can make payments such as parking, photos (Atakul, 2014a). The Philips Museum in Eindhoven has created a game installation called *Mission Eureka* on Philips 100-year history of invention. In the game, which aims at an interactive museum tour for groups of 4 or 8 and above, participants can discover how LED lights work or how X-rays work through with various games and puzzles through iPads and iBeacons (Atakul, 2014b).

In summary, tools such as QR codes, NFC, beacon add value to the tourist experience by providing connections between the physical and digital world. They provide benefits to businesses in informing customers, speeding up transactions, gathering information about customers, and gamification.

## 3D printing in tourism

3D printers transform 3D objects designed in a virtual environment into tangible objects in solid form. With 3D printing technology, a required apparatus can be printed, an object scanned with a 3D scanner can be printed, a drawn design can be prototyped, and even created as a product (Klein et al., 2014; Jung & tom Dieck, 2017). 3D printing technology is a type of rapid prototyping technology that uses photo-stream and paper lamination technology through a digital technology material printer and configures objects by layer by layer with powder materials such as metal or plastic. For this reason, it can greatly shorten the product development process, reduce the production costs, and improve production efficiency. Initially, 3D printing technology was mainly used to produce models in the fields of mold manufacturing and industrial design (Klein et al., 2014). With the advancement of science and technology, global 3D printing technology is mainly used in products in automotive, aerospace, architecture, medicine, industrial machinery products, jewellery design, artistic creation, and other fields. In the future, 3D printing technology will be used in more fields with the advancement of technology and updating of materials. The built-in material of the 3D digital printer is liquid, dust, etc. The printed object is in 3D (Du, 2020). In the tourism sector, 3D printers are used to make personalized meals, shortening the production time of hand-crafted dishes, and make touristic souvenirs and hotel construction.

The environmentally friendly hotel chain Habitas has developed a concept for building 3D printed flat-pack hotels. A modular housing technique was used using 3D printing technology to build hotel rooms. The company packs the basic structures of the rooms flat and sends them to the location where the hotel will be built. With this technique, approximately 100 rooms can be produced per month. From 2020, Habitas plans to build ten to twelve more hotels in Asia. Habitas aims to reduce the cost of building hotels using pre-built 3D printed flat pack designs in Mexico. The founding partner of the company expects hotels to be built in six to nine months and to give a return on investment within two years. The hotel company plans to become the "Club Med for Millennials" and expand into Asia, the Middle East, and Africa (Harangozó, 2020). In 2015, Lewis Grand Hotel (lewisgrand.com) in the Philippines created the world's first 3D printed hotel suite. The suite consists of a two-bedroom 130-square-meter accommodation villa, and the villa has a fully functional living room and a jacuzzi, which took about 100 hours to complete. According to Tablang (2015), 3D printing can save 60% on building costs, and by adding 3D printed parts, the weight of aircraft can be reduced. On that note the airline company Airbus (airbus.com) plans to create a fully 3D printed aircraft by 2050 (Johnson, 2016).

Food Ink is a conceptual pop-up dinner restaurant where food meets art and technology. Technologies such as 3D printing and virtual reality are used to provide the best interactive edible experience in the restaurant. Food Ink is the world's first 3D printing restaurant that brings together architects, artists, chefs, designers, and engineers. The restaurant creates dishes using 3D printers from anything that can take the form of a paste, such as hummus, chocolate mousse, crushed peas, goat cheese, or pizza dough. Food Ink's mission is to explore the intersection between food and technology-powered user experience (foodink.io/, 2020).

**Table 2.1:** Advantages and challenges of smart trends in tourism and hospitality

| | ADVANTAGES | CHALLENGES |
|---|---|---|
| IoT | Used to develop smart metering, smart supply chains, smart transportation, smart grid, and smart traffic light system.<br>Offers real time big data, accurate data collection.<br>Used to build smart environments in destinations or hotels.<br>Practical personal control of hotel rooms (with internet- enabled heating, lighting, and television).<br>Allows self check-in/check-out in hotels and airports.<br>Energy-saving, maintenance, repairs, and detailed understanding of users through analysis of data in real time.<br>Connects physical and digital things to achieve greater value for tourists and businesses.<br>Allows continuous interaction with tourists on different platforms (mobile, kiosk, sensors etc.). | Data privacy problems, misuse, and theft of personal information collected from IoT technologies.<br>Installation cost.<br>Overdependence on sensors.<br>User's adaptation. |
| Recognition technology | Helps identify criminal situations, catching criminals, increasing security.<br>Reduces payment, order, passport, and reservation queues.<br>Eliminates the problem of losing cards and forgetting passwords by using long and complex passwords.<br>Service automation and reduction of personnel costs, reduction of human error.<br>Personalization of the services.<br>Data collection and data analysis (with voice recognition, face recognition, eye recognition, movement recognition, emotional recognition). | Consumer privacy, unauthorized collection of consumer information.<br>Identity theft or theft of customer information.<br>Unique biometric details cannot replace while a compromised credit card can be replaced.<br>Possible problems with identifying certain groups of people, such as children, and some skin tones and facial shapes.<br>Requires approval or participation from the user. |

| | | |
|---|---|---|
| VR | Marketing and presentation of destinations, historical and touristic values, and hotels.<br>Promotion and marketing of tourism services.<br>Sale of tours, making reservations.<br>Information provided before tourism experience and helping decision making. | Unknown health effects.<br>Possible harms of VR headset to the eyes.<br>User's adaptation.<br>In tourism, some applications are still experimental.<br>VR tools are still expensive for the general user.<br>User addiction to the virtual world. |
| AR | Marketing and presentation of destinations, historical and touristic values, and hotels.<br>Promotion and marketing of tourism services.<br>Tourist guide and city guide service.<br>Provides information and facilitateactivities throughout the travel experience.<br>Creates an interactive advertisement for tourism products. | Requires approval or participation from the user.<br>No standards for AR.<br>Consumer privacy, unauthorized collection of consumer information.<br>Can cause accidents while using in an outdoor setting.<br>Can cause digital fatigue, addiction to the virtual world. |
| Robotics | Eases dangerous and difficult work.<br>Provides personalized service by processing the data obtained throughout the experience.<br>Provides 24/7 customer service.<br>Reduces the effort of customer representatives for frequently asked questions.<br>Offers customized pricing and promotions.<br>Saves in employee effort and number.<br>Increases the added value of talents.<br>Responds to the need for periodic workforce instantly. | Lacks creativity.<br>Lacks personal approach.<br>Might be perceived as a threat by human employees (e.g. Neo-Luddism movement).<br>Still high costs<br>No instant reflexes like people in emergencies, other than pre-programmed actions.<br>Takes time for users to adapt. |
| AI | Segments the consumers and creates different marketing content for each customer segment.<br>Personalizes campaigns and services.<br>Provides analysis and reporting in a short time.<br>Shows the big picture and determines the strategies accordingly.<br>Almost zero risks of making mistakes. | Lack of having the necessary skills in tourism.<br>Investments in data and technologies are required to build applications.<br>Requires a high budget.<br>Lack of the ability to know and manage the right processes.<br>Contains very complex systems. |

| | Advantages | Challenges |
|---|---|---|
| AI (cont) | Serves as a virtual assistant, concierge robots, chatbots, digital assistance, and voice-activated services.<br>Collects information about customers on many issues such as travel options, location information, destination preferences, hotel ratings, payment methods, vacation, and hotel preferences. | |
| Big Data | Better decision support.<br>Personalization of services and better customer relationship and satisfaction.<br>Revenue management.<br>Identifies real-time errors and the root causes of problems, reduces risks, supports decision making.<br>Demand forecasting.<br>Increases productivity and reduces costs.<br>Analysing customers' travel options, location information, destination preferences, hotel ratings, payment methods, holiday, and hotel preferences etc. and using them for marketing purposes. | Privacy of customer data, data security issue.<br>Data discrimination or customer discrimination.<br>Very comprehensive process to evaluate big data, requires pretreatment steps: cleaning, reduction, and transmission.<br>Data obtained from many different environments; hence difficult to integrate in different formats.<br>Difficult to meet the software and hardware requirements of large data operations.<br>Needs extensive study and planning to manage data stacks.<br>Strategies needed to prevent reliability violations in data flow.<br>Lack of qualified staff. |
| Blockchain | Reduces integration costs.<br>Eliminates the intermediary or third party, no commission to intermediaries.<br>Data integrity, decentralized business models, the data is immutable and transparent.<br>Data security, secure and transparent transactions.<br>Ease and speed of past transactions, review.<br>Increases customer satisfaction.<br>Designs digital identity, baggage tracking, loyalty programs, e-wallet, secure money transfer.<br>Gathers tourist information and identifies it at all times in the experience and makes instant follow-up throughout the tourist experience.<br>Follow-up of online customer review | Lack of registry interoperability.<br>Poor user experience.<br>Lack of tested applications.<br>Deficiencies in developer tools.<br>Not affordable blockchain applications for every business.<br>Lack of specialized personnel and knowledge in this field.<br>Lack of trust in new technology providers.<br>Legal limitations for applications. |

| | | |
|---|---|---|
| QR code, NFC, Beacon | Wirelessly and contactless transferring data. Location based marketing, real-time marketing, one to one targeting. Large amount of information provided by QR codes to the user, different from NFC and Beacon. Direct sales and payment allowed by NFC and beacon. Cost efficient QR codes when compared to NFC and beacon. QR code generators easily accessible online and usually free. Easy to measure and track the actions triggered via QR code, NFC and beacon. The business scans the customer information so that the customer's information such as location and previous purchase behaviour is accessed. Bidirectional communication provided by NFC and beacon. Personalized promotion, suggestions, and coupons provided to the user by NFC and beacon. QR code, NFC and beacon provide both business and customers with the right information at the right place at the right time. The information provided in NFC and beacon can be updated in real time. | An application to be downloaded to use the QR codes and beacon. Broken web link in QR code. The possibility of corrupt web link when QR code is scanned. Lack of information about QR code, NFC and beacon by users. Possible security attacks. NFC unsuitable for large amount of data transfers. Less demand and popularity. User's adaptation. Requires approval or participation from the user. Not affordable: NFC and beacon technologies for small companies. |
| 3D PRINTING | Freedom of design; allows the production of objects that cannot be produced with the traditional production method. Personalized physical products (food, chocolate, clothing, souvenirs or even hotel rooms). Fast and cost efficient production. | Limited user experience and lack of knowledge of 3D object designing for the printer. Copyright issue, with 3D printing copying issue arises. Still expensive 3D printing tools. |

## Conclusion

Tourism has changed with the widespread use of technologies such as AI, IoT, cloud computing and blockchain. Thanks to these technologies, large and open data sets can be obtained from larger sources. This comprehensive, different data obtained can be monitored with big data technologies, and can be analyzed reliably, quickly and in real time. Information about stakeholders is obtained by processing open data from smart city platforms. This information makes it possible to offer new services and a personalized tourist experience. Many destinations, including Barcelona and Dubai, have carried out studies that improve the tourist experience and stakeholders in the tourism industry using open data within the smart city.

In the near future, tourists will be able to visit where they want to go through VR, and if they like, they will be able to make reservations to the destinations through VR. A digital assistant can even find the hotel for them, make a reservation, and pay the money. Speaking with Google Assistant, they will be able to prepare their holiday suitcases and create the sunglasses that they want with 3D print. When arriving at the airport, the beacons will guide their phone or smartwatch about where the plane will depart. Check-in operations can be made easily via the barcode sent by the airlines to the smart watch. In passport control, they can pass quickly with face recognition. They will be able to track their luggage on their phone with blockchain. When they reach the smart hotel, check-in can be done via mobile phone, smart bracelet or kiosk, and they will be able to open the room door with a mobile phone, smart bracelet, or smart watch. They will be able to get service from the robots working in the hotel, and food served by robots made with 3D printers in the restaurant. While visiting the hotel, thanks to beacon technology on the phone, discount notifications of the hotel's spa or bar will come, and the payment will be made with crypto money. When they leave the hotel, they will be able to access the information they need in the destination with augmented reality, QR codes, NFC and beacon technologies. With Google Glass they even will be able to listen to the information they want, chat with family in 3D hologram and remotely control their smart home. Moreover, if lost, their location can be sent to the hotel's help center with their smart watch or smart bracelet. With the drone video, the best moments of the trip will be saved in the cloud memory. Finally, on the way back home, they will be able to go to the airport by a driverless vehicle.

While augmented and virtual reality technology is mostly used for content marketing and improving customer experience, operations that require human intervention and a lot of time to learn can be automated with AI technology (machine learning, ChatBots/TravelBots and robot technology). Thus, processes are accelerated, quality and performance are increased, and cost is reduced. With IoT, all touristic activities are linked with each other. Voice technology provides voice commands to customers, and unlimited and fast Wifi access increases customer satisfaction. With wearable device technology, customers can also get more personalized and unified services.

# References

Alexis, P. (2017) R-Tourism:Introducing the potential impact of robotics and service automation in tourism, *"Ovidius" University Annals, Economic Sciences Series*, 17(1)

Atakul, B. (2014a) Disney De Artık IBeacon Kullanıyor, Retrieved from http://www.teknolo.com/disney-ibeacon/.

Atakul, B. (2014b). Müze Turu Için IBeacon Oyunu, Retrieved from http://www.teknolo.com/ibeacon-muze-oyunu/.

Atalay, M. & Çelik, E. (2017) Artificial intelligence and machine learning applications in big data analysis, *Mehmet Akif Ersoy Üniversitesi Sosyal Bilimler Enstitüsü Dergisi*, 9(22), 155–172. doi:10.20875/makusobed.309727

Balkan, E. (2019) Yapay Zeka, Büyük Veri ve Pazarlama Devrimi. Retrieved from https://kobitek.com/yapay-zeka-buyuk-veri-ve-pazarlama-devrimi.

Bergstein, B. (2004), *Biometric Technology Getting More Action in Consumer Applications*, Associated Press, New York, NY, August 11

Bi, L., Feng, Z., Liu, M. & Wang, W. (2008) Design and implementation of the airline luggage inspection system base on link structure of QR code, In *Proceedings 2008 International Symposium on Electronic Commerce and Security* (pp. 527–530). IEEE. 10.1109/ISECS.2008.200

Bilginer, B. & Ljunggren, P. L. (2011) Near Field Communication, (Unpublished Master's thesis). Lund University, Sweden.

BLE Mobile Apps (2018) Use of Beacon Technology in Travel and Tourism Industry, Retrieved from https://www.blemobileapps.com/blog/use-beacon-technology-travel-tourism- industry/.

Boden, R. (2013a). Madhya Pradesh to offer NFC info, Retrieved from https://www.nfcworld. com/2013/04/29/323771/madhya-pradesh-to-offer-nfc-info/

Boden, R. (2013b). Spanish hotel delivers guest information via NFC, Retrieved from https://www. nfcworld.com/2013/07/24/325127/spanish-hotel-delivers-guest-information-via- nfc/

Boucher, P. (2017) *How blockchain technology could change our lives: In-depth analysis*, European Parliament.

Bova, R. (2018) How could blockchain transform the way we travel? TravelChain CEO explains. Retrieved from https://cointelegraph.com/news/how-could-blockchain-transform-the-way-we-travel-travelchain-ceo-explains Accessed 13 June 2022

Brar, K. (2019) Hotels using big data to check out guests. Retrieved from https://www.tnp.sg/news/ views/hotels-using-big-data-check-out-guests

Brisena, M. Z., Hirata, F. I., Lopez Juan de, D. S., Garcia, E. J., Cota, C. N. & Hipolito, J. I. N. (2012). Using RFID/NFC and QR-code in mobile phones to link the physical and the digital world. In *Interactive Multimedia*. InTech.

Buhalis, D. & Karatay, N. (2022). Mixed Reality (MR) for Generation Z in cultural heritage tourism towards metaverse. In: Stienmetz, J.L., Ferrer-Rosell, B., Massimo, D. (eds) *Information and Communication Technologies in Tourism 2022*. Springer, Cham. https://doi.org/10.1007/978-3-030-94751-4_2

Buhalis, D., Harwood, T., Bogicevic, V., Viglia, G., Beldona, S. & Hofacker, C., (2019) Technological disruptions in services: Lessons from tourism and hospitality, *Journal of Service Management*, 30(4), 484-506 https://doi.org/10.1108/JOSM-12-2018-0398

Buhalis, D. (2020), Technology in tourism - from information communication technologies to eTourism and smart tourism towards ambient intelligence tourism: a perspective article, *Tourism Review* 75(1), 267-272 https://doi.org/10.1108/TR-06-2019-0258

Buhalis, D. & Sinarta, Y. (2019) Real-time co-creation and nowness service: lessons from tourism and hospitality. *Journal of Travel & Tourism Marketing*, 36(5), 563-582.

Buhalis, D. & Moldavska, I. (2022), Voice assistants in hospitality: using artificial intelligence for customer service, *Journal of Hospitality and Tourism Technology*, https://doi.org/10.1108/JHTT-03-2021-0104

Buhalis, D., Papathanassis, A. & Vafeidou M., (2022) Smart Cruising: smart technology applications and their diffusion in cruise tourism *Journal of Hospitality and Tourism Technology*, https://doi.org/10.1108/JHTT-05-2021-0155

Cackett, D. (2016) *Information Management and Big Data, A Reference Architecture*, White paper. Redwood Shores: Oracle Corporation.

Çeltek, E. (2015) Augmented reality advertisements in tourism marketing, In Taşkıran, N. Ö., & Yılmaz, R. (Eds.), *Handbook of Research on Effective Advertising Strategies in the Social Media Age* (pp. 125-146). IGI Global. http://doi:10.4018/978-1-4666-8125- 5.ch007

Çeltek, E. (2017) QR code advertisements in tourism marketing, In Yılmaz, R. (Eds.), *Narrative Advertising Models and Conceptualization in the Digital Age* (pp. 269-289). IGI Global. http://doi:10.4018/978-1-5225-2373-4.ch015

Çeltek, E. (2019) Advantages of augmented reality, virtual reality, QR code, Near Field Communication, geo-tagging, geo-fencing, and geo-targeting for marketing tourism, In *Smart Marketing With the Internet of Things*, IGI Global, pp. 94-113.

Çeltek, E. (2020) Progress and development of virtual reality and augmented reality technologies in tourism: a review of publications from 2000 to 2018, In Çeltek, E. (Ed.), *Handbook of Research on Smart Technology Applications in the Tourism Industry* (pp. 1-23). IGI Global. http://doi:10.4018/978-1-7998-1989-9.

Chaouchi, H. (2013) *The Internet of Things: Connecting Objects to the Web*, Wiley.

Cheung, C.W., Tsang I.T. & Wong, K.H., (2017) Robot avatar: a virtual tourism robot for people with disabilities, *International Journal of Computer Theory and Engineering, Singapore*, 9(3), 229-234.

Clark, S. (2011) Museum of London adds NFC. Retrieved from https://www. nfcworld. com/2011/08/16/39129/museum-of-london-adds-nfc/

Clark, S. (2012) Sydney picks NFC and QR codes to guide visitors around The Rocks. Retrieved from https://www.nfcworld.com/2012/07/02/316609/ sydney-picks-nfc-and-qr- codes-to-guide-visitorsaround-the-rocks/

Clark, S. (2014) Rio gets 5,000 NFC tags. Retrieved from https://www.nfcworld. com/2014/06/20/329851/ rio-gets-5000-nfc-tags/

Coleman, J. (2011) QR codes: What are they and why should you care? *Kansas Library Association College and University Libraries Section Proceedings*, 1(1), 16–23. doi:10.4148/culs.v1i0.135

Crook, J. (2014) Starwood introduces robotic butlers at Aloft Hotel in Cupertino, Retrieved from https://techcrunch.com/2014/08/13/ starwood-introduces-robotic-butlers-at-aloft-hotel-in-palo-alto/

Davenport, T. H. (2013) *At the Big Data Crossroads: turning towards a smarter travel experience*, Amadeus.

Dinçer, A. (2020) Hollanda'nın Dev Havayolu KLM Blockchain Kullanmaya Başladı. Retrieved from https://kriptokoin.com/ hollandanin-dev-havayolu-klm-blockchain-kullanmaya-basladi/

Dragović, N., Stankov, U. & Vasiljević, Đ. (2018) Contactless technology as a factor of tourism industry development-a review of current practices and future directions, *Economic Themes*, 56(2), 179-202.

Drummond, M. (2016) 5 Great ways airlines are using internet of things. Retrieved from w3.accelya.com/blog/5-great-ways-airlines-are-using-the -internet-of-things.

Du, Y. (2020, March). The promotion of intangible cultural heritage tourism creative products' development through 3D printing technology. In 4th *International Conference on Culture, Education and Economic Development of Modern Society* (ICCESE 2020) (pp. 354- 357). Atlantis Press.

Elisabeth E., Nock R. & Célimène F. (2013) Demonstrator of a tourist recommendation system, In: Bhatnagar V., Srinivasa S. (eds) *Big Data Analytics*. (pp. 171- 175) BDA. Lecture Notes in Computer Science, vol 8302. Springer

EY. (2019) *Turizm Sektörü Dijitalleşme Yol Haritası*. Türkiye.

Feliu, C. (2019) Big data case study: 5 relevant examples from the airline industry, Retrieved from https://blog.datumize.com/5-relevant-examples-of-a-big-data -case-study-from-the-airline-industry

Fes, N. (2018) Blockchain in tourism: hope or hype, Retrieved from https:// www.tourism-review.com/blockchain-in-tourism-world-news10635

foodink.io (n.d)/ The World's First 3d-Printing Restaurant, http://foodink.io/

Gupta, S. (2019) Blockchain in Tourism, Retrieved from https://www.appfutura. com/blog/blockchain-in-tourism---explained/

Ham, M. (2018) Blockchain Altyapılı Dijital Kimlik Sistemi, Retrieved from medium.com/@finartz_com/blockchain-altyap%C4%B1l%C4%B1-dijital -kimlik-sistemi-2e21bc8556ad

Harangozó, O. (2020) Co-founders of Uber and Tinder are backing a '3D Printed' hotel start-up, Retrieved from 3dprintingindustry.com/news/co-founders-of- uber-and-tinder-are-backing-a-3d-printed-hotel-start-up-168408/

Hristova, Y. (2020) Face recognition for the hospitality industry, Retrieved from https://roombre.com/en/blog/hotel-technology/face-recognition-for-the- hospitalityindustry.html

Iansiti, M. & Lakhani, K. R. (2017) The truth about blockchain, *Harvard Business Review*, (January–February 2017) 118–127.

Ivanov, S. & Webster, C. (2017). Designing robot-friendly hospitality facilities, *Proceedings of the Scientific Conference "Tourism. Innovations. Strategies"*, 13-14 October 2017, Bourgas, Bulgaria, pp. 74-81.

Ivanov, S., Webster, C. & Berezin, K. (2017) Adoption of robots and service automation by tourism and hospitality companies, *Revista Turismo and Desenvolvimento*, 27/28, 1501– 1517.

Johnson, J. (2016) 3D printing is set to change the travel industry as we know it, Retrieved from www.cntravellerme.com/content/293-a-new-dimension

Jung, T.H. & tom Dieck, M.C. (2017), Augmented reality, virtual reality and 3D printing for the co-creation of value for the visitor experience at cultural heritage places, *Journal of Place Management and Development*, 10(2), 140-151. https://doi.org/10.1108/JPMD-07-2016-0045

Karabegovic, I. & Dolecek, V. (2017). The role of service robots and robotic systems in the treatment of patients in medical institutions. In M. Hadzikadic, & S. Avdakovic (Eds.), *Advanced Technologies, Systems, and Applications – Lecture Notes in Networks and Systems*. Switzerland: Springer International Publishing AG. doi:10.1007/978-3-319-47295- 9_2

Karampatsou, M. (2018) Big Data in Tourism, (Unpublished master's thesis). School Of Economics, Business Administration, & Legal Studies, Greece.

Kayıkçı, M. B. & Bozkurt, A. K. (2018) Dijital Çağda Z Ve Alpha Kuşağı, Yapay Zeka Uygulamaları Ve Turizme Yansımaları. *Sosyal Bilimler Metinleri*.

Keleş, A., Keleş, A. & Akçetin, E. (2017) Pazarlama Alaninda Yapay Zekâ Kullanim Potansiyeli Ve Akilli Karar Destek Sistemleri", *Electronic Turkish Studies*, 12(11), 109-124.

Klein, S., Avery, M., Adams, G., Pollard, S. & Simske, S. (2014), *From Scan to Print: 3D Printing as a Means for Replication*, HP Laboratories, pp. 2-6.

Kudyba, S. (2014) *Big Data, Mining and Analytics: Components of Strategic Decision Making. Publisher*, Taylor Francis. doi:10.1201/b166

## 40 Smart Cities and Tourism

Kumar, A., Liu, R. & Shan, Z. (2019) Is blockchain a silver bullet for supply chain management? technical challenges and research opportunities, *Decision Sciences* 51(1) pp.1–30. https://doi.org/10.1111/deci.12396

Lai, K. Y., Cheng, L. S., Yee, L. S., Leng, L. W., & Ling, T. P. (2015). WeeliciousCuisine Quick Response (QR), *International Conference on E-Commerce* (ICoEC).

Leppert, J. (2017). Comparing Carnival's ocean medallion versus MSC for me, Retrieved from https://www.travelpulse.com/news/cruise/comparing-carnival-socean-medallion-versus- msc-for-me.html.

Levine, D.E. (2000), Voice security: biometrics keeps information secure, *Audio Technologies*, 6(8), 60-3.

Love, D. (2014) The Cupertino Hotel across the street from Apple has a robot butler, Retrieved from www.businessinsider.com/aloft-hotels-botlr-robot-2014-8

Manyika, J., Chui, M., Brown, B., Bughin, J., Dobbs, R., Roxburgh, C. & Byers, A.H. (2011). *Big Data: The next frontier for innovation, competition, and productivity*, McKinsey Global Institute. MG

Marakos, P. (2015) Implementing QR code in museums and archaeological sites. In *International Workshop on Virtual Archaeology: Museums & Cultural Tourism*, Delphi, Greece.

Mccarthy, A. (2019) Humans get hired at the world's first robot hotel as the machines just can't keep up, Retrieved from https://www.lonelyplanet.com/news/2019/01/23/robot-hotel- japan-human-staff/.

Mills, J.E., Meyers, M. & Byun, S. (2010) Embracing broadscale applications of biometric technologies in hospitality and tourism: Is the business ready?, *Journal of Hospitality and Tourism Technology*, 1(3), 245-256. https://doi. org/10.1108/17579881011078377

Monino, J.-L. & Sedkaoui, S. (2016) *Big Data, Open Data, and Data Development*, Vol. 3. London, UK: ISTE, Ltd. Hoboken, NJ: John Wiley.

Nam, K., Dutt, C. S., Chathoth, P. & Khan, M. S. (2019). Blockchain technology for smart city and smart tourism: latest trends and challenges. *Asia Pacific Journal of Tourism Research*, 24(2) 1-15.

Nergiz, A. (2019). Etihad, Blockchain Konusunda Winding Tree Ile İşbirliği Yapıyor. Retrieved from https://www.havayolu101.com/2019/08/09/etihad-blockchain-konusunda- winding-tree-ile-isbirligi-yapiyor/

Oculus.com (2020) Experiences, Retrieved from https://www.oculus.com/experiences/quest/

Oğuzlar, A. (2011) *Temel Metin Madenciliği*, Bursa, Turkey: Dora.

Özcan, D. (2020) *Blokzincir Mimarisi ve Merkezi Olmayan Uygulamalar*, Pusula Yayıncılık

Pan, X. & Hamilton, A. F. D. C. (2018) Why and how to use virtual reality to study human socialinteraction: The challenges of exploring a new research landscape. *British Journal of Psychology*, 109(3), 1–23. doi:10.1111/bjop.12290 PMID:29313958

Pesonen, J. & Horster, E. (2012) Near field communication technology in tourism, *Tourism Management Perspectives*, 4, 11-18.

Pilkington, M. (2017) Can blockchain technology help promote new tourism destinations? the example of medical tourism in Moldova. *Social Science Research Network*. Available at SSRN: https://ssrn.com/abstract=2984479.

Pizam, A., Ozturk, A. B., Balderas-Cejudo, A., Buhalis, D., Fuchs, G., Hara, T., Meira, J., Revillae, M., Sethi, D., Sheng, Y., State, O., Hacikaraa, A. & Chaulagain, S., (2022), Factors affecting hotel managers' intentions to adopt robotic technologies: A global study. *International Journal of Hospitality Management*, 102, 103139. https://doi.org/10.1016/j.ijhm.2022.103139

Poilabs (2015) Beacon Teknolojisi,Turizm sektörünün gelecekteki pazarlama aracı mı olacak? Retrieved from https://blog.poilabs.com/tr/beacon-teknolo-jisi-turizm-sektorunun- gelecekteki-pazarlama-araci-mi-olacak/.

Rejeb, A. & Rejeb, K. (2019) Blockchain technology in tourism: applications and possibilities, *World Scientific News* 137 (2019) 119-144. Available at SSRN: https://ssrn.com/abstract=3480457

Revfine.com (2019) 8 Examples of robots being used in the hospitality industry, Retrieved from https://www.revfine.com/robots-hospitality-industry/

Revfine.com (2020) How can voice control benefit the travel industry? Retrieved from https://www.revfine.com/voice-control-travel-industry

Rouillard, J. (2008) Contextual QR Codes. In *Proceedings of the Third International Multi-Conference on Computing in the Global Information Technology* – ICCGI, 50-55, Conference Publishing Services of IEEE Computer Society, 51.

Ryu, K. H. & Lee, M. S. (2016) A study on smart tourism based on face recognition using smartphone, *International Journal of Internet, Broadcasting and Communication*, 8(4), 39-47.

Saulat, A. (2018) Four ways AI is re-imagining the future of travel. Retrieved from www. mindtree.com/blog/four-ways-ai-re-imagining-future-travel

Schönberger, V. M. & Cukier, K. (2013*). Büyük Veri - Yaşama, Çalışma ve Düşünme Şeklimizi Dönüştürecek Bir Devrim*, Çev. Banu Erol. İstanbul, Turkey: Paloma.

Skyscanner. (2017) The World's most hi-tech hotels. Retrieved from https://www.skyscanner.net/news/inspiration/the-worlds-most-hi-tech-hotels/.

Stylos, N., Zwiegelaar, J. & Buhalis, D. (2021), Big data empowered agility for dynamic, volatile, and time-sensitive service industries: the case of tourism sector, *International Journal of Contemporary Hospitality Management*, 33(3), 1015-1036. https://doi.org/10.1108/IJCHM-07-2020-0644

Tablang, K. (2015) Manila's Lewis Grand Hotel unveils the first 3D-printed hotel room, Retrieved from https://www.forbes.com/sites/kris-tintablang/2015/09/28/lewis-grand- hotel-unveils-first-3d-printed-hotel-room-philippines/#1c443da82872

tom Dieck, M. C. & Jung, T. H. (2017). Value of Augmented Reality at cultural heritage sites: A stakeholder approach, *Journal of Destination Marketing & Management*, 6(2), 110–117. doi:10.1016/j. jdmm.2017.03.002

Tripventure.soft112.com, (2018) Retrieved from https://tripventure. soft112.com,

Tung, V.W.S. & Law, R., (2017) The potential for tourism and hospitality experience research in human-robot interactions, *International Journal of Contemporary Hospitality Management*, (29),10, 2498-2513.

Tussyadiah, I. P., Wang, D., Jung, T. H. & tom Dieck, M. C. (2018) Virtual reality, presence, and attitude change: Empirical evidence from tourism, *Tourism Management*, 66, 140-154. doi:10.1016/j. tourman.2017.12.003

Willie, P. (2019) Can all sectors of the hospitality and tourism industry be influenced by the innovation of Blockchain technology. *Worldwide Hospitality and Tourism Themes*, 11, 112- 120.

World Travel and Tourism Council (2018a) Four Ways Biometrics Are Making Travel Smarter. Retrieved from https://medium.com/@WTTC/four-ways-biometrics-are-making- travel-smarter-47ea99333b f4

World Travel and Tourism Council (2018b) How can new technologies help deal with overcrowding? Retrieved from https://medium.com/@WTTC/ how-can-new-technologies- help-deal-with-overcrowding-dda554fb164b

Xu, F., Nash, N. & Whitmarsh, L. (2020) Big data or small data? A methodological review of sustainable tourism. *Journal of Sustainable Tourism*, 28(2) 144-163.

Yalçınkaya, P., Atay,. T. A. Y. & Karakaş, E. (2018) Akıllı Turizm Uygulamaları. *Gastroia: Journal of Gastronomy And Travel Research*, 2(2), 85-103.

Yamaguchi, A., Hashimoto, M., Urata, K., Tanigawa, Y., Nagaie, T., Maki, T. & Sonehara, N. (2017). Beacon-based tourist information system to identify visiting trends of tourists, *Journal of Robotics, Networking and Artificial Life*, 4(3), 209-212.

Yazici, M., Kamga, C. & Singhal, A. (2013). A big data driven model for taxi drivers' airport pick-up decisions in New York City. In IEEE International Conference on Big Data, pp. 37–44. IEEE. 10.1109/ BigData.2013.6691775

# 3 From Smart City 1.0 to Smart City 3.0:
## Deep understanding of the smart cities concept and evolution

*Diogo Correia and Leonor Teixeira*

## Introduction

The mobilization of people led cities to rapid growth within a short period. This paradigm brought several issues, since many cities were not prepared to face the rapid population growth and the worldwide migration to urban areas. Streets have not grown because of this quick urbanization; green parks have not extended, and city boundaries were kept in the same place. Therefore, cities have a considerable challenge in accommodating the growth experienced. Technology and consequently Smart Cities emerged to answer such challenges. In the 1960s emerged the "informational or cybernetically planned cities". In the 1980s, technologies were sought to promote "computable or networked cities" (Gabrys, 2014). In the 1990s, the Smart City concept was associated with information and communication technologies (ICTs) for the first time, expecting them to be in the center of urban management (Aurigi, 2006; Bastelaer, 1998; Gibson et al., 1992; Graham & Aurigi, 1997; Tan, 1999).

Until 2010, the number of Smart City studies reported in the literature was scarce. Only after the emergence of the Smart City projects supported by the European Commission, was the proliferation of writings and academic publications on the topic noted (Jucevičius et al., 2014). From then onwards, the Smart City expression started to be widely adopted. Figure 3.1 portrays the search results of "Smart City" or "Smart Cities" expressions from Scopus.

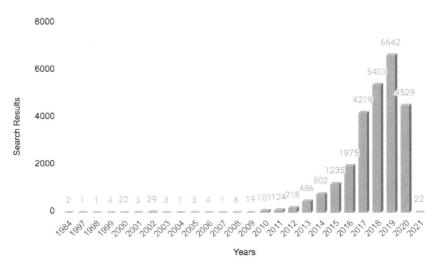

**Figure 3.1:** - Scopus Search Results for "Smart City" or "Smart Cities"

It is apparent in the literature that the smart city concept has been evolving. It is no longer in the first stage where technology companies led research and cities' transformation. Moreover, the focus changed from technology diffusion to meet corporate and economic interests, to break silos and focus on people, governance, and policies (Robert et al., 2017). Simultaneously, citizens passed from a passive role to urban development and planning co-creators (Mainka et al., 2016). Based on a narrative literature review, this paper details the evolution of the concept, highlights the associated comprehensions and terms, and proposes a common understanding of the Smart City concept.

## Theoretical background: Smart City concept evolution

In the beginnings of the Smart City conceptualisation, the term was associated with a futuristic city, where technology would be predominant. It is a fact that technology is ever more present in our daily lives. However, what seemed to be a movement to implement technology without any plan quickly has shifted to a problem-solving ideology. Table 3.1 states and resumes the evolution of the Smart City concept from Smart City 1.0 to the Smart City 3.0.

The first Smart City stage – Smart City 1.0 – was seen as the possibility of providing citizens with information and services via the integration of Information and Communication Technologies (ICT) into the city's infrastructure. It was provided a techno-centric interpretation of cities, where ICTs were the goal and not the means (Ahvenniemi et al., 2017).

| Concept | Sources |
|---|---|
| **Smart City 1.0** | |
| A city that uses ICTs to collect data to improve its critical infrastructures and services' efficiency. | (Hall et al. 2000; Harrison et al. 2010) |
| **Smart City 2.0** | |
| A city that starts with the human capital, motivating citizens to create and flourish their lives, using ICT to increase the quality of life and the city's social, economic, and environmental sustainability. | (Ahvenniemi et al. 2017; Angelidou 2014; Barrionuevo, Berrone, and Ricart Costa 2012; Caragliu, del Bo, and Nijkamp 2009; Chen 2010; Hollands 2008; Mohanty, Choppali, and Kougianos 2016; Neirotti et al. 2014; Rios 2008) |
| **Smart City 3.0** | |
| A city that uses ICT to promote citizen engagement and active participation, allowing continuous interactions, where the strategy is collaboratively created with them and relevant stakeholders. | (Albino, Berardi, and Dangelico 2015; Van der Graaf and Veeckman 2014; Trivellato 2017) |

**Table 3.1:** The three Smart City stages

Cities realized that the vision led by technology companies lacked the context. Municipalities' budgets served to test, and develop solutions in laboratories and closed rooms, without relating these to citizens' real needs. The lack of policymakers' knowledge to realize cities as open and interoperable systems and the political wish for quick news led them to become dependent on proprietary technological solutions. Over time it created a dependency on private companies, not allowing cities to integrate other stakeholders and systems into their strategy and infrastructure. After Hollands (2008) criticized cities for not taking into account the people, the concept started to strive for human and social capital (Caragliu et al., 2009). Smart City's understanding was inflicted because of the world's financial crisis and popular acknowledgment of the global warming effects. From these extreme events, emerged concerns regarding sustainability and citizens' quality of life. United Nations' Sustainable Development Goals, and the Green Deal, brought cities a decarbonization mindset, adopting green and sharing-based policies focused on citizens' quality of life (European Commission, 2019; UN, 2018).

The transition period from the Smart City 1.0 to the Smart City 2.0 between 2008 and 2012 was notorious. The focus shift from "What" to "Why", from technology to its purpose, from only hardware and software development to answering people's needs. Thus, it evolved to an understanding of a Smart City as a city that crossed traditional infrastructure with ICTs to collect real-time data and optimize services by integrating and analyzing information.

ICTs turned to be seen as a means and not an end in themselves (Nam & Pardo, 2011). Due to the emergence of social networks and the constant criticism that policymakers have faced since 2010, they started to perceive the need to design thinking and participatory development methodologies. The emergence of the smartphone and associated technologies provided citizens with the chance to be more active, use word of mouth to report issues, problems and occurrences in real-time. Being more informed about the decision-making processes increased the scrutiny of the decisions taken by policymaking. Therefore, municipalities began to involve citizens from the design phase.

The Smart City 3.0 developed collaborative cities in a co-creation perspective (Cohen, 2015). Smart City initiatives are no longer just *for* the citizen but created *with* the citizen. This led to adding a new dimension, "co-creation", to the previous ones: technology, people, and sustainability. After 2014, the citizens' role moved to active contributors of the city's strategy, empowering them to be part of the co-creation process at the different stages and enhancing the participatory engagement (Correia & Feio, 2020). Co-creation was first seen as a way for citizens to collaborate with cities to solve specific urban environment issues (Choque et al., 2019). This finally moved to a participatory approach involving citizens and other stakeholders in design thinking.

## Conceptualising Smart Cities evolution

Smart City is an ambiguous concept. Many researchers have discussed its understanding and proposing several definitions (Batty et al., 2012; Bibri & Krogstie 2017; Hollands 2008; Nam &Pardo 2011; Venkat Reddy et al., 2017) Narrative literature research was conducted to find and study the variations of the Smart City concept. Two phases were considered. The first aimed to collect as many variations of the concept as possible. In the second phase, each variation was analyzed to understand its specific meaning and relation to the Smart City concept. The review of definitions was evaluated via Scopus using the combinations of the keywords "smart", "cit*", "concept", and "definition". From this search, about 4000 papers were obtained. From these, 600 abstracts were read and, 250 of those deserved a more in-depth analysis. Through forward and backward citation tracking and analysis, other related variations of the concept were possible. Every term was taken into consideration. The comprehension of each variation was translated in a sentence and was subjected to a thematic analysis to associate with the respective Smart City stage and focus. The ones which could be identified as having a specific meaning associated with the topic were included in Table 3.2. The others, where the definition was not evident, deserved a brief

## Variations of the concept across the three stages

While in the first Smart City stage, the focus was on technology, the second was on people and sustainability. In the third stage, the focus is on co-creation and co-design. Table 3.2 summarizes and aggregates the variations of the literature organized through the three stages.

Table 3.2 corroborates Smart City's initial focus. The embeddedness of technologies and devices into the urban space enabled anyone to access and exchange information at any place and time. Over the years, 2D and 3D digital and cyber tools were made available for policymakers' visualization and simulation. The technical improvements were accompanied by social concerns reflected in the "Creative City", "Humane City", "Knowledge City" and "Learning City" understandings, which pushed for the involvement of the community. The emerging variations of the Smart City concept also helped to understand its proper evolution. The efficiency of services and infrastructures, reducing resource demand to promote city's sustainability, and combat climate change is central to the variations that constitute the "Sustainability" phase. Increasingly, citizens have been empowered by cities' willingness to build cities for them, whose inclusion and participation became highly relevant to the Smart City strategy's success.

Through Smart City 2.0 and Smart City 3.0, the presence of the technology is scarce and used only as a mechanism. The learnings can also explain that from initial mistakes. It is possible to identify the ghost cities' phenomenon in the literature to explain that technology implementation to improve quality of life and sustainability is insufficient. Citizens need to feel part of the process and identify themselves with their surrounding environment and urban development (Calzada & Cobo, 2015). Thus, participatory methodologies are evolving and being applied to urban planning strategies. Following the clarification of each concept's meaning through qualitative analysis, there is a lack of understanding of each one's literature presence. Subsequently, a quantitative analysis was followed. Each term was searched separately (e.g., "Ubiquitous Cit*"). Within the results obtained, were searched the combination with the Smart City concept (e.g., "Ubiquitous Cit*" AND "Smart Cit*"). The results are shown in Figure 3.2.

**Table 3.2:** Smart city concept variations

| | | Variation | Focus | Sources |
|---|---|---|---|---|
| Smart City 1.0 | Technology | Cyber City | 3D virtual model space using ICT as preconditions of practical action and city control | (Komninos 2011) |
| | | Digital City | Municipal ICT infrastructure that connects the community and enables access to public services | (Yovanof and Hazapis 2009) |
| | | E-city or Electronic City | Presenting different civic services 24/7 using ICT | (Tohidi and Jabbari 2011 |
| | | Hybrid City | The intersection of the virtual with the physical reality | (Streitz 2019) |
| | | Information City | Process and distribution of information through web portals | (Anthopoulos and Fitsilis 2010) |
| | | Innovative City | Focus on innovation | (Scheel and Rivera 2013) |
| | | Intelligent City | ICTs and people together to enhance the innovation, learning, knowledge, and problem solving | (Komninos 2009, 2011) |
| | | Mobile City | Mobile devices and applications for the provision of services and access to information | (Walravens 2012) |
| | | Networked City | Technological design and morphology of cities integrated and ordered by infrastructure networks | (Monstadt and Schramm 2017) |
| | | Real-time City | Real-time actions supported by control centers | (Kitchin 2014) |
| | | Sensing City | Data collection to provide a portrait of the city's details | (Zhu et al. 2017) |
| | | Sentient City | Cities able to produce some level of transference through correlation and measurement | (Shepard 2011) |
| | | Ubiquitous City | Devices interconnected, enabling anyone in any place with any device at any time do anything desired | (Anthopoulos and Fitsilis 2010) |
| | | Virtual City | A user interface to the services through a real 3D model of the city | (Linturi, Koivunen, and Sulkanen 2000) |
| | | Wired City | Use of computer and communications (C&C) technology for the provision of services | (Targowski 1990) |
| | | Wireless city | Wireless infrastructure technologies making Internet access available | (Ganapati and Schoepp 2008) |

| | | | | |
|---|---|---|---|---|
| | People | Creative City | Find innovative and creative solutions with the local community | (Ponzini and Rossi 2010) |
| | | Humane City | Sociable, cooperative, and human-centered city | (Streitz 2011) |
| | | Knowledge City | The encouragement of the nurturing of knowledge and investing in education, training, and research | (Yigitcanlar, O'Connor, and Westerman 2008) |
| | | Learning City | Involvement of stakeholders and the encouragement of citizen participation placing innovation and learning | (Longworth 2006) |
| Smart City 2.0 | Sustainability | Compact City | Growth is balanced with social inclusion and careful use of natural resources | (Artmann et al. 2019) |
| | | Eco-city | Ecological preservation - next generation of infrastructures and environmentally friendly buildings | (Kenworthy 2006) |
| | | Green City | Zero-emission and zero-waste urban design | (Lehmann 2010) |
| | | Liveable City | Citizens enjoy a high quality of life and improved standards of living | (Mase 2012) |
| | | Low carbon City | Minimization of the human-inflicted carbon footprint | (Sahni and Aulakh 2014) |
| | | Resilient City | Capacity to absorb, learn and adapt | (Desouza and Flanery 2013) |
| | | Smart Sustainable City | Supported by ICT, meeting the needs of citizens without compromising the needs of future generations | (ITU 2015) |
| | | Sustainable City | Long term improvement of environment, social equity & well-being | (Hiremath et al. 2013) |
| | | Zero Carbon City | CO2 and greenhouse gases zero emission | (Kennedy and Sgouridis 2011) |
| Smart City 3.0 | Co-creation & Co-design | Inclusive City | Social capital of urban development, promoting inclusion in public services or involving citizens into co-designing | (Paskaleva 2011) |
| | | Happy City | Citizen's happiness, engagement in planning and decision-making | (Costa, Machado, and Gonçalves 2019) |
| | | Open City | City's data available for all the stakeholders and its involvement in the designing process | (Degbelo et al. 2016) |
| | | Smart Community | Uses technology to solve social and business needs to reinvent cities for the development of economy and society | (Mase 2012) |

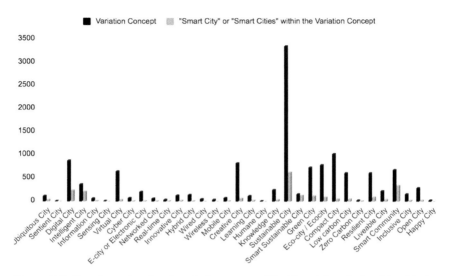

**Figure 3.2:** *Search results of each variation concept (Black) and the relationship with the "Smart City" concept (Grey)*

The detailed search results on Scopus are represented in Table 3.3, divided into three groups: from 0 to 50 scientific articles, from 51 to 500 articles, and more than 500 articles. From the analysis of Table 3.3, it is noticeable that "Sustainable City", with 623 results, is the term with the most significant number of published papers searching with the "Smart City". However, to have a rigorous perspective on this subject, it is necessary to get the results in relative terms.

After detailing the search results, it was possible to make a comparison between searches. It allows the understanding of the most related Smart City variations by analyzing the relationship between the number of results obtained by the Variation Concept and its combination with the term "Smart Cit*". This can be calculated by the following formula:

$$\text{Relationship (\%)} = \frac{\text{"Smart Cit*" AND "[Variation Concept]" Search Results}}{\text{"[Variation Concept]" Search Results}} \times 100$$

| "[Variation Concept]" | "Smart Cit*" AND "[Variation Concept]" |
|---|---|
| **0 - 50** | |
| Sentient City (12), Sensing City (15), Real-time City (40), Wired City (50), Wireless City (45), Humane City (14), Zero Carbon City (24), Happy City (27) | Ubiquitous City (44), Sentient City (5), Information City (18), Sensing City (5), Virtual City (40), Cyber City (11), E-city/Electronic City (14), Networked City (11), Real-time City (15), Innovative City (25), Hybrid City (19), Wired City (4), Wireless City (7), Mobile City (9), Learning City (25), Humane City (6), Knowledge City (37), Zero Carbon City (9), Liveable City (39), Inclusive City (32), Open City (29), Happy City (5) |
| **51 - 500** | |
| Ubiquitous City (122), Intelligent City (377), Information City (68), Cyber City (75), E-city/Electronic City (216), Networked City (65), Innovative City (134), Hybrid City (144), Mobile City (79), Learning City (118), Knowledge City (255), Smart Sustainable City (162), Liveable City (226), Inclusive City (166), Open City (299) | Digital City (245), Intelligent City (214), Creative City (63), Smart Sustainable City (137), Green City (120), Eco-city/Ecocity (88), Compact City (53), Low Carbon City (52), Resilient City (94), Smart Community (354) |
| **+ 500** | |
| Digital City (876), Virtual City (655), Creative City (825), Sustainable City (3343), Green City (737), Eco-city/Ecocity (794), Compact City (1029), Low Carbon City (620), Resilient City (621), Smart Community (681) | Sustainable City (623) |

**Table 3.3:** Detailed search results on Scopus

The comparison results of each term given by the previous equation are represented in Figure 3.3. The respective percentage demonstrates the relationship degree between the Variation Concept results and Smart Cities. From Figure 3, it is possible to note that the "Smart Sustainable City" term is the most related to the "Smart City", followed by the "Intelligent City" and the "Smart Community", both above 50 per cent. However, this can be explained by the fact that these are recent terms. Therefore, it was necessary to study when they emerged in the literature and when they were associated with the Smart City term. This would allow understanding if it were already impacted by Smart Cities when the term emerged.

52    Smart Cities and Tourism

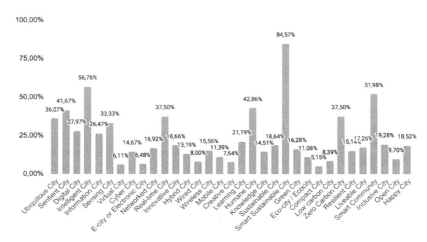

**Figure 3.3:** Relationship between the Search Results of the Raw Term and within Smart Cit*

Figure 3.4 demonstrates that the "Smart Sustainable City" concept emerged not just after the "Smart City" but was the only one impacted from the beginning. Considering that Smart Cities emerged in the 1990s, Figure 3.4 shows that most of the various concepts that emerged after that era were impacted shortly after. It also shows that the terms "Digital Cities", "Intelligent Cities", Information Cities", "Virtual Cities" and "Cyber Cities" were the first to be impacted in 2000. Despite their older existence, all concepts after 2010 were associated with Smart Cities. This can be explained by what Figure 3.1 previously showed about the growth of Smart Cities noticed after 2010.

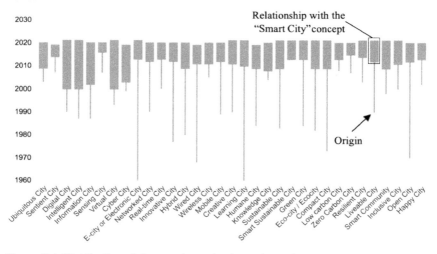

**Figure 3.4:** Distribution of the search results throughout the years

The literature also mentions other variations in which the meaning is not exact and lacks academic recognition. These are Ambient Cities (Andrejevic 2005), Cities as Internet–of–everything (Kyriazis et al., 2013), Business City (Cathelat, 2019), Multimedia City (Boll & Utz, 2003), Flexi City, Cyberville (Mohanty et al., 2016), MESH City, Teletopia (Venkat Reddy et al., 2017), Talented City (Karaköse & Yetiş, 2017), Telicity (Silva et al., 2018), Greentopia, New Media Community (Cheung, 1991), Technocities (Downey & McGuigan, 1999), Cooperative City, Self-aware City, Transient City (Streitz, 2019), Slim City, Transition Town, Resilient City, Negative Carbon City (Bibri & Krogstie, 2017), Broadband City/Broadband Metropolis associated to the implementation of broadband technology

## The future of Smart Cities

The Smart City concept has evolved. In the literature can be noted three stages with different focused dimensions: technology, people and sustainability, and co-creation and co-design. This paper studied more than 30 existing variations of the Smart City concept within the literature and their relationship with the Smart City term. From an analysis of the obtained search results on Scopus, it was noticeable that Sustainable Cities were the most present term in the literature in absolute terms. However, when combined with Smart Cities, the most related concept was Smart Sustainable Cities followed by Intelligent Cities and Smart Community. The year when the concepts emerged and the time they were associated with Smart Cities was also analyzed.

The evolution of the concept led Smart Cities to be rooted in three axes: Sustainability, Innovation, and Quality of Life (Correia et al., 2020). The two significant Smart City future developments are the: 1) development of technologies and interoperability between systems, and 2) participatory development methodologies for the engagement of citizens and stakeholders. Cities are increasingly adopting an open data ideology to enable third parties to develop new applications, emerging new inter-organizational partnerships built around developing and implementing data-driven governance projects (Shelton et al., 2015). Cities realize the potential of integration and interoperability of solutions. However, strategic planning remains a rather abstract idea (Angelidou, 2014). Without planning, cities cannot define infrastructure layers and combat the lack of integration and standardization among sectors. Cities should promote standards to facilitate third parties' integration and application development.

The need for a frame of reference is evident. A collaborative dimension of governance in co-design, co-creation, and co-production has to be considered for more significant crossover information (involving stakeholders) and faster processes (Anttiroiko et al., 2014). The emergence of participatory technological-based methodologies will fill the gap between decision-makers and citizens, and the rest of the stakeholders. Big data analytics and artificial intelligence will enhance accurate real-time decision-making based on the embeddedness of technology in urban furniture (Stylos et al., 2021; Buhalis & Sinarta, 2019). This will allow the prediction and monitoring of city events and improve planning. 5G, IoT, vehicular communications, cloud, and edge computing will enhance solutions' responsiveness and allow connectivity among cities' infrastructures and devices. Data privacy issues and ethics will emerge and the need for blockchain and smart contracts technologies. Technological advancements of Industry 4.0, shared by Smart Cities, will walk side-by-side with social and ethical constraints, and the improvement of citizen's quality of life concerns.

Despite the different understandings and variations, it is vital to promote a standard Smart City concept to guide cities throughout the implementation, following up, and regulation. Therefore, based on the performed study, Smart Cities are cities supported by ICT, co-designed with citizens, to promote social, environmental, and economic sustainability and improve citizens' quality of life. Following the concept's clarification, it is necessary to study the crucial metrics and Key Performance Indicators (KPI) to assess Smart Cities and perform continuous measurements. There are also missing gaps in Smart Cities' strategic planning and participatory methodologies. Therefore, a standard framework must also be developed to guide cities during the Smart City planning and implementation process.

# References

Ahvenniemi, H., Huovila, A., Pinto-Seppä, I. & Airaksinen, M. (2017). What are the differences between sustainable and smart cities? *Cities* 60, 234–45. http://dx.doi.org/10.1016/j.cities.2016.09.009.

Albino, V., Berardi, U. & Dangelico, R.M. (2015). Smart Cities: Definitions, Dimensions, Performance, and Initiatives. *Journal of Urban Technology* 22(1), 3–21. http://dx.doi.org/10.1080/10630732.2014.942092.

Andrejevic, M. (2005). Nothing comes between me and my CPU: Smart clothes and 'ubiquitous' computing. *Theory, Culture & Society* 22(3), 101–19.

Angelidou, M. (2014). "Smart City policies: A spatial approach. *Cities* 41, S3–11. http://dx.doi.org/10.1016/j.cities.2014.06.007.

Anthopoulos, L. & Fitsilis, P. (2010). From digital to ubiquitous cities: Defining a common architecture for urban development. *Proceedings - 2010 6th International Conference on Intelligent Environments, IE 2010*: 301–6.

Anttiroiko, A.V., Valkama, P. & Bailey, S.J. (2014). Smart cities in the new service economy: building platforms for smart services" *AI and Society* 29(3), 323–34.

Artmann, M., Kohler, M., Meinel, G., Gan, J. & Ioja, I-C. (2019). How smart growth and green infrastructure can mutually support each other — a conceptual framework for compact and green cities. *Ecological Indicators* 96(June), 10–22. http://dx.doi.org/10.1016/j.ecolind.2017.07.001.

Aurigi, A. (2006). New technologies, same dilemmas: Policy and design issues for the augmented city. *Journal of Urban Technology* 13(3), 5–28.

Barrionuevo, J.M, Berrone, P. & Ricart Costa, J. (2012). Smart cities, sustainable progress: opportunities for urban development. *IESE Insight* (14), 50–57. https://www.ieseinsight.com/docImpresion.aspx?id=1392.

Batty, M. Axhausen, K.W., Giannotti, F., Pozdnoukhov, A., Bazzani, A., Wachowicz, M., Ouzounis, G. & Portugali, Y. (2012). Smart cities of the future. *European Physical Journal: Special Topics* 214(1), 481–518.

Bibri, S.E. & Krogstie, J. (2017). Smart sustainable cities of the future: An extensive interdisciplinary literature review. *Sustainable Cities and Society* 31, 183–212. http://dx.doi.org/10.1016/j.scs.2017.02.016.

Boll, S. & Utz, W. (2003). MediÆther — an event space for context-aware multimedia experiences categories and subject descriptors. ETP '03, 21–30.

Buhalis, D. & Sinarta, Y., (2019), Real-time co-creation and nowness service: lessons from tourism and hospitality, *Journal of Travel & Tourism Marketing*, 36(5), 563-582. https://doi.org/10.1080/10548408.2019.1592059

Calzada, I. & Cobo, C. (2015). Unplugging: Deconstructing the smart city. *Journal of Urban Technology* 22(1), 23–43. http://dx.doi.org/10.1080/10630732.2 014.971535.

Caragliu, A., del Bo, C. & Nijkamp, P. (2009). Smart cities in Europe. *Journal of Urban Technology* 18(2), 65–82.

Cathelat, B. (2019). Smart cities: Shaping the society of 2030. https://unesdoc. unesco.org/ark:/48223/pf0000367762.

Chen, T. (2010). Smart grids, smart cities need better networks." *IEEE Network* 24(2), 2–3.

Cheung, C.W. (1991). Regional innovation strategies and information society: A review of government initiatives in Japan. *Asian Geographer* 10(1), 39–61.

Choque, J., Diez, L., Medela, A. & Muñoz, L. (2019). Experimentation management in the co-created smart-city: Incentivization and citizen engagement. *Sensors (Switzerland)* 19(2): 1–17.

Cohen, B. (2015). The 3 generations of smart cities. https://www.fastcompany. com/3047795/the-3-generations-of-smart-cities.

Correia, D. & Feio, J. (2020). The smart city as a social policy actor. In *International Conferences ICT, Society, and Human Beings.*

Correia, D., Teixeira, L. & Marques, J. (2020). Triangular pyramid trunk: the three axes of the smart city assessment tool. *WIT Transactions on Ecology and the Environment* 241: 79–90.

Costa, R., Machado, R. & Gonçalves, S. (2019). 806 Ambient Intelligence – Software and Applications, 9th International Symposium on Ambient Intelligence *Guimarães: Innovative and Engaged City*. Springer International Publishing. http://link.springer.com/10.1007/978-3-030-01746-0.

Degbelo, A., Granell, C. Trilles, S., Bhattacharya, D., Casteleyn, S. & Kray, C. (2016). Opening up smart cities: citizen-centric challenges and opportunities from GIScience. *ISPRS International Journal of Geo-Information* 5(2).

Desouza, K.C., & Flanery, T.H. (2013). Designing, planning, and managing resilient cities: a conceptual framework. *Cities* 35, 89–99. http://dx.doi.org/10.1016/j.cities.2013.06.003.

Downey, J. & McGuigan, J. (1999). *Technocities*. SAGE Publications Ltd.

European Commission. (2019). *The European Green Deal*.

Gabrys, J. (2014). Programming environments: Environmentality and citizen sensing in the smart city. *Environment and Planning D: Society and Space* 32(1), 30–48.

Ganapati, S. & Schoepp, C.F. (2008). The wireless city. *International Journal of Electronic Government Research* 4(4), 54–68.

Gibson, D. V., Kozmetsky, G. & Smilor, R. W. (1992). *The Technopolis Phenomenon: Smart Cities, Fast Systems, Global Networks,* Roman & Littlefield.

Graham, S. & Alessandro, A. (1997). Urbanising Cyberspace? *City* 2(7), 18–39.

Hall, R.E. & Bowerman, B., Braverman, J., Taylor, J., Todosow, H. & Wimmersperg, U. (2000). "The Vision of a Smart City." *2nd International Life Extension Technology Workshop, Paris, France* https://www.researchgate.net/publication/241977644_The_vision_of_a_smart_city.

Harrison, C., Eckman, B., Hamilton, R., Hartswick, P., Kalagnanam, J., Paraszczak, J. & Williams, P. (2010). Foundations for smarter cities. *IBM Journal of Research and Development* 54(4).

Hiremath, R.B. , Balachandra, P., Kumar, B., Bansode, S.S. & Murali, J. (2013). Indicator-based urban sustainability - a review. *Energy for Sustainable Development* 17(6), 555–63. http://dx.doi.org/10.1016/j.esd.2013.08.004.

Hollands, R.G. (2008). "Will the real smart city please stand up? Intelligent, progressive or entrepreneurial?" *City* 12(3), 303–20.

ITU. (2015). Agreed Definition of a Smart Sustainable City, *Focus Group on Smart Sustainable Cities, SSC–0146 Version Geneva*, 5–6 May. https://www.itu.int/en/ITU-T/focusgroups/ssc/Pages/default.aspx.

Jucevičius, R., Patašienė, I. & Patašius, M. (2014). Digital dimension of smart city: Critical analysis. *Procedia - Social and Behavioral Sciences* 156, 146–50.

Karaköse, M. & Yetiş, H. (2017). A cyberphysical system based mass-customization approach with integration of Industry 4.0 and Smart City, In D.B

Rawat (ed.). *Wireless Communications and Mobile Computing*. https://doi. org/10.1155/2017/1058081.

Kennedy, S. & Sgouridis, S. (2011). Rigorous classification and carbon accounting principles for low and zero carbon cities. *Energy Policy* 39(9), 5259–68. http://dx.doi.org/10.1016/j.enpol.2011.05.038.

Kenworthy, J.R. (2006). The Eco-City: Ten key transport and planning dimensions for sustainable city development. *Environment and Urbanization* 18(1), 67–85.

Kitchin, R. (2014). The real-time city? Big data and smart urbanism. *GeoJournal* 79(1), 1–14.

Komninos, N. (2009). Intelligent cities: towards interactive and global innovation environments, *International Journal of Innovation and Regional Development* 1(4).

Komninos, N. (2011). Intelligent cities: variable geometries of spatial intelligence. *Intelligent Buildings International* 3(3), 172–88.

Kyriazis, D., Varvarigou, T., White, D., Rossi, A., & Cooper, J. (2013) Sustainable smart city IoT applications: heat and electricity management & eco-conscious cruise control for public transportation. In: 14*th IEEE international symposium and workshops on a world of wireless, mobile and multimedia networks*. IEEE, pp 1-5.

Lehmann, S. (2010). Green urbanism: formulating a series of holistic principles. *Sapiens* 3(2).

Linturi, R., Koivunen, M.R. & Sulkanen,J. (2000). Helsinki Arena 2000 - Augmenting a real city to a virtual one. *Lecture Notes in Computer Science* 1765 LNCS, 83–96.

Longworth, N. (2006). *Learning Cities, Learning Regions, Learning Communities: Lifelong Learning and Local Government*, Routledge.

Mainka, A., Castelnovo, W., Miettinen, V., Bech-Petersen, S., Hartmann, S. & Wolfgang, S. (2016). Open innovation in smart cities: civic participation and co-creation of public services. *Proceedings of the Association for Information Science and Technology* 53(1), 1–5. doi: 10.1002/pra2.2016.14505301006.

Mase, K. (2012). Information and communication technology and electric vehicles - paving the way towards a smart community. *IEICE Transactions on Communications* E95-B(6), 1902–10.

Mohanty, S. P., Choppali, U. & Kougianos, E. (2016). Everything you wanted to know about smart cities. *IEEE Consumer Electronics Magazine* 5(3), 60–70.

Monstadt, J. & Schramm, S. (2017). Toward the networked city? translating technological ideals and planning models in water and sanitation systems in Dar Es Salaam. *International Journal of Urban and Regional Research* 41(1), 104–25.

Nam, T. & Pardo, T.A. (2011). Conceptualizing Smart city with dimensions of technology, people, and institutions. In *ACM International Conference Proceeding Series*, 282–91.

## 58   Smart Cities and Tourism

Neirotti, P., Marco, A., Cagliano, A.C.,  Mangano, G. & Scorrano, F. (2014). Current trends in Smart City initiatives: Some stylised facts. *Cities* 38, 25–36. https://doi.org/10.1016/j.cities.2013.12.010.

Paskaleva, K.A. (2011). The Smart City: A nexus for open innovation? *Intelligent Buildings International* 3(3), 153–71.

Ponzini, D. & Rossi, U. (2010). Becoming a creative city: the entrepreneurial mayor, network politics and the promise of an urban renaissance. *Urban Studies* 47(5), 1037–57.

Rios, P. (2008). *Creating the Smart City*, University of Detroit Mercy.

Robert, J., Kubler, S., Kolbe, N., Cerioni, A., Gastaud, E. & Främling, K. (2017). Open IoT ecosystem for enhanced interoperability in smart cities - example of Métropole de Lyon. *Sensors (Switzerland)* 17(12): 1–21.

Sahni, S. & Aulakh, R.S. (2014). Planning for low carbon cities in India. *Environment and Urbanization ASIA* 5(1), 17–34.

Scheel, C. & Rivera,A. (2013). Innovative cities: In search of their disruptive characteristics. *International Journal of Knowledge-Based Development* 4(1), 79–101.

Shelton, T., Zook, M. & Wiig, A. (2015). The 'actually existing smart city.' *Cambridge Journal of Regions, Economy and Society* 8(1), 13–25.

Shepard, M. (2011). *Sentient City: Ubiquitous Computing, Architecture, and the Future of Urban Space*. The MIT Press.

Silva, B.N., Khan, M. & Han, K. (2018). Towards sustainable smart cities: a review of trends, architectures, components, and open challenges in smart cities. *Sustainable Cities and Society* 38, 697–713. https://doi.org/10.1016/j.scs.2018.01.053.

Streitz, N. (2019). Beyond 'smart-only' cities: redefining the 'smart-everything' paradigm. *Journal of Ambient Intelligence and Humanized Computing* 10(2), 791–812. http://dx.doi.org/10.1007/s12652-018-0824-1.

Streitz, N. (2011). Smart cities, ambient intelligence and universal access. *Lecture Notes in Computer Science* 6767 LNCS(PART 3), 425–32.

Stylos, N., Zwiegelaar, J. & Buhalis, D. (2021), Big data empowered agility for dynamic, volatile, and time-sensitive service industries: the case of tourism sector, *International Journal of Contemporary Hospitality Management*, 33(3), 1015-1036. https://doi.org/10.1108/IJCHM-07-2020-0644

Tan, M. (1999). Creating the digital economy: strategies and perspectives from singapore. *International Journal of Electronic Commerce* 3(3), 105–22.

Targowski, A.S. (1990). Strategies and architecture of the electronic global village. *Information Society* 7(3), 187–202.

Tohidi, H. & Jabbari, M.M. (2011). The main requirements to implement an electronic city. *Procedia Computer Science* 3: 1106–10. http://dx.doi.org/10.1016/j.procs.2010.12.180.

Trivellato, B. (2017). How can 'smart' also be socially sustainable? insights from the case of Milan. *European Urban and Regional Studies* 24(4): 337–51.

UN. (2018). Sustainable Development Goals. https://www.un.org/sustainabledevelopment/sustainable-development-goals.

van Bastelaer, B. (1998). Digital cities and transferability of results." *Proceedings of the 4th EDC Conference on Digital Cities* (October), 61–70.

Van der Graaf, S. & Veeckman, C. (2014). Designing for participatory governance: assessing capabilities and toolkits in public service delivery. *Info* 16(6), 74–88.

Venkat Reddy, P., Siva Krishna, A. & Ravi Kumar,T. (2017). Study on concept of smart city and its structural components. *International Journal of Civil Engineering and Technology* 8(8), 101–12.

Walravens, N. (2012). Mobile business and the smart city: developing a business model framework to include public design parameters for mobile city services. *Journal of Theoretical and Applied Electronic Commerce Research* 7(3), 121–35.

Yigitcanlar, T., O'Connor, K. & Westerman, C. (2008). The making of knowledge cities: Melbourne's knowledge-based urban development experience. *Cities* 25(2): 63–72.

Yovanof, G.S. & Hazapis, G.N. (2009). An architectural framework and enabling wireless technologies for digital cities & intelligent urban environments. *Wireless Personal Communications* 49(3), 445–63.

Zhu, D., Wang, N., Wu, L. & Liu, Y. (2017). Street as a big geo-data assembly and analysis unit in urban studies: a case study using Beijing taxi data." *Applied Geography* 86, 152–64. http://dx.doi.org/10.1016/j.apgeog.2017.07.001.

# 4 Smart sports in smart cities

*Ekaterina Glebova and Michel Desbordes*

Urban habitants' lifestyles have rapidly evolved through the emerging technologies, the digitalization of the economy, and new consumption patterns, means of modern transportation. Sport is an integral part of a healthy lifestyle and this fact is considered for smart cities development. Smart cities are related to sports and recreation areas in many direct and indirect aspects (Atali, 2018). There are many cases when cities successfully activate development through sport as cities are facing complex challenges in attaining constant development within the context of sports and healthy lifestyles (Blasi et al., 2022). Smart cities' sports infrastructure encompasses facilities, systems, goods, and services that enable the sports and healthy lifestyle leisure. They use data and technology to engage people to do sports, promote sports culture and physical activity, organize sports events of various scales, create efficiencies, optimize resources, improve sustainability, create economic development, and enhance the quality of life for people in the city.

This chapter focuses on the three main categories of actors: (1) Sports environment user, a citizen practicing the physical activity and using sports facilities, (2) Team player or athlete, who practices as part of a club, amateur or professional (3) Sports Fan, Spectator or/and follower, a person who is interested in sports content consumption (live or mediatory watching). The chapter supports the development of strategies that connect sport and cities. It provides a theoretical basis to learn and analyze the interrelation of sports and the concept of smart cities, followed by real examples. It discloses the current state of technologies, infrastructure, and culture of sports in modern smart cities, defining the main constructs. The chapter also explores the role of sports in smart cities. It discloses how sports may affect on smart city and how urban development fosters the sports industry. By distinguishing different types of sports, urban infrastructure and their nature and purposes, it provides a comprehensive review of the nature, features, and dimensions of sports in the smart city framework. It also addresses development issues and trends in sports in terms of urban maintenance and development and recognizes the importance of new technologies' wide dissemination and their effect on the sports industry. Urban sports are a marketing tool influencing city and country brand image. Exploring the obstacles and opportunities for sports infrastructure deployment can define future directions for smart cities.

## Sports development and integration in urban life

The concept of the smart city is at the forefront of innovation in urban development and is an increasingly popular topic for urban planners internationally (Nilssen, 2019). Social innovation relates to two aspects of the smart city literature: (1) quality of life in the smart city and (2) leisure in the smart city. While technological advancement is at the core of innovation, not all new technology constitutes social innovation (Tjønndal & Nilssen, 2019). The global trend is to use cultural sports and entertainment facilities for urban development initiatives (Barghchi et al., 2010).

Contemporary sports culture embraces different fields, directions, and organizations, shaping a complex structure (Rainoldi et al, 2022). At first, we distinguish sports practice (doing sports) and sports as entertainment (sports spectacle and related activities). Second, in terms of smart city projects, management and development, we see the point in contrasting professional sports (Campbell, 1999) and sports for all (Pancic & Mitic, 2016). Figure 4. 1 let us identify key constructs of the 'sports in smart city' concept.

**Figure 4.1:** Key 'sports in smart city' constructs

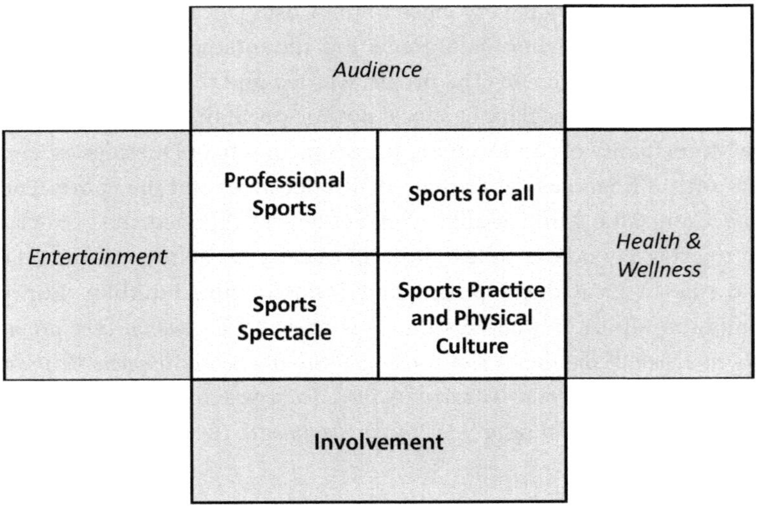

Sports are developing continuously in the framework of smart cities, involving all the audiences and embracing entertainment and public health purposes. Sport can be considered as an urban development tool as urban development is activated through sports. Developing a sports as a process of making a city 'smarter' in the majority of cases includes the development of sports infrastructure and culture as a part of a 'smart' lifestyle for habitants (Baroncelli & Ruberti, 2022). Smart cities' development also makes sports smarter through integration of infrastructure, including Sport public spaces and sports venues, to an ecosystem with future perspectives (Tomino & Perić, 2022). By promoting sports, cities care about inhabitants, attract guests and investments and reveal genuine potential. Sport is promoted as an activity by creating public spaces in the city. By organizing events in iconic places, cities are showcasing their attractiveness even beyond sport, boosting tourism and economy, and developing the city (or even country) image (Djamballah et al., 2015; Hautbois et al., 2020; Perić et al, 2022). Becker and Wicken (CAUTHE Conference, 2013) noticed that *"sport participation has an inherent travel component"*. However, Banyai and Potwarka (2011) argue that the Olympic image does not have a substantial impact, and the rate of revisits to the destination is low. Accordingly, Law et al. (2014) conclude that a sporting mega-event *"does not provide a substantial benefit without effective marketing strategies"* in a city ('place') on all the stages of this event.

As an example, The Riudecanyes lake is located in the Province of Tarragona, Catalonia region, Spain. Its surroundings have both cultural and landscape components, which seems to be a perfect environment for sport and recreational activities. The project 'Riudecanyes Adventure' is focused on the creation of new sports natural park and ran from January 2014 to July 2015. The location is very close to the Costa Dorada, a popular tourist area. In Riudecanyes there is a green and mountainous landscape, in the pre-coastal mountain chain. The project was led and managed by the Riudecanyes Adventure Association, a local not-for-profit organization composed of the Municipality of Riudecanyes, the Municipality of Duesaigües, and the community of Regantes del Pantano de Riudecanyes and the Sports Council of Baix Camp, the Municipality of Argentera also joined the Association. This project is a good example of how sport can play an important and even crucial role in local development and infrastructure building. European Commission report emphasizes that this project *"has shown very promising results in terms of the number of users and environmental impacts. It promotes the use of the reservoir and its surroundings, by organizing sports activities and promoting awareness and respect for the environment"* (European Commission, 2016).

## Creating sport public spaces in the city

A city can't exist without infrastructure. A smart city requires a smart infrastructure. It includes two main categories: sports spaces and clusters and sports venues, often overlapping. Sports infrastructure and smart sports venues include new generation stadiums, sports venues, facilities, sports culture engagement. In order to prevent and combat obesity and loneliness cities need to promote physical activities and sharing social experiences (Duparc, 2019a). Often cities develop 'sport city zones' and either concentrated as a cluster or disseminated infrastructure for sports training open for all. These zones can also attract spectators, participants, and attention from outside the city, increasing tourism arrivals and helping to promote the city's brand image and international reputation. For example, The Queen Elizabeth Olympic Park (www.queenelizabetholympicpark.co.uk/) seems to encourage a broad range of London inhabitants for physical activity. It offers the public to access affordable swimming and cycling facilities. The public spaces also encourage cycling, walking, and running.

Valle and Kompfer (2013) found three key reasons why the importance of urban space for sport is increasing. First, sport becomes more and more individual, including a reduction in participation in sports clubs. Training does not take place at sports complexes on the outskirts of the city or in enclosed anonymous sports facilities only, but also fitness clubs and private studios, and crowded places in public spaces. It comes together with personalization, brought by big data, mobile apps, and connectivity (Glebova et al., 2020b). The second reason, according to Valle and Kompfer (2013), is *"the fact that contemporary lifestyle is more and more focused on being active and healthier"*. This has led to a growth of demand and supply in sports products and services: fitness centers, yoga studios, personal coaching for amateurs, sport tourism, and sport fashion. Definitely, it influences urban development, making sports services and facilities more common and sophisticated. Sport is switching its role from a 'necessary physical exercise', turning into a kind of 'fun'. Sport visibility becomes more important as *"it leads us to the third reason: the urban environment, because public space is used daily by sport people, or sport is used for city marketing"* (Valle & Kompfer, 2013).

Stadia and sport facilities are part of the critical infrastructure. *"The definition of a sports facility is different from open recreational areas, such as golf courses to an indoor arena, dome, and single-purpose or multi-use stadia. Traditionally, the sport facility was a modest facility with a capacity of perhaps a few hundred, serving a small local community and forming part of the social fabric, along with the religious building, and town hall. The new Olympic movement was proclaimed in 1894 and held its first competition in Athens in 1896. Ever since, sports have emerged in their modern forms and the facilities have evolved into one of the greatest public building forms of the twentieth century, regarded, at its best, as an essential and positive element of civic life."* (Barghchi et al., 2010)

Urban development brings new life and upgrades to existing sport facilities, and fosters the building of new stadiums as a part of the city and infrastructure, delivering a new level of sports culture. With continuous improvements in urban sports infrastructure, entertainment systems, and internet connectivity occurring all the time, smart city habitants can build sports experiences fitting their preferred specifications, 24/7 at any place (Glebova et al., 2020a,b; Yang & Cole, 2022) and free of charge. Consequently, sports venues are in process of competing to attract the public. Glebova et al. (2020a) have defined nine main areas of stadia upgrades brought by digitalization and technologies:

1. Multipurpose nature of facilities,
2. Modular infrastructure,
3. Seating,
4. Heating, ventilation, and air conditioning (HVAC),
5. Access, safety, and smart ticketing,
6. Social media, mobile and immersive experiences,
7. Restoration and collaborations,
8. Outsourcing,
9. Stadium connectivity.

Smart transport is a part of sports city life as: *"Intelligent mobility is one of the focus areas in smart cities, in the coming years there will be a further dynamic development of new technologies in road transport, in particular in the field of information and telecommunications techniques"* (Lewicky et al., 2020). There are a few kinds of smart transport that not only promote physical activity but also foster sustainable development and ecology, for example, bicycles, scooters, skates, rollers, and other mobility tools functioning by humans exercising without producing any air pollution. The wide dissemination of these mobility tools requires infrastructure and ecosystem: special roads and routes, parking, rent, sharing and repair services, connected systems, and culture. For example, in Spain, Barcelona's 'Bicing' shared bicycle system (https://bicing.barcelona) provides 6,000 bicycles that can be used for short trips around the city. Bicycle pickup stations are located close to public transportation hubs and parking areas, for users' convenience. In addition, for smart parking spaces, Barcelona city deploys wireless sensors under roads to navigate drivers to available parking spaces.An app provides an opportunity to pay for parking and *"supplies parking data for use by different smart city systems"*.

In terms of city development, the challenge is to ensure that sports facilities zones are accessible to a diverse range of citizens. It concerns a variety of infrastructure and inclusive design for providing an opportunity to access sports spaces, facilities, and entertainment for every city habitant, regardless of age, gender, disability, and other demographic features. For example, for the inhabitants of the east part of London which, according to the park's official website, is *"the most diverse area in the country"*, Queen Elizabeth Olympic Park represents an opportunity to embrace the spirit of the Games and use it to create new opportunities in the long term. On the official website, they state: *"Our goal is to make sure that the Park is a great example of the best principles of accessibility and inclusive design so that it can be enjoyed by everyone regardless of disability, age, gender, sexual orientation, race or faith."* (Queen Elizabeth Park, n.d.)

Access and inclusion therefore of sports culture in smart cities follow the philosophy of 'Equal access to sports'. Creating inclusivity of sports culture and diversity (Godfrey et al., 2019) in sports is one of the key elements of any smart sport, either professional, amateur, or physical activity. The role of cities in the development of gender equity in sports initiatives has been crucial to their success; and modern cities and urban culture are becoming the *"incubators for problem-solving, testing new and innovative solutions in order to face social and economic challenges"* (Duparc, 2019b), including gender inequity problem. Over the last decade, the issue of women's opportunities and participation in sports has been addressed by a large number of stakeholders across multiple sectors, including urban development. As a result, an impressive number of initiatives have emerged providing women equal opportunities to access sport. There are many well-known organizations and initiatives that aim to promote the role of women in society. The sports field is not an exception: Women Sport International (womensportinternational. org); Global Sports Week; European women and sport (http://ewsports. over-blog.com); the International Working Group on Women and Sport and the International Association of Physical Education and Sport for Girls and Women(https://iwgwomenandsport.org); UNESCO's initiative which aims at establishing a Global Observatory for Women, Sport, Physical Education, and Physical Activity (Unesco (n.d)). However, the problem about gender inequity in sports is still pressing in a few Muslim countries (Pfister, 2010; Amara, 2012).

Sports and physical activity must be open to all citizens regardless of their age. The city plays a key role in all ages' inclusivity, providing a special infrastructure and fostering sports events and communities organization for youth and elders. The case study generated by Tjønndal and Nilssen (2019) is an interesting example: *"Bodø is municipality of 51 000 inhabitants and is located in the northern part of Norway .... In 2018 Bodø Municipality introduced a new concept called Digital Kveld – or "Digital Evening" – in the city's public library. Digital Kveld is hosted every Wednesday and Sunday, is free of charge, and is open to children aged 9–14. The purpose of Digital Kveld is to provide local children with a meeting place in which to play computer games or PlayStation and to learn how to use different digital tools without having to buy expensive computer programs or gaming consoles. As an expansion of Digital Kveld, Bodø Municipality hosted its very first e-sport competition in November 2018 (Digital Kveld, 2018). Around 150 local children took part in the e-sport tournament, with competitions being held in OverWatch, Golf with your Friends, Fortnite, Minecraft, FIFA, Mario Kart 8, and Super Smash Bros WII U. Like Digital Kveld, participation in the e-sport competition was free of charge.*

*E-sports and events like Digital Kveld have been met with some resistance in the media when discussed in relation to more traditional sports. The arguments against e-sports often revolve around the fact that these activities do not involve physical activity and are therefore not considered to be health-promoting in the same way as other sports. ... Most e-sports do not involve physical activity with the exception being games such as Wii Sports and new games using VR technology. [However] engaging children and youth in research on leisure activities of Norwegian youth has demonstrated that e-sports have some positive health benefits in terms of social and mental health. ... Playing games online with peers opens up a whole new world of possibilities in terms of digital friendships and digital communities. Gaming and e-sports provide some Norwegian youth with increased feelings of belonging and acceptance amongst like-minded peers. Although this research is still limited in Norway, the potential mental health benefits of playing esports should not be overlooked when exploring social innovation and quality of life in smart cities"* (Tjønndal & Nilssen, 2019). Gamification therefore needs to be explored further (Xu et al., 2017, Xu et al., 2016).

# Using technology

## Sports mobile applications

There are many changes in the service field, sports, and customer experiences brought by mobile applications (apps). Mobile apps became essential in sports culture, as the apps became the 'quintessence' of new technologies, offering integrated user interface and connectivity, delivering a new level of customer experiences and functioning for all the stakeholders (Glebova et al, 2020a,b; Schut & Glebova, 2022). Apps let city habitants stay connected, updated in terms of news, measure sports performance and analyze it, watch sports and do shopping from any location, and many more in real time (Buhalis et al., 2019; Buhalis & Sinarta, 2019; Buhalis & Foerste, 2015).

The important feature of apps is the possibility to consolidate all the information and services in a single place (Schut & Glebova, 2022), just at the fingertips of each customer.

The power of data and social media in terms of sports provide unique advantages of apps are not limited to consolidation only. Connectivity between all the stakeholders gives an opportunity to collect and analyze data. It helps companies and organizations to better know their client in detail, and fosters the delivery of more personalized and higher-quality customer experiences. Social media apps provide a platform for communications and sharing social experiences, developing new tools and features. As social media consumption (SMC) has grown as a major platform of sports spectatorship (Daehwan et al., 2019), sports teams and leagues are concerned about the shift of sport consumers' preference from spectatorship to SMC (Luker, 2012), which raises an important open question: Does SMC 'cannibalize' stadium attendance? Mobile apps can be dedicated to a sports club, event, brand, and tool for metrics, social media, or even all of these together. However, we outline the most typical features/content for sport mobile apps:

- User account
- Social media linkage
- Ticket sale
- Brand store
- Loyalty club/ payment
- Team
- New
- Notifications
- Chat
- Live streaming
- Immersive experiences

An interesting example of a sports mobile app is Urban Sports Club (https://urbansportsclub.com). This has an exclusively digital membership, which means a user can only check in to sports with the app. Users can download the app for free from the Google Play Store or the App Store and it requires a working internet connection. There is a range of sports activities on the Urban Sports Club website or directly in-app. When a customer arrives at a venue, he/ she can check in by scanning the Urban Sports Club QR code displayed near the entrance. More than 8000 sports venues in nine countries (Belgium, Denmark, Finland, France, Germany, Italy, Norway, Portugal, and Spain) available for these app users.

In terms of active participation "L8star Fitness Tracker" helps with "heart rate blood pressure, monitor real-time pedometer, calorie counter, sports activity tracker, sleep monitoring, sedentary and call reminder for iOS and Android:

- "Fitness Tracker embraces pedometer, calorie counter, distance, track your all-day activities, providing sports data immediately. This fitness tracker will vibrate when receiving a phone call or a message. Sedentary reminder for body relaxing. Shake wrist to take photos, daily waterproof for rainy days, or hands washing.

- Heart Rate and Blood Pressure Monitor Measuring heart rate, and blood pressure each hour automatically, and it can also be measured by APP manually, provides an opportunity to monitor health conditions at any time (not for medical purposes).

- Sleep monitor. This fitness tracker will monitor the whole sleeping status by analyzing the deep sleep and light sleep, helps to improve sleep quality. Syncs the sleep data to the APP chart. It can also wake up consumers by vibration alarm clock function. It's suitable for kids, women, and men.

- App 'L8STAR' from APP store or Play Store connects fitness tracker to a smartphone by Bluetooth".

## Immersive technologies and mixed reality for sports

The term 'immersive technologies' (extended reality, XR) is used to refer to several different technologies, such as virtual reality (VR), augmented reality (AR), and mixed reality (MR) (Handa et al., 2012). The immersive technologies' role in sports performance and consumption is increasing, and virtual, augmented, and mixed reality deployment is widely experienced in sports. It provides options for training and sports spectating, making it more interactive and interesting. It lets a consumer virtually travel through distance and even time, becoming a part of any event or environment (Glebova, 2020). For example, the "Zwift"(zwift.com) app blends the fun of video games with the intensity of serious training, helping the consumer get faster and exercise more effectively. It's a choice of training plans, group rides, races, and real-time analytics. Real-time performance tracking and analytics will revolutionise sport participation (Buhalis & Sinarta, 2019) AR is one of the powerful interactive tools to demonstrate real-time performance tracking in analytics in sports, useful in any type of sports activity: performance, training, coaching, and spectating. The continuous advances in wireless (sensor) and mobile technologies activate new opportunities in the development of sports applications. Sensor devices are getting smaller, less bulky, and smarter, possible for more efficient methods for the acquisition of performance data. The diversity, powerfulness, networking ability, and handy design of mobile devices allow the implementation of effective monitoring and instant intervening routines. Innovations help to enhance the sports spectating experience: new camera perspectives, voice assistance (Buhalis & Moldavska, 2021), live and post-game analyses, virtual reality solutions, and new performance statistics (Glebova, 2020). The metaverse will revolutionise all this by providing an immersive experience for both active and passive sports participation (Dwivedi, et al, 2023).

## Conclusions: Sports-friendly city: building the philosophy

Sport is an important part of a smart city, embracing different forms of pastime: sports training, sport tourism, professional sports, entertainment, and events of various scales. The smart city concept goes beyond a set of infrastructure, facities and technologies. There are many great examples across the world demonstrating how public and private sector actors participate in building infrastructure and the philosophy of smart sport in a smart city. In sports, it's difficult to overestimate the importance of co-creation experiences. Hence, technologies play a crucial role: "*Achieving nowness service requires a layer of infrastructure using smart technologies that integrate the real-time service ecosystems. These include sensors and beacons, big data management, cloud computing, Decision Support Systems, Artificial Intelligence, and Machine Learning. These hardware and software technologies collect and analyze information dynamically as well as trigger several processes in real-time. ICTs act as the catalysts in an agile ecosystem to enhance real-time service performance based on the brand's specific objectives*" (Buhalis & Sinarta, 2019).

Tjønndal & Nilssen (2019) explore Barnetråkk as a digital tool used in Bodø, Norway. It was developed to map children's movements and experiences in public spaces in urban areas in Bodø, designed to engage children and youth in urban planning so that their opinions and experiences can be incorporated into urban development. "*It allows children to digitally map their daily walking routes to school and mark places along the way – or in the city in general – that they associate with joy (such as play, sport, and leisure activities) and danger (traffic, scary places, or areas with scary adults and/or animals). Barnetråkk helps urban planners, public sector agencies, and local politicians to see how children use the public spaces in their neighborhoods, what they enjoy about their city, and what they would like to change. This methodology can therefore be seen as innovative, in that it makes use of children's voices in urban planning through the use of new digital technology*". It's an example of how local authorities can

## 70 Smart Cities and Tourism

incorporate children's participation in urban planning (Tjønndal & Nilssen, 2019). As another example, in September 2019, the City of Montréal, Canada released a list of 19 projects to improve the sporting offer on the territory. The city invests to finance borough initiatives conceived to develop and improve the city sports facilities and improve the service offered to Montréalers. These projects are *"part of a comprehensive city strategy which relies on active design and expresses a strong commitment to support access to sport for all"* (Duparc, 2019a).

In the framework of internet connectivity and user-friendly interfaces, smart city ecosystems should empower sports lovers to enjoy their favorite activities in a more comfortable way than before, employing sports tracking and analytics, modern sports facilities, online coaches, and much more, powered by user-friendly mobile apps. Making urban sports smarter can integrate the city sports ecosystem, closely interrelated with all other city constructs and fields, fostered by innovations and city development. Sports culture must therefore be built to engage a wide diversity of city inhabitants and guests to get involved. The entire ecosystem, including sports-friendly culture and philosophy, functioning for all the stakeholders: public and private actors, sports startup community, professional teams and athletes, and city inhabitants and guests, should embrace the culture and appropriate philosophy and sports must be a part of this philosophy.

## References

Amara M. (2012). The Arab World in the global sporting arena: An Islamic perspective. In: M. Amara, *Sport, Politics and Society in the Arab World. Global Culture and Sport.* Palgrave Macmillan, London

Atalı, L. (2018). Akıllı Şehirler ve Spor. *Herkese Bilim ve Teknoloji Dergisi.Sayı: 96, s:14-15.*

Banyai, M. & Potwarka, L.R. (2011). Assessing destination images of an Olympic host city using social media, *European Journal of Tourism Research,* 5 (1).

Barghchi, M., Omar, D. & Aman M.S. (2010). Sports facilities in urban areas: trends and development considerations. *Review Paper, Pertanika Journal of Social Science and Humanities* 18(2)

Baroncelli, A. & Ruberti, M. (2022). Smart sport arenas make cities smarter. In *Managing Smart Cities* (pp. 89-104). Springer, Cham.

Blasi, S., Gobbo, E. & Sedita, S. R. (2022). Smart cities and citizen engagement: Evidence from Twitter data analysis on Italian municipalities. *Journal of Urban Management* 11(2) 153-165.

Buhalis, D., Harwood, T., Bogicevic, V., Viglia, G., Beldona, S. & Hofacker, C., (2019), Technological disruptions in Services: lessons from tourism and hospitality, *Journal of Service Management*, 30(4), 484-506 https://doi.org/10.1108/JOSM-12-2018-0398

Buhalis, D. & Sinarta, Y., (2019), Real-time co-creation and nowness service: lessons from tourism and hospitality, *Journal of Travel & Tourism Marketing*, 36(5), 563-582 https://doi.org/10.1080/10548408.2019.1592059

Buhalis, D. & Foerste, M. (2015). SoCoMo marketing for travel and tourism: Empowering co-creation of value. *Journal of Destination Marketing & Management*, 4(3), 151-161. https://doi.org/10.1016/j.jdmm.2015.04.001

Buhalis, D. & Moldavska, I. (2021). Voice assistants in hospitality: using artificial intelligence for customer service. *Journal of Hospitality and Tourism Technology*.

Campbell, H.S. (1999). Professional sports and urban development: a brief review of issues and studies, *Review of Regional Studies*, 29(3), 272-292

CAUTHE Conference (2013). *Conference Handbook of Book Abstracts*, 11-14 February New Zealand.

Djaballah, M., Hautbois C., & Desbordes M. (2015). Non-mega sporting events' social impacts: A sense making approach of local governments' perceptions and strategies. *European Sport Management Quarterly*, 15(1), 48–76.

Duparc, M. (2019a). Urban sports, *Smart cities and sport publication summit, 2019.* Lausanne, Switzerland. http://www.smartcitiesandsport.org/summit-2019/ accessed 01.05.2020

Duparc, M. (2019b). Women in sport, *Smart cities and sport publication summit, 2019*. Lausanne, Switzerland. http://www.smartcitiesandsport.org/summit-2019/ accessed 01.05.2020

Dwivedi,. Y., Hughes, L., Baabdullah, A., Ribeiro-Navarrete, S., Giannakis, M., Al-Debei, M, Dennehy, D., Metri, B., Buhalis, D., Cheung, C., Conboy, K, Doyle, R., Goyal, D.P, Gustafsson, A., Jebabli, I., Young-Gab Kim, Kim, J., Koos; S., Kreps, D., Kshetri, Kumar, V., Oui, K., Papagiannidis, S., Pappas, I., Polyviou, A., Park, S., Pandey, N., Queiroza, M., Raman, R., Rauschnabel, R., Shirish, A., Sigala, M., Spanaki, K., Wei-Han Tana, G., Tiwari, M., Viglia, G., Fosso Wamba, S. (2023), Metaverse beyond the hype: Multidisciplinary perspectives on emerging challenges, opportunities, and agenda for research, practice and policy, *International Journal of Information Management*, 66, 102542, https://doi.org/10.1016/j.ijinfomgt.2022.102542

European Commission (2016). *Study on the Contribution of Sport to Regional Development through the Structural Funds*. Good practice case studies. July.

Glebova, E. (2020). Définir la réalité étendue dans les sports : limitations, facteurs et opportunités, in Desbordes M. & Hautbois C., *Management du sport 3.0, Spectacle, fan experience et digital, Economica*.

Glebova, E., Desbordes, M. & Geczi, G. (2020a). Changes in stadia sports spectators' customer experiences, *Physical Education, Sport, Science (PSS), Testnevelés, Sport, Tudomány (TST)*.

## 72 Smart Cities and Tourism

Glebova, E., Desbordes, M. & Geczi, G. (2020b). Relocations of sports spectators' customer experiences. *Physical Education, Sport, Science (PSS), Testnevelés, Sport, Tudomány (TST)*.

Godfrey, M.J., Kim, J., Eluère, M. & Eys, M. (2019). Diversity in cultural diversity research: a scoping review. *International Review of Sport and Exercise Psychology*. May, DOI: 10.1080/1750984X.2019.1616316

Handa M., Aul, E. G. & Bajaj S. (2012). Immersive technologies, challenges and opportunities, *International Journal of Computing & Business Research*, 1-11.

Hautbois, C., Djaballah, M. & Desbordes M. (2020). The social impact of participative sporting events: a cluster analysis of marathon participants based on perceived benefits. *Sport in Society*, 23(2), 335-353. doi: 10.1080/17430437.2019.1673371

Law, R., Buhalis, D. & Cobanoglu, C. (2014). Progress on information and communication technologies in hospitality and tourism. *International Journal of Contemporary Hospitality Management*, 26(5), 727-750.

Lewicki, W., Stankiewicz, B. & Olejarz-Wahba A. (2020). The role of intelligent transport systems in the development of the idea of smart city. In book: *Smart and Green Solutions for Transport Systems*. 16th Scientific and Technical Conference "Transport Systems. Theory and Practice 2019", DOI: 10.1007/978-3-030-35543-2_3

Luker, R. (2012). Shifting interest by age, gender gives MMA a fighting chance. *Street & Smith's Sports Business Journal*, 15(24), 17.

Nilssen, M. (2019). To the smart city and beyond? Developing a typology of smart urban innovation. *Technological Forecasting & Social Change*, 142, 98–104. doi:10.1016/j.techfore.2018.07.060

Pancic, S. & Mitic, D. (2016) *The Best Practicies Sport for All*, UDK 796.1

Perić, M., Badurina, J. Đ. & Wise, N. (2022). Sports tourism and event impacts. In N. Wise & K. Maguire (eds.) *A Research Agenda for Event Impacts*. Edward Elgar Publishing.

Pfister, G. (2010). *Women and sport in Islamic countries*. DOI: 10.7146/ffi. v1i1.31586

Queen Elizabeth Park (n.d.) https://www.queenelizabetholympicpark.co.uk/our-story/transforming-east-london/accessibility, last access 03.05.2020

Rainoldi, M., Ladkin, A. & Buhalis, D. (2022). Blending work and leisure: a future digital worker hybrid lifestyle perspective. *Annals of Leisure Research*, 1-21.

Schut, P-O. & Glebova, E. (2022). Sports spectating in connected stadiums: mobile application Roland Garros 2018. *Frontiers in sports and active living*, 4:802852. doi: 10.3389/fspor.2022.802852

Tjønndal, A. & Nilssen, M. (2019). Innovative sport and leisure approaches to quality of life in the smart city, *World Leisure Journal*, 61(3), 228-240, DOI:10.1080/16078055.2019.1639922

Tomino, A. C., & Perić, M. (2022). Sport-tourism running events in the post-COVID-19 world: Any sign of change? *Academica Turistica-Tourism and Innovation Journal, 15*(1).

Unesco (n.d) https://unesdoc.unesco.org/ark:/48223/pf0000153990_eng, last access 05.05.2020

Valle, D. & Kompfer V. (2013). Sport in the City. *CASCAIS* – dcv/vk.

Xu, F., Buhalis, D. & Weber, J., (2017), Serious games and the gamification of tourism, *Tourism Management* 60, 244-256 http://www.sciencedirect.com/science/article/pii/S0261517716302369

Xu, F., Tian, F., Buhalis, D., Weber, J. & Zhang, H., (2016), Tourists as mobile gamers – gamification for tourism marketing, *Journal of Travel and Tourism Marketing, 33*(8), 1124-1142 http://dx.doi.org/10.1080/10548408.2015.1093999

Yang, C., & Cole, C. L. (2022). Smart stadium as a laboratory of innovation: Technology, sport, and datafied normalization of the fans. *Communication & Sport, 10*(2), 374-389.

# Part II:
# Smart Tourism and Smart Tourists

# 5 Advances in smart destination management and public governance:
## Tourism innovation ecosystems for digital transformation

*Carlos Romero-Dexeus, Aurkene Alzua-Sorzabal, Diana Gómez-Bruna, Francisco Femenia-Serra and Edurne Vidal López-Tormos*

## Introduction

Since 2015, the 'smart destination' (SD), drawn on the smart city concept, has been spreading all over the world (Buhalis, 2019). Smart destinations impact urban strategies and tourism destination planning and management. They are in vogue, not only in scientific research, but also in public government policies and projects (Battarra et al., 2016; Gretzel, 2018). This trend responds to the need for regions to face an increasing number of challenges under growing social and economic uncertainty. They also illustrate the necessity to improve the performance of local public governments and help local companies improve tourists' satisfaction and citizens' lives. Many organizations, cities and regions have embraced the idea of 'smartness' as a potential solution for their problems. This is based on the ideal of making a more intensive use of technologies while creating better life conditions, safeguarding the environment and increasing the quality of life (Cohen, 2012).

Since the emergence of the British seaside resort in the late 19th and early 20th century, every generation has witnessed a technological breakthrough that has revolutionized the tourism industry and destinations (Buhalis et al., 2019). The present situation is characterized by a deep digital transformation, accelerated as a result of the COVID-19 irruption. Digital transformation is more powerful, transformative and with longer term implications than previous transformations (Benckendorff et al., 2019; Xiang, 2018). All societies, corporations, cities and regions must prepare for the change caused by the current technological revolution and digitalization (Buhalis & Wagner, 2013).

Regarding tourism, the new context intensifies the diversification of services and processes (Buhalis, 2019). Applied to territories, it stresses the diffusion of smartness in small but highly productive units that rely on new technologies linked to the process of service co-creation. It also requires greater awareness of the need to preserve the quality of local natural and cultural environments. The new market conditions will continue to encourage the emergence of additional disruptive forces and business models that, from within or outside the tourism sector, will affect the tourism ecosystem progress (Buhalis et al., 2019). This challenges the traditional organizational structures of destinations and requires reengineering of business operations and public management. The innovation capacity offered by technology to destinations and companies also opens a new scope of opportunities to improve the management of all tangible and intangible elements that shape the tourist experience (Lamsfus et al., 2015); through value co-creation and engagement in customer citizenship behavior in the hospitality and tourism context (Assiouras et al., 2019). As destination management organizations (DMOs) become aware of new technologies, managers and leaders struggle to prioritize the technologies to select and deploy (Femenia-Serra & Ivars-Baidal, 2019). Destination leaders know that these technologies will likely impact their work areas and that it is important to stay ahead of the curve. But DMOs do not always have a clearly defined goal for each implemented technology. In these cases, there is a need for experts' support on decision making processes to choose technologies which warrant the use of their often-limited resources.

This chapter tackles the research problem of how city governments can take ownership of smart city/smart destination projects to ensure that they create value for residents and local organizations. Therefore, it focuses on the value smart services create and how local governments can ensure that value is created and delivered. To address these issues, the chapter presents the research project undertaken in the framework of the Observatory for the Digitization of Tourist Destinations (DIGITUR) in Spain. This was an initiative launched in 2019 by the Spanish Secretary of State for Tourism, and was driven by Segittur (the Spanish state company dedicated to the management of innovation and tourism technologies) in collaboration with Exceltur (a non-profit Spanish organisation that integrates the 34 leading Spanish private tourism sector operators). This novel initiative has been fully funded by the Ministry's budget.

The objective of DIGITUR is to promote the digitization of Spanish tourist destinations. As a starting point, it addresses those key areas or critical problems of destinations where technology can allow management improvements on the tourist experience, competitiveness and sustainability of the destination. DIGITUR aims to encourage the development of digital transformation in Spanish tourist destinations, within the framework of the recently created Smart Tourism Destinations Network of Spain (SDs Network). It takes advantage of the new opportunities offered to destinations using new solutions and tools, as well as those developed in the smart cities' framework, to respond to current tourism issues and future challenges.

This chapter illustrates the relevance of the actions in the framework of smart destination policies aimed at activating national innovation systems. In tourism systems, innovation is generally considered to be closely linked to knowledge management of all relevant contexts (Buhalis, 2022). In smart destinations, knowledge transfer is implicit in its conceptualization (Gretzel et al., 2015). Smart destinations therefore can be understood as collections of linked innovations, aimed at facing the highly competitive and unpredictable market for tourism services (Williams et al., 2020). DIGITUR is an example of the Spanish strategy to develop environments that will boost innovation across the tourism sector. Segittur acts as an innovation hub for tourism in Spain that fosters and coordinates the digital transformation of the SDs Network members, including over 150 Spanish tourism destinations. The network approach provides a unique setting to knowledge sharing, data exchange and co-creation.

## Innovative ecosystems as platforms for value co-creation

Technology is driving a rapid shift towards network-based social and economic models. In tourism, the value of the experience is not only created by the firm and its customers, but is also embedded in a larger social and physical context of what is being experienced (Hoarau & Kline, 2014; Prahalad & Ramaswamy, 2004). Value can be co-created by all stakeholders involved during the practice of the experience, when knowledge is shared between them (Boes et al., 2016; Vargo et al., 2015). This co-creation of value allows knowledge transfer, as customers, providers and other actors are engaged. Therefore, both information technology capacity and knowledge sharing are of great significance to tourism organizations of all kinds and need to be facilitated by using appropriate platforms (Zhang et al., 2018). Most organizations are somewhat aware of the exponential advances in networking and emerging technologies. However, the very basis for the success of the contemporary technology and other industries is fundamentally based on user co-creation within real time contexts (Buhalis & Sinarta, 2019). The institutions that make it possible to transform the vast user-generated input into socially and economically valuable products and services have become the key ingredient of economic and social change (Lember et al., 2019).

Social media and the advances of ICT technologies have transformed the way regional and city brands reach out and engage with consumers. The new technological environments enable customers and residents alike to engage in a dialogue, co-create and enhance the speed and agility of their services (Buhalis & Sinarta, 2019). The latest thinking about digitally enabled co-production or co-creation is related to the idea of government as platforms (Lember, 2018). Smart city frameworks and tourism ecosystems as platforms bring together different services, applications, and technologies, as well as all types of stakeholders (Zhang et al., 2018). However, tourism ecosystems are not simply the technological infrastructure that is used to facilitate tourism services. The new technological framework, that includes social media, mobile technologies and IoT, transform the experience co-creation and co-production processes. The real-time data and artificial intelligence, based on contextual data, provides management and marketing tools to stakeholders in co-creation dynamics to satisfy both visitors and residents (Buhalis & Sinarta, 2019).

The implementation of tourism innovative ecosystems or platforms is a complex process that goes far beyond technology itself (Williams et al., 2020). It is closely related to knowledge and governance of destinations and hence calls for new organizational structures, skills, new leadership forms and transformation of public-private relationships. In this sense, the existence of a support network that comprises a multiplicity of autonomous, interdependent, and self-organizing actors, that are integrated in an environment without borders, seems fundamental (Vargo et al., 2017). This approach assumes that city governments, often expressed as DMO in the domain of tourism, are central players in smart destinations and in the smart city. Smart city governance requires innovative decision-making models, new government capacities, and collaborative networks, also defined as "smart governance" (Pereira et al., 2018). Public programmes devoted to support destinations in their digitalization process focus on smart governance as one of the ultimate goals of policies and actions. This set of ideas is very present in smart destination programmes launched by public institutions in Spain, as the leading country in this field. In the following section, we examine the importance of governance in the context of smart destinations and how this philosophy has influenced the implementation of projects such as DIGITUR.

## Rethinking governance in smart destination ecosystems

Governance is a fundamental element of smart destinations, as a framework to adapt to the digitalization process in tourism and as a destination management approach (Ivars-Baidal et al., 2019). Traditional understanding of governance is linked to public transparency in decision making and policy implementation, citizens' participation in policies, coordination between different stakeholders, collaboration between public and private institutions, co-responsibility and efficiency (Closa Montero, 2003). In tourism, governance has relevance due to the spatial concentration of manifold stakeholders with different agendas (Buhalis, 2022). The applicability of governance ideas in this field builds on the need to rely on strong public-private partnerships. To attain sustained success, the cooperation between administration, businesses and local communities is required (Vera et al., 2011; Pulido & Pulido, 2014). In smart destinations (SDs), while these principles remain, new factors have been introduced and impose the need to rethink existing frameworks for destinations' governance. These new elements that make necessary a new approach to governance include the accelerated adoption of technologies by different actors in the smart tourism ecosystem and the generation of tourism-related big data (Buhalis, 2020; Gretzel, Werthner et al., 2015).

Smart destinations reengineer tourism destination management (Pearce, 2014; Jovicic, 2017). The concept builds on smart cities and includes some of the ideas that guide smart cities, such as the need to develop greener, more connected, efficient, and more liveable spaces. Beyond this origin, smart destinations are characterized by the efforts to collect, aggregate, analyse and distribute relevant big data that comes from sources such as social media, public and organizational activities, individual tourists and physical infrastructures, among others (Stylos et al., 2011). Transforming these big data into key information for decision making is one of the main objectives of smart tourism development (Gretzel, Sigala et al., 2015). In smart destinations, technology becomes embedded in physical spaces of tourist areas and becomes the link between the different agents of the ecosystem (Gretzel, Werthner et al., 2015; Koo et al., 2016). SDs also aim at enhancing experiences thanks to higher levels of connectivity and availability of data on tourists, their preferences, behaviours, and profiles (Buhalis & Sinarta, 2019). This opens new possibilities for experience personalisation and co-creation between DMOs, businesses and tourists themselves (Femenia-Serra et al., 2019). In line with these overall objectives, smart destinations' DMOs apply a set of specific smart solutions aimed at enhancing visitor experiences but also at improving destination marketing and management (Ivars-Baidal et al., 2019). Technologies and solutions available to DMOs vary from basic tools such as websites, mobile apps, or social media analytics, to more complex systems and instruments, including sensors, public Wi-Fi networks, automated services, advanced information and recommendation systems, etc.

However, smart tourism destinations experience multiple challenges that are key to both the tourist experience and to destination resilience, including: product design, revitalization and integration of the value chain, preservation of local identity, marketing, accessibility policies, mobility systems, load capacity management, security, tourism space management, flow management signage, etc. The use of technology might be helpful in solving or ameliorating the variety of problems, but technology adoption does not necessarily mean a real, rapid improvement in all the processes related to destination management and governance (Buhalis, 2019). While new technology can be utilized to help businesses and destinations run more efficiently and productively, some organisations may not be initially willing to accept new technologies or cannot implement them due to limitations in financial, human or technical resources (Femenia-Serra & Ivars-Baidal, 2019). Destinations need to avoid falling into the belief that technology can solve every problem. Technological solutions cannot and should not replace policies that give solution to deep social and environmental problems, often attached to tourism activity. DMOs should manage a complex situation in which decision making is extremely difficult. They require assistance by other organizations and public programmes to ensure the protection of the public interest and the progress of their territories.

## Case study: DIGITUR in Spain

The DIGITUR case study demonstrates the relevance of knowledge and innovation agents in tourism systems to support destinations and help overcome their challenges. The DIGITUR project focuses on developing knowledge-based services, and training in digital transformation of destinations. Rapidly evolving technology has changed the way consumers interact with destinations as well as the way organisations interact with each other and do business. In many situations, the selection of different technologies to be implemented in a destination is subject to divergent interests and tensions that must be acknowledged. Assuring the public interest, participation, and transparency in the implementation of smart solutions and technologies in destinations presents a different set of challenges (Femenia-Serra & Ivars-Baidal, 2020). Tourist territories and the organizations governing them often face the pressure of private companies that lobby for public investments in their products and services. In line with this, DIGITUR was conceived to support local destinations to boost and accelerate the digital transformation processes so that the tourist and citizen experience and the performance of the areas could be enhanced.

The DIGITUR methodology consists of learning from real-life applications and involvement of multiple stakeholders. The shared knowledge generation process is conducted in two phases. In the first, the initial steps consist of searching and identifying good practices regarding digital transformation of tourist places. For that purpose, an experts panel from the tourism and hospitality sector is consulted and different sources of data and documentation from national and international organizations are identified.

The areas in which the opinions of experts and best practices are sought include product design, dynamization and integration of the value chain, preservation of local identity, commercialization, accessibility policies, mobility systems, load capacity management, security, tourism space management, signage in flow management, etc. In this process, two different action paths are put in place. In the first of these, the aim is to identify those critical issues of destination management that can benefit from the incorporation of different technologies.

### Phase I: Identification of key issues

In this phase in addition to identifying those critical issues for destination management, different problems that affect the local society and the territory were observed, focusing on the management and interaction with the local society and the environment in the value proposition to travellers and in the municipal public services.

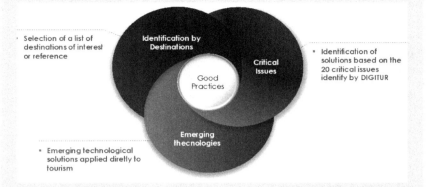

To do so, DIGITUR carried out four focus groups that included the participation of experts in urban and vacation destination management and experts in digital transformation of companies in the sector. These sessions allowed the identification of 20 key topics in destination management as illustrated in Table 5.1.

**Table 5.1:** Challenges in destination management

1. Difficulty in interacting with the traveller at the destination.
2. Difficulty in attracting desirable segments that match strategic goals.
3. Waste of economies of scale for technological adoption.
4. Insufficient use of digital marketing.
5. Lack of data availability for tourism management.
6. Lack of real-time information for tourism management.
7. Lack of integration of the destination's differential offer in its value proposition.
8. Insufficient coherence in content and messages sent to the market.
9. Lack of participatory tourism governance
10. Little digital adoption by tourism SMEs.
11. Difficulty in evaluating the satisfaction of the visitor after the trip.
12. Inefficient management of tourist mobility.
13. Lack of sharing economy management and the phenomenon of housing for tourist use.
14. Need to improve response to citizens' security problems.
15. Lack of knowledge on the competitive position of the destination.
16. Congestion of citizens and tourists in space and tourist attractions.

82  Smart Cities and Tourism

17. Insufficient measures to mitigate ecological footprint.

18. Uneven distribution of wealth generated by tourism.

19. Negative perception of tourism by residents.

20. Lack of tools for the management of environmental resources.

**Phase II: Guidebook of good practices and technological solutions**

Once the critical issues were identified, the second phase of the project consisted in preparing a guidebook of good practices and technological solutions that would support the knowledge implementation needs of managers in tourist destinations. The guidebook was set by looking at four dimensions of good practices through four channels: (i) expert recommendation; (ii) destination; (iii) technology; (iv) critical issues.

After a first consultation round with experts related to destination management and technology, and after examining the practices of a large sample of cities and destinations that are well-positioned in smart cities and destinations rankings, a final list comprising a total of 243 destinations was developed, as illustrated in Table 2. These destinations were classified according to their specialization in four categories. The performed selection showed that Europe was the region with the highest number of best practices, particularly in "cultural and urban" destinations.

**Table 5.2:** Selection and number of good practices by region and type of tourist destination. Source: Segittur (2019)

| | Europa | Asia | Americas | Africa | Oceania | Total |
|---|---|---|---|---|---|---|
| Culture & Urban | 53 | 25 | 18 | 9 | 2 | 107 |
| Beach | 22 | 23 | 22 | 15 | 2 | 84 |
| Niche | 12 | 5 | 9 | 1 | 3 | 30 |
| Nature & Sports | 5 | 6 | 7 | 3 | 1 | 22 |
| Total | 92 | 59 | 56 | 28 | 8 | **243** |

Along with the good practices search, an analysis was also carried out looking at those technologies with the highest levels of application to the tourism sector based on the identified critical issues. Similarly to Buhalis et al., (2019) the identified technologies included: Big data and analytics, artificial intelligence, IoT (Internet of things), augmented reality, virtual reality, blockchain, QR / NFC / RFID codes, drones / UAV, mobile positioning data, mobile applications and 'superapps', open data and data sharing, gamification, shared platforms, business intelligence, and digital marketing. As shown in Table 5.2, technologies related to big data and analytics, mobile applications and superapps, and business intelligence are the most prevalent among all those identified.

In order to have a more global vision of the implemented technological solutions in destinations, it was also considered necessary to identify how frequently technological solutions had been developed for each of the critical issues identified in the first phase of the programme. In Figure 5.2, the ranking of the critical issues for which more technological solutions were being applied is presented. As illustrated, *"Difficulty in evaluating the satisfaction of the visitor after the trip"* (# 11) and *"Difficulty in interacting with the tourist at the destination"* (# 1) were high in the ranking, while the *"Lack of management of the phenomenon of housing for tourist use"* (# 13) received little attention despite their relevance.

Once all the practices were identified, technologies were prioritized based on a *Prioritization Methodology*. This methodology assessed to what extent each of the good practices contributed to improve both the destination and its relationship with the tourist, in the different phases of the trip, and the relationship between the destination, local society, and the territory. Four other criteria were added to complete the assessment, namely: the degree of the technological innovation and its value proposition; scalability, that is, the ability to adapt to different territories; the degree of maturity of the solution, that is, a solution previously tested successfully; and ease of implementation, considering cost, deadlines, and degree of necessary technical knowledge. As a result, a guidebook was published, comprising the 33 identified good practices. These represent examples of various digital solutions that stand out for their innovation and applicability to the management of Spanish destinations, reaching the different types of tourist destination and covering all the critical issues identified in the first phase developed by the Observatory. The guidebook also incorporates a technical sheet with exhaustive information on each of the identified good practices. The technical document begins with a descriptive section, which provides a global vision of the practice, identifying the critical issues it addresses, the time of the travel cycle or the management dimension of the destination to which it applies, the technology used, the destinations in which it has been implemented and its impact on the 17 UN Sustainable Development Goals. The second section of the document provides details about the outcomes of the implementation of the technology, while the third and final section evaluate the effectiveness of the implemented practice (Segittur, 2019).

## Figure 5.2: Ranking of critical issues for which more technological solutions were applied

**Table 2. Most applied technologies according to critical issues identified in the management of tourist destinations**

| Critical Issues | Big Data Analytics | Mobile Apps | Business Intelligence | Open Data | Shared Plataforma | Artificial Intelligence | Mobile Data | IoT | QR | Gamification | AR | VR | Drones | Blockchain | Summary |
|---|---|---|---|---|---|---|---|---|---|---|---|---|---|---|---|
| #1 Interaction | O | O | | | | O | | | O | O | O | O | | | 50% |
| #2 Segments | O | O | O | O | | | O | | O | O | | | | | 50% |
| #3 Econ. Scale | O | | O | O | O | | O | | | | | | | | 36% |
| #4 Marketing | O | O | O | | | | | | | O | O | O | O | | 50% |
| #5 Data | O | O | O | O | O | O | O | O | | | | | | | 57% |
| #6 Real time | O | O | O | O | O | O | O | | | | | | | | 50% |
| #7 Integration | O | | O | O | | | | | | | | | | O | 29% |
| #8 Posts | O | | O | O | O | | | | | | | | | | 29% |
| #9 Governance | | O | O | O | O | | O | O | O | | | | | | 50% |
| #10 SMEs | O | O | O | O | O | | | | | | | | | | 36% |
| #11 Assessment | O | O | O | O | | O | | | | | | | | | 36% |
| #12 Mobility | | O | | | O | | O | O | O | | | | | | 36% |
| #13 Tourist rentals | O | | | | | O | | | | | | | | | 14% |
| #14 Security | | O | | | | O | O | O | | | | | | | 29% |
| #15 Position | O | | O | O | | | | | | | | | | | 21% |
| #16 Congestion | O | O | O | | | O | O | O | | | | | | | 43% |
| #17 Ecolology | O | O | | | | | | O | | O | O | O | O | | 50% |
| #18 Inequality | O | O | | | O | O | O | | | | | | | | 36% |
| #19 Tourismphobi | | O | | | O | | | | | | | | | | 14% |
| #20 Environment | O | O | O | | O | O | | O | | | | | O | | 50% |
| Summary | 85% | 75% | 65% | 50% | 50% | 45% | 40% | 40% | 20% | 20% | 15% | 15% | 15% | 5% | |

## Conclusions

This chapter advances the concept of smart destination management and smart public governance by presenting and discussing recent contributions. It attempts to operationalize these dimensions based on the empirical knowledge provided by the DIGITUR case study in Spain. This case is representative of how destinations are transitioning towards a digital scenario in which the concepts of governance and innovation are inevitably involved and reshaped. Smart tourism destinations, as a working framework, have captured attention and have become the object of multiple policies and actions, including the creation of networks, such as the Spanish one. In these networks and smart ecosystems, knowledge is generated in a collaborative way. It is more necessary than ever before to ensure a public-driven implementation of solutions and technologies.

Based on the lessons derived from the DIGITUR case, the identification of best practices and instruments in digital transformation can enhance current understanding of value co-creation within the smart destination's ecosystem. By exploring the key role of knowledge transfer, this chapter sheds light on the mechanisms boosting innovation through a manager's active engagement in tourism destinations. DIGITUR integrates dynamic knowledge by linking practices and new technologies in the network so that the process can provide practitioners and policymakers with deeper insights and support to cope with the associated challenges and uncertainty. For practitioners and participants of the network, the need to build a common vision of digitalization to enhance the interaction and performance of the destinations is emphasized. Participants in the study mentioned some challenges related to the difficulties interacting with the traveller at the destination, complexity, and barriers to take advantage of economies of scale for technological adoption, or challenges to integrate the offer differential of the destination in its value proposition. The case illustrates the need to provide a framework for co-production and co-creation processes to enhance the place competitiveness. Citizens and tourism stakeholders participate actively in delivering and designing the services they receive. Smart city technological infrastructures can be useful to help coordinate co-production and co-creation, by allowing for more efficient information flows and providing support functions (e.g., stakeholders can have real-time access to and exchange of information or use various digital products). Real-time data collection and provision can provide local communities opportunities to enhance the dialogue between visitors and residents in new models of service delivery (Buhalis & Sinarta, 2019).

Even if technology is at the core of the DIGITUR action, institutions play a leading role in resource integration and value creation processes since the local organizations can enable or constrain exchanges. This case study provides an opportunity for broadening the scope of innovation to also include social structures (i.e., institutions and institutional arrangements) that guide knowledge transfer actions among multiple actors at the tourism destination. DIGITUR enables policymakers and managers to apply a systems perspective that considers the interaction among all actors. Moving forward the smart destination network emerges as an innovative environment in which actors engaged in complementary and interdependent resource integration and value creation practices.

Tourism destination organizations, tourism operators, and business models need to adapt to rapidly changing urban environments and encompass a more holistic approach and increase the local capacities through the user/community Involvement. Citizens are not only recipients but also actors of smart destination value proposition. The information presented reveals the importance of having a public-private partnership (PPPs) in place. From a tourism perspective, long-term agreements between the governments and private partners are needed. Smart city investment should be aligned with a tourism destination's strategic priorities and citizens' needs. The idiosyncratic nature of destinations, and the necessary scalability of these actions aimed at innovation, illustrate that future studies should pay attention to those city and regions that face even more challenges when adapting to smart tourism ecosystems. The development of smart destination policies and actions has followed a clear urban bias until now. Therefore, it would be interesting to carry out actions outside these types of territories. Typologies of smart cities can help to better understand where each tourism destination stands (OECD, 2019), and foster, peer-to-peer dialogues to make urban governance more effective and closer to the local needs. A shift of digital innovation will support small and medium enterprises (SMEs) and engagement of citizens in smart cities and regions.

# References

Assiouras, I., Skourtis, G., Giannopoulos, A., Buhalis, D., & Koniordos, M. (2019). Value co-creation and customer citizenship behavior. *Annals of Tourism Research*, 78, 102742.

Battarra, R., Gargiulo, C., Pappalardo, G., Boiano, D.A. & Oliva, J.S., (2016) Planning in the era of information and communication technologies. Discussing the "label: Smart" in South-European cities with environmental and socio-economic challenges. *Cities*, 59, 1-7.

## 5: Advances in smart destination management and public governance 87

Benckendorff, P. J., Xiang, Z. & Sheldon, P. J. (2019) *Tourism Information Technology*. Wallingford: CABI

Boes, K., Buhalis, D. & Inversini, A., (2016) Smart tourism destinations: ecosystems for tourism destination competitiveness, *International Journal of Tourism Cities*, 2(2), pp. 108-124. https://doi.org/10.1108/IJTC-12-2015-0032

Buhalis, D., (2022), Tourism management and marketing in transformation: Introduction and editor's statement, in Buhalis, D., (ed) *Encyclopedia of Tourism Management and Marketing*, Edward Elgar Publishing.

Buhalis, D. (2019) Technology in tourism-from information communication technologies to eTourism and smart tourism towards ambient intelligence tourism: a perspective article, *Tourism Review* 75(1), 267-272

Buhalis, D., Harwood, T., Bogicevic, V., Viglia, G., Beldona, S. & Hofacker, C. (2019) Technological disruptions in Services: lessons from tourism and hospitality', *Journal of Service Management*, 30(4), 484-506

Buhalis, D., & Sinarta, Y. (2019) Real-time co-creation and nowness service: lessons from tourism and hospitality. *Journal of Travel & Tourism Marketing*, 36(5), 563-582.

Buhalis D., & Wagner R. (2013) E-destinations: Global best practice in tourism technologies and applications. In: Cantoni L. & Xiang Z. (eds) *Information and Communication Technologies in Tourism*. Springer, Berlin. https://doi. org/10.1007/978-3-642-36309-2_11

Closa Montero, C. (2003) El libro blanco sobre la gobernanza, *Revista de Estudios Políticos*. Centro de Estudios Políticos y Constitucionales (España), 119, 485–503.

Cohen, B. (2012) *What Exactly Is A Smart City?*, Fast Coexist. Available at: http://www.fastcoexist.com/1680538/what-exactly-is-a-smart-city.

Femenia-Serra, F. & Ivars-Baidal, J. A. (2019) DMOs surviving the smart tourism ecosystem, in *Travel and Tourism Research Association's European Chapter Conference*. Bournemouth (United Kingdom).

Femenia-Serra, F., Neuhofer, B. & Ivars-Baidal, J. A. (2019) Towards a conceptualisation of smart tourists and their role within the smart destination scenario, *The Service Industries Journal*, 39(2), 109–133. doi: 10.1080/02642069.2018.1508458.

Gretzel, U., Sigala, M., Xiang, Z & Koo, C. (2015) Smart tourism: foundations and developments, *Electronic Markets*, 25(3), 179–188. doi: 10.1007/s12525-015-0196-8.

Gretzel, U., Werthner, H., Koo, C. & Lumsfus, C. (2015) Conceptual foundations for understanding smart tourism ecosystems, *Computers in Human Behavior*, **50**, pp. 558–563. doi: 10.1016/j.chb.2015.03.043.

Hoarau, H. & Kline, C. (2014) Science and industry: Sharing knowledge for innovation. *Annals of Tourism Research, 46*, 44-61.

Ivars-Baidal, J. A., Celdrán-Bernabeu, M.A., Mazón, J. & Perles-Ivars, Á. (2019) Smart destinations and the evolution of ICTs: a new scenario for destination management?, *Current Issues in Tourism*, 22(13), 1581–1600. doi: 10.1080/13683500.2017.1388771.

Jovicic, D. Z. (2017) From the traditional understanding of tourism destination to the smart tourism destination, *Current Issues in Tourism*, 22(3), doi: 10.1080/13683500.2017.1313203.

Koo, C., Yoo, K., Lee, J. &, Zanker, M., (2016) Special section on generative smart tourism systems and management: Man-machine interaction, *International Journal of Information Management*, 36(6), 1301–1305. doi: 10.1016/j.ijinfomgt.2016.05.015.

Lamsfus, C., Martín, D., Alzua-Sorzabal, A. & Torres-Manzanera, E., (2015) Smart tourism destinations: An extended conception of smart cities focusing on human mobility. In *Information and Communication Technologies in Tourism 2015* (pp. 363-375). Springer, Cham.

Lember, V., Brandsen, T. & Tõnurist, P. (2019) The potential impacts of digital technologies on co-production and co-creation. *Public Management Review*, 21(11), 1665-1686.

Lember, V. (2018) The role of new technologies in co-production, In Brandsen, T., Steen, T. & Verschuere, B. (eds) *Co-production and Co-creation: Engaging citizens in public service delivery*. Routledge, 115-127

OECD. (2019). *1st OECD Roundtable on Smart Cities and Inclusive Growth.*

Pearce, D. G. G. (2014) Toward an integrative conceptual framework of destinations, *Journal of Travel Research*, 53(2), 141–153. doi: 10.1177/0047287513491334.

Pereira, G. V., Parycek, P., Falco, E., & Kleinhans, R. (2018) Smart governance in the context of smart cities: A literature review, *Information Polity*, 23(2), 143-162.

Prahalad, C. K., & Ramaswamy, V. (2004) Co-creation experiences: The next practice in value creation. *Journal of interactive marketing*, 18(3), 5-14.

Pulido, J. I. & Pulido, M. C. (2014) ¿Existe gobernanza en la actual gestión de los destinos turísticos? Estudio de casos, *Pasos*, 12(4), 685–705.

Segittur (2019) *Guía de Buenas Prácticas y Soluciones Tecnológicas para la Transformación Digital de los Destinos*, Madrid: Ministerio de Industria, Comercio y Turismo.

Stylos, N., Zwiegelaar, J. & Buhalis, D. (2021), Big data empowered agility for dynamic, volatile, and time-sensitive service industries: the case of tourism sector, *International Journal of Contemporary Hospitality Management*, 33(3), 1015-1036.

Vargo, S.L., Koskela-Huotari, K., Baron, S., Edvardsson, B., Reynoso, J. & Colurcio, M., (2017) A systems perspective on markets–Toward a research agenda, *Journal of Business Research*, 79, 260-268.

Vargo, S.L., Wieland, H. & Akaka, M.A., (2015) Innovation through institutionalization: A service ecosystems perspective, *Industrial Marketing Management*, 44, pp.63-72.

Vera, J. F., Palomeque, F.L., Marchena, M.J. & Clavé, S.A. (2011) *Análisis territorial del turismo y planificación de destinos turísticos*. Valencia: Tirant Lo Blanc.

Williams, A.M., Rodriguez, I. & Makkonen, T., (2020) Innovation and smart destinations: Critical insights, *Annals of Tourism Research*, 83, p.102930.

Zhang, H., Gordon, S., Buhalis, D. & Ding, X. (2018) Experience value cocreation on destination online platforms. *Journal of Travel Research*. 57(8), 1093-1107.

Xiang, Z., (2018) From digitization to the age of acceleration: On information technology and tourism, *Tourism Management Perspectives*, 25, 147-150.

# 6 Smart tourists in smart cities

*Tomáš Gajdošík*

## Introduction

Smart cities pursue efficiency, contribute to citizen value co-creation and sustainability, and improve the quality of life of their residents. This concept also impacts other industries and sectors that offer services to people that do not reside in the city, such as tourists (Sánchez-Corcuera et al., 2019). Therefore, smart city development must take into account not only the business and environment-related domains but also the cumulative use of urban resources for citizens and tourists (Romão et al., 2018).

Smart cities, as knowledge centres managing information, technology and innovation (Caragliu et al., 2011) are essential to respond to the voices of citizens (Kim et al., 2021). They have also become a differential element in decision-making of many tourists. Participation in tourism is becoming a vital part of new global lifestyle. In order to satisfy the growing demand of tourists, the authorities in various cities aim to see tourists as temporary citizens, trying to create value for them. Thanks to smart technologies, tourism is spilled into all areas of the city. Hence, the lines between residents and tourists are being blurred. This results into the convergence between 'everyday' and 'touristic' in the urban context (Gretzel & Koo, 2021).

Tourists are increasingly more active and have higher expectations in terms of tourism engagement with local resources looking for authentic experiences (Antón et al, 2019). The widespread adoption and extensive use of information technologies have resulted in a radical shift in tourist behaviour, creating a new market segment – smart tourists (Gajdošík, 2020). Smart tourists are profiting from the use of cutting-edge technologies (Shen et al., 2020a) that smart city infrastructure can offer (Um & Chung, 2021) Therefore, smart cities play a crucial role in satisfying the demand of these smart tourists.

## Smart tourists as temporary citizens in smart cities

Cities have become global economic hubs, driving growth and innovation, while attracting more and more people who come to live, do business and discover them. The people component in smart cities is critical to their development (Heaton & Parlikad, 2019), as smart cities are developed for people. This social approach highlights the value creation for citizens and communities. Value creation is based on effective and systematic bid data analysis and optimisation of networks, which requires active involvement and participation in city-related issues (Stylos et al., 2021). For citizens, it might offer better insights into city life, support everyday living and decision making, and empower alternative visions of city development (Wolff et al., 2020) Citizens and local communities should be constantly connected, technology savvy, sufficiently creative and empowered (Hedlund, 2012; Buhalis & Amaranggana, 2014). Such a behaviour seamlessly connects people with the city services and creates value by solving city related problems with the aid of technology.

Smart cities are also the world's greatest tourism destinations (Table 6.1). Nearly half of global international travel takes place in cities, for business, pleasure, art and culture as well as medical and educational reasons (WTTC, 2019). Tourists are drawn to the vibrancy, excitement and diversity of the offer in cities. Regarding service innovation (Buhalis et al., 2019) implemented in smart cities, the culture and tourism sectors have become critical for all services offered in smart cities (Um & Chung, 2021).

As tourism shapes the city development, smart cities have started to consider tourists as temporary citizens, where tourism is an inseparable part of the city (Barcelona, 2017). The term 'temporary citizen' has been used because tourists are no longer only consumers. Thanks to real-time information and connection with city stakeholders, they co-create their experience and are becoming 'prosumers' (Buhalis & Sinarta, 2019). Therefore smart cities should consider tourists as temporary citizens and ensure that city policies promote the engagement of visitors and residents to build a city for all (UNWTO, 2018). Residents and tourists should also be central to the debate as the primary recipients of value (Koo et al., 2019) through the process of smart city development.

**Table 6.1:** Tourism activity in selected cities

| City | Tourist arrivals | Direct T&T GDP (US$ bn) | Direct T&T GDP (% of city GDP) | International tourist spend (US $ bn) |
|---|---|---|---|---|
| Paris | 19,760,800 | 35.6 | 4.1 | 14.8 |
| New York | 14,010,000 | 26.0 | 3.5 | 21.0 |
| Tokyo | 10,443,100 | 23.1 | 2.4 | 21.7 |
| London | 19,559,900 | 18.2 | 1.9 | 17.5 |
| Singapore | 19,760,800 | 13.7 | 4.0 | 19.9 |
| Barcelona | 7,016,600 | 9.3 | 5.2 | 15.2 |
| Seoul | 9,105,900 | 4.7 | 1.3 | 9.9 |
| Amsterdam | 8,835,400 | 5.5 | 4.0 | 10.4 |
| San Francisco | 2,987,500 | 5.2 | 3.1 | 5.0 |

*Source*: Processed based on WTTC, 2019 and Euromonitor International, 2019.

# Behaviour of smart tourists and implications for smart cities

With a tendency toward shorter and more frequent trips, smart cities emerge as the ideal destinations offering compelling experiences to the increasingly demanding tourists. The built smart infrastructure in smart cities, the use of the Internet of Things, cloud computing, big data analytics, as well as the widespread adoption of mobile devices offering ubiquitous connectedness (Buhalis, 2020), has led to that fact that some tourists started to behave smarter and the smart tourist market segment was created (Gajdošík, 2020). The characteristics of a smart tourist are summarized as follows (Table 6.2):

**Table 6.2:** Characteristics of a smart tourists

| Description | Author(s) |
|---|---|
| Exigent and well informed tourists, who are interested in the sustainability and responsibility of the destination they visit, yet treat the environment with elevated sensibility and responsibility, as well. The smart tourist wants to interact with the destination. Due to this engagement, they become co-creators and co-promoters of the destination. | Gahr et al. (2014) |
| A tourist heavily reliant on information and communication technologies, who undertakes in-depth information searches, and is very active on social media. Smart tourists are seeking customised and personalised offerings as well as mindful of value for money and safety and environmental matters | Ghaderi et al. (2018) Fan et a. (2019) |
| A tourist who benefits from smart tourism by utilising various information technologies available at a smart tourist destination. | Gretzel et al. (2018) |

| | |
|---|---|
| A tourist who uses personalised and contextualised services, engage and explores the destination and is in search for authentic and immersive experience during all stages of travel. | Buhalis and Sinarta (2019) |
| A tourist being more knowledgeable of the destination, more demanding, better connected. A smart tourist is more likely to share information, with a greater capacity for making recommendations and placing greater importance of user-generated content. Smart tourists differ from previous tourists, as they have become more dependent on information technology; self-service and reservation tools and they value easier access to technology, better value for their money, and greater variety, flexibility, personalisation and safety. | González-Reverté (2019) Buhalis, and Amaranggana (2015) |
| A tourist who, by being open to sharing his or her data and making use of smart technologies, interacts dynamically with other stakeholders, co-creating in this way an enhanced and personalised smart experience. This tourist is open to innovations, social and pro-active and finds his or her natural environment in the smart tourism ecosystem and the smart destination. | Femenia-Serra et al. (2019a) Fan et a. (2019) |
| A member of a profiling market segment, who is accustomed to use information technologies during all the trip experience phases. The willingness to co-create and share data leads to the need of personalised solutions, while reviews, authentic experiences and user-generated content are more crucial than in other segments in destination selection process. | Gajdošík (2020) |
| A tourist that has at his/her service all digital tools provided by technologies to make every aspect of his/her life smarter and contribute to the wellbeing of the places visited. Smart tourists often behave in a sustainable and responsible way because they connect with local actors and resources. | Shen et al. (2020b) |

These characteristics emphasise mainly (1) the use of information technologies while travelling; (2) experience co-creation and data sharing; and (3) focus on sustainability. For a smart tourist, technology represents an opportunity to actively participate in city activities and to take part in the construction of its own experience (Prebensen et al., 2013). The smart tourist is no longer isolated in a limited zone of knowledge while traveling but is empowered to reach out to local communities, other travellers and their own network of contacts before during and after the actual trip (Fan et al., 2019). By using the mobile device and location-based services, tourists can exchange information in real time, be active in conversations and personalise their experience (Buhalis & Foerste, 2015). This connected, better informed and engaged tourist is dynamically interacting with the destination, leading to the need of co-creating tourism product and adding value for all tourism stakeholders (Neuhofer et al., 2012; Buhalis & Sinarta, 2019).

**94** Smart Cities and Tourism

However, smart tourists do not merely use smart technologies for their own enjoyment and sake. They can engage with local resources and develop a sustainable behaviour during their journey, becoming the co-creators of responsible experiences and sustainable co-managers of vulnerable tourism resources in a destination (Shen et al., 2020b).

Smart tourists are co-designers, co-marketers, co-advertisers, co-promoters and co-distributors of tourism experience (Sigala, 2018; Buhalis & Sinarta, 2019). Smart tourists show proactiveness in terms of contents and communication with a range of stakeholders. They are active managers of their own experience, not only consumers. This makes them also co-producers and developers of tourism activity in a city with an economic impact (Navío-Marco et al., 2018). This new type of a tourist often wants to have a super-connected experience (Femenia-Serra et al., 2019b), actively participates in activities (Prebensen et al., 2013) and is in the search of authentic and immersive experiences (Buhalis & Sinatra, 2019; Fan et al., 2019). Hence, smart tourists bring more effectiveness, transparency, loyalty and economic value to a destination and thus they are worth focus on (Gajdošík, 2020).

Although smart tourists are important stakeholders of smart cities (Sigalat-Signes et al., 2020), smart cities stakeholders often have limited knowledge about their behaviour or even misconceptions. Therefore, the aim of this contribution is to focus on the smart tourists' behaviour and provide implication for development of smart cities.

The empirical analysis is based on the two-step questionnaire survey. The first step was done in 2018 by obtaining information form 5,975 tourists. These tourists were classified into segments, leading to the identification of the smart tourist market segment (Gajdošík, 2020). The sample of 840 smart tourists use smart technologies to co-create their experience through smart technologies and share data with stakeholders. Further, the members of this segment were contacted with a more in-depth survey in 2019. Finally, 499 complete responses were obtained from smart tourists. The surveys were conducted in Slovakia, a country recognized as a digital challenger (Novak et al., 2018) and a place where the use of Internet services and integration of digital technology are at the average of the European Union counties (European Commission, 2019).

## The use of information technologies by smart tourists

Smart cities are ideal places for smart tourists, as their built smart information infrastructure that enables to provide real-time information for tourists. Information technologies should enhance experience of a smart tourist by giving all the related real-time information about the destination and its services in the planning phase, enhance access to real-time information to assist tourists in exploring the destination during the trip and prolong engagement to relieve the experience by proving the descent feedback after the trip (Buhalis & Amaranggana, 2015). The behaviour of smart tourists, when comparing with other (non-smart) tourist segments considering the use of information technologies, differs in all trip experience phases (Fan et al., 2019). Smart tourists are keener to use information technologies in all phases. The specific technologies and statistical differences between smart tourists and other tourists reveal the opportunities for smart cities development (Table 6.3).

**Table 6.3:** The use of specific technologies during trip experience phases

| | Total | Non smart | Smart | Kruskal-Wallis | |
|---|---|---|---|---|---|
| | N= 5976 | N= 5136 | N= 840 | $\chi^2$ | p value |
| | Mean | Mean | Mean | | |
| Planning and booking | | | | | |
| IDS/OTA | 1.56 | 1.49 | 2.02 | 107.695 | 0.000 |
| Hotel web site | 1.59 | 1.54 | 1.94 | 87.73 | 0.000 |
| Destination web site | 1.26 | 1.2 | 1.65 | 103.739 | 0.000 |
| Sharing economy platform | 0.39 | 0.36 | 0.57 | 35.643 | 0.000 |
| Meta search | 0.61 | 0.57 | 0.85 | 148.051 | 0.000 |
| Staying in a destination | | | | | |
| Digital map | 1.24 | 1.19 | 1.56 | 148.051 | 0.000 |
| Mobile app | 0.53 | 0.42 | 1.22 | 795.437 | 0.000 |
| Hotel web site | 0.86 | 0.79 | 1.27 | 255.311 | 0.000 |
| Destination web site | 0.77 | 0.69 | 1.21 | 306.749 | 0.000 |
| Augmented reality | 0.16 | 0.12 | 0.42 | 354.818 | 0.000 |
| smart cards | 0.41 | 0.32 | 0.99 | 696.289 | 0.000 |
| Wearables | 0.19 | 0.14 | 0.50 | 397.025 | 0.000 |
| Sharing the experiences | | | | | |
| Sharing on social media | 1.02 | 0.89 | 1.83 | 795.093 | 0.000 |

Note: The evaluation was on the scale 0 – never, 1 – sometimes, 2 – often, 3 – regularly.

In the pre-trip phase, tourists use information technologies for searching information, planning the trip and booking services. During planning and booking, the internet distribution systems (IDS) or online travel agencies (OTA) belong to the most used technologies by smart tourists (Buhalis & Foerste, 2015). Other tourist segments prefer hotel website on the first place. The destination website is used quite often by smart tourists, while only sometimes by other tourist segments. This creates opportunities for changing tourism websites in smart cities to smart portals providing convenience to smart tourists by filtering suitable information, and learning from the processes to provide users with explicit and customised information (Zhang et al., 2018; Gajdošík, 2020).

In order not to get lost in an unfamiliar environment, smart tourists use information technologies to solve problems in real time, provide flexibility and experience enrichment. These tourists use quite often a digital map while staying in the destination. The mobile app gained much more importance by smart tourists than by other tourist segments. This useful technology enables the concentration of all the important tourist information about the city as a destination on a one place and can support the co-creation and personalisation of the experience. Therefore, smart cities should create mobile apps that incorporate the most common requirements of smart tourists, including cutting-edge technologies, such as digital maps with real-time position monitoring, augmented reality and social media integration.

The differences in the use of smart cards and wearables are also very evident between smart tourists and other tourist segments. Smart cards can reveal important information about tourist behaviour in the destination (e.g. movement, product and services used) and promote the most important tourism offer. Smart tourists can focus more on experiencing rather than searching for tourism attractions and finding the appropriate transport mode. Although wearables are sometimes used by smart tourists, these devices are predicted to have a significant impact on the interaction with the surroundings of a destination (Tussyadiah, 2014), thus creating opportunities for smart cities development.

The use of social media to share the experience is very common for smart tourists (Fan et a.l, 2019). Smart tourists trust reviews and recommendation of other tourists published on social media. For the majority of smart tourists (55.8%) sharing the photos, videos and status updates enhance the overall tourism experience. Moreover, 80.3% of smart tourists write reviews. Writing and publishing post-trip experiences can help tourists to strengthen and build experience, and at the same time have an impact on the decision-making of other tourists (Shen et al., 2020a). Therefore, smart cities should implement news feeds and integrate their social media channels in their online presence.

The comparison of smart tourists and other segments, in terms of technology use, confirmed the higher technology acceptance and use in the segment of smart tourists. If a tourist does not want to be confused in an unfamiliar environment and wants to have a personalised experience, the use of smart technologies in inevitable. Figure 6.1 presents the most important smart technologies for smart tourists. Smart tourists were asked to give their opinion regarding the expected degree of impact of selected technologies on tourism development and anticipate the period of maximum impact in tourism.

**Figure 6.1:** Evaluation of smart technologies by smart tourists

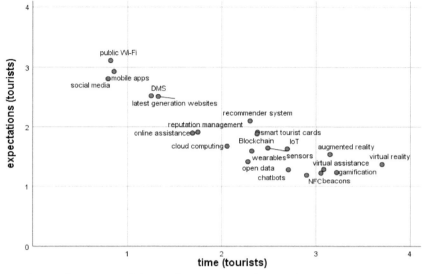

Note: **Expectation** – expected degree of impact measured on a scale: 0 – no impact, 4 – very high impact.
**Time** – anticipated period of maximum impact measured on a scale: 0 – today, 2 – short term /2-5 years/, 5 – medium term /5-10 years, 10 – long term /10 years and more.

Social media, public Wi-Fi, latest generation websites, as well as mobile apps are considered by smart tourists as the technologies with the highest impact, as these technologies are already implemented in smart cities. However, they should be enriched by location-based services, real-time conversation and AI-based applications. Technologies enhancing tourist experience (smart cards, recommender systems, online assistance, chatbots, virtual assistance, wearables, augmented and virtual reality) have been predicted to have slightly lower impact and cities should implement them soon to satisfy the demand of smart tourists. Technologies related to data management and storage, such as destination management system, e-reputation management, cloud computing, Blockchain and open data are also considered as technologies with medium expected impact. These technologies are prerequisites of big data analytics that can analyse and interpret data on tourist behaviour in a destination. Therefore, if a smart city wants to offer a personalised tourism product, it must start to use these technologies. To attract smart tourists, smart cities should, together with their destination management organisations (DMOs), invest more on their enabling technologies, keep their official tourism website up-to-date and better manage their online reputation.

## 98  Smart Cities and Tourism

The biggest advantage of smart cities is their built smart network and sensing infrastructure. Smart tourists consider the sensing and network technologies (NFC, beacons, sensors) as being more important. The effect of these technologies can be augmented using the Internet of Things, allowing collected data to be transferred to data management systems. The analysis of the smart tourists' opinions on smart technologies revealed which technologies to implement in order to support smart tourist behaviour. Smart technologies represent the interconnection and collaborative progress of various technologies simultaneously (Shen et al., 2020a), not just the use of single technology separately.

## Experience co-creation and data sharing

The second specific feature of a smart tourist is the higher focus on experience co-creation and willingness to share data with stakeholders in a destination. When choosing a destination, smart tourists consider reviews, price and the offer of authentic experience (Table 6.4). Tourists see reviews as more reliable source of information than other sources (Xiang & Gretzel, 2010). Price levels is still one of the most important factors in decisions about whether, and where, to undertake trips (Forsyth & Dwyer, 2009). The third most important factor is the offer of an authentic experience.

**Table 6.4:** Factors influencing the choice of a destination

| Factors | Total | Non smart | Smart | Chi-square test | |
|---|---|---|---|---|---|
| | N= 5976 | N= 5136 | N= 840 | $\chi^2$ | p value |
| | (%) | (%) | (%) | | |
| Reviews | 81.00 | 79.00 | 88.00 | 34.493 | 0.000 |
| Price | 88.00 | 88.00 | 86.00 | 3.974 | 0.046 |
| The offer of authentic experience | 50.00 | 49.00 | 55.00 | 12.378 | 0.000 |
| Recommendations from family and friends | 37.00 | 36.00 | 41.00 | 6.276 | 0.012 |
| Official photos and videos | 33.00 | 32.00 | 37.00 | 7.719 | 0.005 |
| Customer photos and videos | 29.00 | 28.00 | 37.00 | 31.921 | 0.000 |
| Ease of reservation process | 31.00 | 31.00 | 34.00 | 4.075 | 0.044 |
| Travel distance | 17.00 | 18.00 | 16.00 | 1.54 | 0.215 |
| Customer service | 5.00 | 5.00 | 9.00 | 22.022 | 0.000 |
| Sustainable principles | 4.00 | 4.00 | 6.00 | 10.44 | 0.001 |

In terms of experience, smart tourists are, more than other tourists, keen on the offer of authentic experience. They prefer mainly the experience in the urban settings (59.8%), adventurous experience (50.9%) and natural experience (41.9%). The high demand of experience in the urban areas gives smart cities a unique position to attract smart tourists. Therefore, the tourism products in smart cities should be transferred to authentic and memorable experiences. The massive use of information technologies by smart tourists serve as a prerequisite for experience co-creation. Smart tourists do not want to be passive information recipients. A clear shift towards active co-creation and personalisation of experience is evident. From the technological point of view, there are several requirements for experience co-creation. First, is the information aggregation based on data from tourists (Neuhofer et al., 2015). Enabling cookies on websites and location-based services in mobile apps or creating an account on a website supports smart tourists to share their data in order to co-create. Smart tourists are quite active in conversations with tourism producers through social media and some smart tourists enable mobile apps to provide personal information from their smartphone (Figure 6.2).

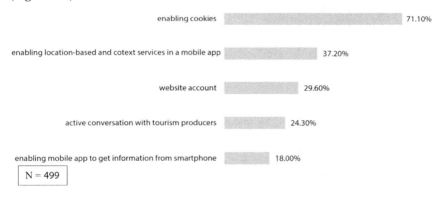

**Figure 6.2:** Using information technologies for experience co-creation by smart tourists

Instead of obtaining data from tourists themselves, a smart city can obtain relevant information about their behaviour from other sources. These sources include sensors, mobile positioning or cards. Smart cities use sensors for monitoring traffic or density of crowds. These sensors can monitor tourist behaviour using cameras, scanners, infrared ports, radio frequency identification, near field communication, Wi-Fi hotspots, beacons and other sensing technologies. Moreover, mobile positioning can be used to track tourist mobile devices. In order to monitor tourist purchase behaviour, tracking the bank or tourist cards is also useful. However, sharing data is influenced by the fear of misusing the data. Although, 29.7% of smart tourists do not have such a fear, 43.4% of smart tourists are afraid of overall privacy evasion and 24.3% do not want their movement to be monitored. This create some challenges for co-creation that smart cities should face. The co-creation of experience also requires that stakeholders are dynamically connected in a system

## 100 Smart Cities and Tourism

to facilitate personalised experiences (Buhalis & Amaranggana, 2015) and real-time synchronization (Neuhofer et al., 2015, Buhalis & Sinarta, 2019). The real-time databases for monitoring and big data analytics implemented in smart cities create the baseline for such a synchronization, thus enabling the real-time experience co-creation.

### Focus on sustainability

Smartness should not be viewed only by lenses of information technology. Respecting sustainable principles is also important. It is predicted that the ethical concerns will have a substantial impact only on a relatively small group of tourists. Information technologies have provided consumers with more powerful tools to plan and evaluate their sustainable behaviour, Therefore the 'new normal' will be an increased standard of sustainability transparency (Sattel, 2015), demanded mainly by smart tourists. Smart tourists are more responsible and behave in a more sustainable way in order to reduce some of the effects of their activities (Shen et al., 2020b). The smart technologies used by smart tourists provide more efficient and effective alternatives in all trip experience phases, thus creating possibilities for sustainable behaviour. The sustainable behaviour of smart tourists includes several activities (Table 6.5).

**Table 6.5:** Sustainable behaviour of tourists

| Trip experience phase | Sustainable behaviour |
|---|---|
| Planning and booking | Choosing destination based on respecting the sustainable principles |
| Staying in a destination | Minimising environmental effects<br>Trying to get to know local culture<br>Support of local economy |
| Sharing the experience | Influencing other tourists to behave in a sustainable way<br>Expressing satisfaction on social media |

In the planning and booking phase, smart tourists should choose their destination based on respecting the sustainable principles. Sustainable principles an important factor of destination choice, only for 6.0% of smart tourists; when compared with other segments (4.0%) (Table 6.4). However, smart tourists are becoming more likely to choose destinations that behave sustainably. Technology enables smart tourists to easily find and compare destinations based on sustainable principles. Therefore, smart cities should communicate their sustainable practices to reach this market segment.

When staying in a destination, 58.1% of smart tourists try to always minimize the negative environmental effects of their travel and 35.9% do it occasionally. If a smart city provides relevant data and technology, the informed smart tourist can make better decisions in a destination by reducing traffic congestion or overcrowding of tourist attractions in peak periods. From the socio-cultural point of view, smart technologies used by smart tourists assist and engage tourists into immersive experiences. Moreover, for almost 26% of smart tourists, getting to know the local culture is the most valuable tourism experience. Smart cities should therefore strengthen the initiatives supporting the residents and avoiding the crowding-out effect in the city centre. In terms of supporting the local economy, it is the smart tourist segment, among other tourist segments, who has the highest additional spending in a destination (Gajdošík, 2020). This spending goes directly to destination stakeholders, supporting the economic pillar of sustainability.

Sharing the experience is also an important part of sustainable tourist behaviour. The majority (80.7%) of smart tourists write reviews about places they visited and thus influence other tourists to behave like them. The regular use of social media for expressing feedback and satisfaction enables stakeholders to improve their services and thus to behave more sustainably. This creates the pressure to implement e-reputation management with text mining and sentiment analysis, as the amount of user-generated content makes it hard to process manually.

## Conclusion

Cities do not only boost economic development, and affect the environment and quality of residents' life, but they are also attractive places for tourists. Smart cities are attractive and have a plethora of tourism activities. The development and massive use of information technologies have changed the way a city is constructed and used by residents and tourists. This is particularly the case after the COVID-19 pandemic, as citizens and travellers learn to operate most functions digitally. Technological solutions and innovations offered by smart cites can satisfy the high requirements and preferences of smart tourists, who use information technologies during all trip experience phases to co-create personalised experience and behave in a more sustainable way. The study provides a better understanding of smart tourist behaviour in the context of smart cities.

The focus on the smart tourist market segment has many advantages for smart cities. It is an economically interesting segment, with high purchasing power, as their consumption in a destination is higher than the consumption of other tourist segments. The massive use of information technologies during all the trip experience phases provides valuable data and strengthens the effectiveness and governance of a smart city. In order to satisfy the smart tourist segment, smart cities should create value propositions during all trip experience phases, based on personalisation, experience enrichment and sustainability. All communication channels should provide tourists with explicit and customised information. Based on the available data on tourists, smart cities can personalise and contextualise their offerings and services to each tourist and customise them according to their requirements. The tourism experience in smart cities should be developed from passive consumption to active co-creation or even self-production using e.g., smart web portals and mobile apps. Smart cities are therefore ideal destinations for smart tourists, who, thanks to technologies, can get to know the city and behave 'like a local'. Therefore, smart cities should govern the city to create engaging life of residents and memorable experience for tourists. Smart cities should act as a magnet not only for creative and smart residents but also for smart visitors. This will create value for all stakeholders and will lead to more sustainable, competitive and resilient cities.

> **Acknowledgements:** The research was supported by the research project VEGA 1/0237/20 Tourism 4.0: Smart and sustainable tourism development in a competitive environment.

# References

Sattel, J. (2015) Future traveller tribes 2030: Understanding tomorrow's traveller. Amadeus, https://amadeus.com/en/insights/blog/tribes2030

Antón, C., Camarero, C., Laguna, M. & Buhalis, D., (2019), Impacts of authenticity, degree of adaptation and cultural contrast on travellers' memorable gastronomy experiences, *Journal of Hospitality Marketing & Management*, 28 (7), 743–764, https://doi.org/10.1080/19368623.2019.1564106

Barcelona, (2017), Barcelona Tourism for 2020. A collective strategy for sustainable tourism, https://ajuntament.barcelona.cat/turisme/sites/default/files/barcelona_tourism_for_2020.pdf .

Buhalis, D., Harwood, T., Bogicevic, V., Viglia, G., Beldona, S. & Hofacker, C. (2019) Technological disruptions in Services: lessons from tourism and hospitality', *Journal of Service Management*, 30(4), 484-506

Buhalis, D. (2020) Technology in tourism-from information communication technologies to eTourism and smart tourism towards ambient intelligence tourism: a perspective article, *Tourism Review*, 75 (1), 267-272.

Buhalis, D. & Amaranggana, A. (2014) Smart tourism destinations, in Xiang, Z. & Tussyadiah, I. (eds) *Information and Communication Technologies in Tourism 2014*, Cham: Springer International Publishing, pp. 553-564.

Buhalis, D. & Amaranggana, A. (2015) Smart tourism destinations enhancing tourism experience through personalisation of services, in Tussyadiah, I. & Inversini, A. (eds) *Information and Communication Technologies in Tourism 2015*, Cham: Springer International Publishing Switzerland, pp. 377-389.

Buhalis, D. & Foerste, M. (2015) SoCoMo marketing for travel and tourism: Empowering co-creation of value, *Journal of Destination Marketing and Management*, 4(3), 151-161.

Buhalis, D. & Sinarta, Y. (2019) Real-time co-creation and nowness service: lessons from tourism and hospitality, *Journal of Travel & Tourism Marketing*, 36 (5), 563-582.

Caragliu, A., Del Bo, C. & Nijkamp, P. (2011) Smart Cities in Europe, *Journal of Urban Technology*, 18 (2), 65-82.

Euromonitor International (2019) Top 100 city destinations: 2019 edition. https://go.euromonitor.com/white-paper-travel-2019-100-cities

European Commission (2019) Digital economy and society index 2019. Country report Slovakia. https://ec.europa.eu/newsroom/dae/document.cfm?doc_id=59906

Fan, D., Buhalis, D. & Lin, B. (2019) A tourist typology of online and face-to-face social contact: Destination immersion and tourism encapsulation/decapsulation, *Annals of Tourism Research*, 78, 102757.

Femenia-Serra, F., Neuhofer, B. & Ivars-Baidal, J. A. (2019a) Towards a conceptualisation of smart tourists and their role within the smart destination scenario, *The Service Industries Journal*, 39 (2), 109-133.

Femenia-Serra, F., Perles-Ribes, J. F. & Ivars-Baidal, J. A. (2019b) Smart destinations and tech-savvy millennial tourists : hype versus reality, *Tourism Review*, 74 (1), 63-81.

Forsyth, P. J. & Dwyer, L. (2009) Tourism price competitiveness, in Blanke, J. & Chiesa, T. (eds) *The Travel and Tourism Competitiveness Report 2009: Managing in a Time of Turbulence.* Geneva: World Economic Forum, pp. 77-90.

Gahr, D., Rodríguez, Y. & Hernández-Martín, R. (2014) Smart destinations . the optimisation of tourism destination management, paper presented at *Seminario de Economía Canaria.* Tenerife, 19-20 June, Islas Canarias, Spain.

Gajdošík, T. (2020) Smart tourists as a profiling market segment: Implications for DMOs, *Tourism Economics*, 26 (6), 1042-1062.

Ghaderi, Z., Hatamifar, P. & Henderson, J. C. (2018) Destination selection by smart tourists: the case of Isfahan, Iran, *Asia Pacific Journal of Tourism Research*, 23 (4), 385-394.

González-Reverté, F. (2019) Building sustainable smart destinations: an approach based on the development of Spanish smart tourism plans, *Sustainability*, 11 (23), 6874.

Gretzel, U., Ham, J. & Koo, C. (2018) Creating the city destination of the future: The case of smart Seoul, in Wang, Y., Shakeela, A., Kwek, A. & Khoo-Lattimore, C. (eds) *Managing Asian Destinations*, Springer, Singapore, pp. 199-214.

Gretzel, U. & Koo, C. (2021) Smart tourism cities: a duality of place where technology supports the convergence of touristic and residential experiences, *Asia Pacific Journal of Tourism Research*, 26 (4), 1-13.

Heaton, J. & Parlikad, A. K. (2019) A conceptual framework for the alignment of infrastructure assets to citizen requirements within a Smart Cities framework, *Cities*, 90 (1), 32-41.

Hedlund, J. (2012) Smart city 2020: Technology and society in the modern city. Microsoft Services.

Kim, B., Yoo, M., Park, K., Lee, K. & Hyun, K (2021) A value of civic voices for smart city: A big data analysis of civic queries posed by Seoul citizens, *Cities*, 108, 102941.

Koo, C., Mendes-Filho, L. & Buhalis, D. (2019) Smart tourism and competitive advantage for stakeholders, *Tourism Review*, 74 (1), 1-4.

Navío-Marco, J., Ruiz-Gómez, L. M. & Sevilla-Sevilla, C. (2018) Progress in information technology and tourism management: 30 years on and 20 years after the internet - Revisiting Buhalis & Law's landmark study about eTourism, *Tourism Management*, 69, 460–470.

Neuhofer, B., Buhalis, D. & Ladkin, A. (2012) Conceptualising technology enhanced destination experiences, *Journal of Destination Marketing and Management*, 1 (1–2), 36-46.

Neuhofer, B., Buhalis, D. & Ladkin, A. (2015) Smart technologies for personalized experiences: a case study in the hospitality domain, *Electronic Markets*, 25 (3), 243-254.

Novak, J., Purta, M., Marciniak, T., Ignatowicz, K., Rozenbaum, K., & Yearwood, K. (2018) *The rise of digital challengers. How digitization can become the next growth engine for Central and Eastern Europe.* http://digitalchallengers.mckinsey.com

Prebensen, N. K., Vittersø, J. and Dahl, T. I. (2013) Value co-creation significance of tourist resources, *Annals of Tourism Research*, 42, 240-261.

Romão, J., Kourtit, K., Neuts, B. & Nijkamp, P. (2018) The smart city as a common place for tourists and residents: A structural analysis of the determinants of urban attractiveness, *Cities*, 78, 67-75.

Sánchez-Corcuera, R., Nunez-Marcos, A. & Sesma-Solance, J., (2019) Smart cities survey: Technologies, application domains and challenges for the cities of the future, *International Journal of Distributed Sensor Networks*, 15.

Shen, S., Sotiriadis, M. & Zhang, Y. (2020a) The influence of smart technologies on customer journey in tourist attractions within the smart tourism management framework, *Sustainability*, 12 (10), 1-18.

Shen,S., Sotiriadis,M. & Zhou, Q. (2020b) Could smart tourists be sustainable and responsible as well? The contribution of social networking sites to improving their sustainable and responsible behavior, *Sustainability*, 12(4), 1-21.

Sigala, M. (2018) New technologies in tourism: From multi-disciplinary to anti-disciplinary advances and trajectories, *Tourism Management Perspectives*, 25 (1), 151–155. doi: 10.1016/j.tmp.2017.12.003.

Sigalat-Signes, E., Calvo-Palomares, R., Roig-Merino, B. & Garcia-Adán, I. (2020) Transition towards a tourist innovation model: The smart tourism destination: Reality or territorial marketing?, *Journal of Innovation and Knowledge*, 5 (2), 96-104.

Stylos, N., Zwiegelaar, J., & Buhalis, D., (2021), Big data empowered agility for dynamic, volatile, and time-sensitive service industries: the case of tourism sector, *International Journal of Contemporary Hospitality Management*, 33(3), 1015-1036. https://doi.org/10.1108/IJCHM-07-2020-0644

Tussyadiah, I. (2014) Expectation of travel experiences with wearable computing devices, in Xiang, Z. and Tussyadiah, I. (eds) *Information and Communication Technologies in Tourism 2014*. Cham: Springer International Publishing Switzerland, pp. 539-552.

Um, T. & Chung, N. (2021) Does smart tourism technology matter? Lessons from three smart tourism cities in South Korea, *Asia Pacific Journal of Tourism Research*, 24 (4), 396-414.

UNWTO (2018) Overtourism? Understanding and Managing Urban Tourism Growth beyond Perceptions.

Wolff, A., Barker, M., Hudson, L. & Seffah, A. (2020) Supporting smart citizens: Design templates for co-designing data-intensive technologies, *Cities*, 101, 102695.

WTTC (2019) *City Travel & Tourism Economic Impact Report*. wttc.org/Research/Economic-Impact

Xiang, Z. & Gretzel, U. (2010) Role of social media in online travel information search, *Tourism Management*, 31 (2), 179-188.

Zhang, T., Cheung, C. & Law, R. (2018) Functionality evaluation for destination marketing websites in smart tourism cities, *Journal of China Tourism Research*, 14 (3), 263-278.

# 7 Co-creating and co-destructing personalised experiences through smart tourism

*Katerina Volchek, Dimitrios Buhalis and Rob Law*

## Introduction

The 4th industrial revolution has pushed the development of smart tourism cities' infrastructure and transformed business processes for value co-creation. The concept of a 'smart city' signifies capabilities for tourism resource optimisation and value co-maximisation through smart technology (Buhalis, 2020). Tourism destinations have long used technology to develop their competitiveness (Buhalis & Wagner, 2013). The rapid development of smart cities opens new space for advancing tourist experience (Buhalis & Amaranggana, 2015). However, the capabilities of smart cities to inform tourism infrastructure and secure value maximisation remain largely underexplored (Matos et al., 2019; Gretzel, 2018). Being dependent on collaboration between tourism businesses and other stakeholders, the process of value co-creation through smart technology can also result in value co-destruction (Vargo & Lusch, 2017). Understanding value co-creation and co-destruction processes in smart tourism cities is crucial for businesses (Pillmayer et al., 2021; Assiouras et al., 2019).

Historically, businesses used market research results and their expertise to interpret tourist requirements and adapt service offerings accordingly in the mid and long term. Personalisation has long been acknowledged among the essential tools to co-create advanced tourist experiences (Ricci et al., 2015). Personalisation refers to a strategy of creating a service with the parameters that are relevant to satisfy the individual needs and demands of a customer (Volchek et al., 2021). The capabilities of tourism service providers to identify real-time tourists' preferences and constraints and distribute services create the potential for delivering relevant, novel and memorable travel experiences. In contrast, irrelevant services offerings are likely to result in customer dissatisfaction. The importance of personalisation, together with a risk of co-destructed experience by an irrelevant service, urges the need for a reliable personalisation strategy to ensure the relevance of a service offering. As a facet of smart tourism cities (Choi et al., 2019), personalisation depends on big data and their infrastructure (Stylos et al., 2021). Accurate recognition of tourists' needs requires tourism service providers to utilise real-time data and a range of analytical techniques (Buhalis & Sinarta, 2019).

Smart tourism cities' infrastructure offers opportunities for reengineering processes and automating many aspects of value co-creation. The growing scope and quality of available relevant data, the increasing interconnectivity of smart technologies, and the advancements in data analytics provide new ways to observe real-time human behaviour and interpret immediate tourist needs (Wise & Heidari, 2019; Stylos et al., 2021). However, a generalised view on utilising smart city infrastructure to advance travel experience through personalisation rather than destroying it, is still missing.

This chapter conceptualises the potential of a smart tourism city to co-create and co-destruct tourist experiences through personalisation. The chapter uses a multidisciplinary approach to integrate tourist behaviour, information system design and service management. The chapter first defines personalisation as a service offering in tourism and explains the reason why it is acknowledged as one of the determinants of advanced tourist experience. The chapter then defines the types of resources required for personalisation. It then applies the concept of layered system architecture to match the resource requirements of successful personalisation with the capabilities of smart city infrastructure. The chapter applies Service-Dominant Logic (SDL) (Vargo & Lusch, 2017) to conceptualise the potential of not only co-creating but also co-destructing tourist experiences through the process of personalisation. It proposes a new resource-based framework that explains the processual view of tourist personalised experience creation by smart tourism cities infrastructure. The proposed framework argues that the relevance of resources, which are contributed by a smart tourism city's stakeholder, determines whether travel experiences are co-created or co-destructed through personalisation. The chapter suggests that adequate coordination between all smart tourism city stakeholders is crucial to realise the capabilities of personalisation to deliver advanced tourist experiences.

## Personalised travel experiences

Service personalisation is a strategy of creating a service offering with features that are suitable for satisfying individual customer's needs (Volchek et al., 2019). Market interactions are motivated by attempts to create value (Akaka et al., 2017). Value for customers is associated with the satisfaction of their personal needs. According to the Porter's focus differentiation strategy (1998), the better the match between personal needs and service offering's characteristics, the higher customer value can be created. Individually designed, personalised and individualised services have a greater potential to maximise customer value, than standardised solutions.

Personalisation in tourism is recognised among the future determinants of travel business competitiveness (Zanker et al., 2019). A distinctive feature of tourist needs is their high dependence on real-time context and situations whilst travelling (Buhalis & Sinarta, 2019). An unexpected crisis situation (both personal or contextual); proximity to an unseen attraction; unexpectedly available time (due to a cancelled meeting, for example); an encounter with new acquaintances; previously unconsidered events, and many more contextual factors can motivate or force tourists to change earlier-defined plans and form new demands on the go. Equally, health situations for travellers or dependants; unexpectedly long distance from the point of interest due to traffic; worsening weather; congestion conditions; Internet connection and network challenges; low battery life, can prevent tourists from realising their individual plans and force last-minute itinerary changes. Increasingly, travellers benefit from highly-relevant service that is responsive to contextual challenges and opportunities in real time. Offerings need to be sufficiently flexible to satisfy their immediate needs and support value co-creation when so many external conditions may disrupt travel plans (Buhalis & Foerste, 2015). This became obvious during the COVID period or when wars or terrorism attacks occurred at destinations or in transit regions.

The main challenge that arises for travel businesses is to react in real-time to the changes in individuals' situations. To keep the service offering relevant, personalisation commonly applies known behaviour traits and formed preferences to offer a relevant service. In addition to pleasure, tourist behaviour is driven by the need for novel, authentic, and memorable experiences (Skavronskaya et al., 2020). Therefore, tourists can switch to a non-typical behaviour, referred to as liminal, for the duration of their trips. This means that tourists can try services that they do not encounter in their daily routines, such as unfamiliar types of accommodation, new types of travel attractions, unusual activities, entertainment and food (Pung et al., 2020). Given the high dependence of tourist needs on a real-time situation, the application of long-term preferences for personalisation may result in irrelevant service offerings, capable of ruining the experience. Tourism service providers need to continuously search for reliable opportunities to recognise immediate tourist needs and develop personalised service offering accordingly in real time.

## Personalisation through smart city infrastructure

Smart tourism cities motivate the collaborative development of processual innovations and the design of new services (Pillmayer et al., 2021). A smart ecosystem refers to complex relationships among people, institutions and technology, designed to optimise the network of relationships between them (Gretzel, 2018). The interconnectivity and interoperability of multiple devices, which became possible due to the advancements in the Internet of Things (IoT), big data, and artificial intelligence (AI), enable ambient intelligence (Buhalis, 2020; Buhalis & Leung, 2018). This creates a space for smart infrastructure-driven collaboration between travel businesses, governments, local communities, and tourists to co-create value for each of them.

Smart tourism city infrastructure revolutionises the opportunities for mass personalisation. The collaboration within smart city ecosystems makes real-time sharing and exchanging resources possible. Thus, personalisation requires information about the tourist internal and external context to interpret individual tourist needs, differentiate service offerings and provide tourists with relevant solutions (Buhalis & Foerste, 2015, Piccoli et al., 2017). As a facet of smart tourism, personalisation aims to benefit from its shared infrastructure, including available data and AI-driven analysis, to develop and deliver advanced tourist experiences (Choi et al., 2019, Buhalis et al., 2019).

Complex processes that drive the development of a smart tourism city ecosystem and enable personalisation are often conceptualised in architectural layers (Gretzel, 2018). They offer a structured way to list core resources and explain their organisation for a defined purpose. Figure 7.1 summarises personalisation as enabled by smart tourism city ecosystems, through architectural layers. Physical, technology, data, business, and experience layers highlight the resources required for value co-creation through personalisation.

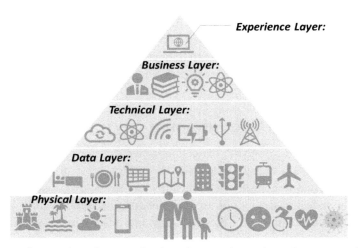

**Figure 7.1:** Co-creation of personalised tourist experience through smart tourism city infrastructure

## Physical layer

The physical layer of a system architecture serves as a background for defining a service and provides critical support for other layers to implement it (Gretzel, 2018). Tourist needs, preferences, and restrictions depend on their internal and external contexts (Buhalis & Foerste, 2015). A physical layer can be used to recognise a real-time tourist situation at a destination towards needs, demands, preferences, and restrictions they might have. Internal context consolidates the individual characteristics, which might affect consumer behaviour. Age, gender, levels of education, income, culture and religious views form relatively stable tourist preferences towards service (Pearce, 2011). For example, representatives of Generations X, Y, Z and Alpha may have distinct requirements for travel experiences. Individual conditions, such as a high level of stress, caught flu or COVID, allergies or disabilities, might create additional requirements or restrictions to the desired experience. Tourist service providers need to know relevant information about an internal tourist context to be able to develop personalised service offerings for each person. The external context factors are any factors that surround a tourist either physically or virtually. They can generate new needs and affect those determined by tourists' internal context. For example, the physical location at a destination and available time can motivate tourists to visit additional attractions. Travelling alone or with family members or friends creates specific demands for travel experiences. Changing COVID-19 regulations may require adjustment of the timetable. New acquaintances or an exciting event can have an immediate effect on the articulated plans, making previously delivered service offerings irrelevant (Buhalis & Sinarta,

2019; Lamsfus et al., 2015). Understanding the tourist external context is critical to supporting them with relevant and up-to-date service offerings. The personalisation strategy at the physical layer aims to recognise those factors of tourist internal and external contexts that determine their needs. Those factors, in turn, are used to define the data and technology required to create personalised services. Personalisation recognises tourists as important stakeholders of smart tourism city infrastructure, who enable the personalisation process, and, therefore, should be engaged from the start.

## Data and technical layers

A distinctive feature of a smart tourism ecosystem is its capacity for human context recognition through collaborative usage of smart city infrastructure and its resources (Xie et al., 2016). Context recognition refers to a process of automatic sensing of data, suitable to describe internal and external contexts of an object and of making inferences about this object based on the collected data (Otebolaku & Andrade, 2016). Data and technical layers are used to conceptualise a system's capabilities to create and deliver its target outcome (Gretzel, 2018). The data layer identifies required data with its sources and ways to acquire, store, process, and mine data. The technology layer represents hardware, software, computational and analytical principles that are required to make use of the data. Together, they create a resource background for service co-creation. The ability of a smart ecosystem to sense and interpret the influential factors of tourist context enables tourism businesses to develop or adjust service accordingly.

Context sensing aims to collect relevant data required for personalisation. In addition to information from tourist profiles and online behaviour (e.g. searched topics and keywords, visited websites), smart tourism ecosystems can utilise environmental sensors embedded in personal tourist devices. Such data as individual geolocation, altitude, acceleration, heart rate and blood pressure, and, increasingly, brain activity can be captured by tourists' personal devices, including smartphones, smartwatches, smart rings and smart clothes (Ardito et al., 2019). After a proper analysis, such data can generate insights about tourists' internal context.

To create a holistic understanding of tourist context, tourism businesses can benefit from the data generated by other destination stakeholders. Maps, timetables of events, opening and busy hours of attractions, shops, restaurants and other points of interest have been made available for tourist service providers planning for a while. Collaboration among travel businesses, road management, police and Internet providers allows aggregation of geolocation data of cars, pedestrians, and public transport passengers, to make inferences about real-time traffic conditions and parking availability in travel areas (Buhalis et al., 2019). Weather monitoring services share real-time weather forecasts and support planning by individuals and weather-dependent transportation such as ferries and airline schedules. Vendors engaged in transportation, hospitality and tourism businesses may exchange data about the immediate availability of hotel rooms and tickets (Mehraliyev et al., 2020; Wise & Heidari, 2019). Sensing the external tourist context through smart tourism city infrastructure opens new opportunities for increasing the relevance of service offerings.

At the stage of making inferences, personalisation aims to acquire information about tourist behaviour patterns and other influential factors required to understand tourist context. Historical and real-time data can be accumulated and continuously updated, forming a pool for analysis, prognosis and scenario building. Collaborations with analytical software providers or research agencies make the capabilities of advanced analytics, including AI, available for tourism businesses (Choi et al., 2019). Data-driven context recognition is capable of identifying real-time tourist behavioural patterns in specific situations (Xiang & Fesenmaier, 2017). Thus, matching longitude, latitude and altitude, received from a tourist smartphone's accelerometer with GPS coordinates allows travel businesses to locate the tourist at a specific shop or restaurant. The number of mobile signals in close proximity with the tourist smartphone enables travel businesses to conclude about the number of people around them. Information can be historical to identify patterns or in real time to explore opportunities. The outcome of tourism context recognition serves as a background for selecting and delivering relevant services to tourists and utilising assets smartly.

The analytical potential of tourism infrastructures has been dramatically extended by the capabilities of AI (Luckey et al., 2020; Koo et al., 2019). Compared with supervised learning, which requires labelled data to identify trends, unsupervised learning can make inferences by extracting trends from previously unlabelled data. This function enables AI to detect events dynamically, which remained unobserved with predefined settings and assumptions. For example, deep reinforcement learning algorithms can be used to detect previously unidentified inconsistencies in planned processes, together with the causes of the problems (Ullah et al., 2020). One of the possible applications of AI is the monitoring of the trends that were not observed earlier, thereby informing the smart city infrastructure about the required changes (Luckey et al., 2020). Collaboration between data and AI providers fuels the potential of travel businesses to advance tourist experience through personalisation.

## Business and experience layers

The business layer refers to a business ecosystem of multiple organisations collaborating for value co-creation (Höpken et al., 2010). It explains the logic and strategy of utilising available resources to develop and deliver services and create customer experiences in the experience layer (Gretzel et al., 2018). In the case of personalisation, the business layer benefits from partners' business strategy to utilise the results of context recognition to inform and drive service adaptation. As a strategy of need satisfaction, personalisation can target adaptation of a core service (Salonen & Karjaluoto, 2016); augmentation of processes (Piccoli et al., 2017); or dynamic innovation to deliver highly relevant value (Buhalis & Sinarta, 2019). Therefore, personalisation does not require a value proposition re-articulated for each customer. Instead, it needs to ensure the relevance of all elements of the marketing mix, including the service and its presentation, communication and delivery within the defined value proposition.

Service automation enables differentiation of service parameters without engaging extra resources (Sigala, 2012; Tussyadiah, 2020). For example, online databases, which store information about available hotel rooms, can automatically group offerings according to defined criteria. As a result, target tourists would be provided with service offerings, such as a specified type of room, price, and extra services as bundles. Such service offerings can be communicated in the most relevant way for these tourists. Travel businesses can design personalised landing website pages so that each of the pages would be shown to users with specific characteristics (Volchek et al., 2019). A responsive user interface enables relevant web content presentation for each type of personal device (Chan et al., 2021). Tourists benefit from the same information, presented in an easy-to-read way, individually designed for them. Cloud computing and constant connectivity allow scheduling direct marketing messages for the moment that is relevant for the tourist (Buhalis & Volchek, 2021; Lei et al., 2020). The role of travel businesses is to define the logic of service differentiation by matching identified tourist needs with service offerings relevant to satisfy them.

The capabilities of smart ecosystems for context recognition and service automation provide travel businesses with new opportunities for advanced personalisation (Gretzel et al., 2015b). Thus, travel businesses can use their expertise and knowledge about tourist needs in a specific context to assume that a certain service offering would satisfy these needs. Then, travel businesses can utilise the results of tourist context recognition to automate the delivery of the service offerings with predefined characteristics to the target tourists. Inferences about tourist contexts and service offering propositions

## 114 Smart Cities and Tourism

can be fully automated and enhanced by AI that is now capable of identifying new context-specific behaviour patterns (Fiorini et al., 2017). Therefore, the engagement of additional technology can expand the potential of travel business ecosystems to further enhance service offering relevance for target customers.

The relevance of the delivered combination of service offerings for immediate tourist need satisfaction creates a background for pleasurable, authentic, novel and memorable experiences (Piccoli et al., 2017). A match between service parameters and customer needs, preferences or restrictions is the underpinning background for the advanced experiences (Choi et al., 2019; Neuhofer et al., 2015). A relevant assumption about tourist needs in a defined context, and the business logic of satisfying these needs with specific service offerings, together with smart tourist city-driven analytics, are the prerequisites for the co-creation of advanced tourist experiences through personalisation.

As a result, smart tourism city infrastructure can engage different stakeholders in planning personalised service offerings dynamically (Buhalis & Sinarta, 2019; Massimo & Ricci, 2020). Collaboration among tourists themselves, tourism and hospitality business, destination management organisation, IT companies, research agencies, governments and other organisations allows the development of a comprehensive understanding of tourist context and an appropriate response. Some data drive planned contextual reactions when issues are expected (e.g. a storm arriving soon or a sport mega-event planned) or unexpected (e.g. car accident or plane crash). Any disengaged stakeholder limits the potential of the collective smart tourism ecosystem to accurately recognise the context, creating risks for personalised service offerings to be realised.

## Personalised experience co-creation and co-destruction through smart city infrastructure

The resource potential of smart ecosystems to provide tourists with real-time personalised services to deliver advanced experiences is evident. However, smart ecosystems face challenges while solutions remain largely underexplored (Ardito et al., 2019; Gretzel et al., 2015a). The personalisation process itself has often been observed as posing a risk of experience co-destruction (Volchek et al., 2019; Smith, 2013).

SDL provides the theoretical explanation for co-created and co-destructed tourist experiences. According to SDL, value does not exist per se. It arises from service capability to generate benefits from an ecosystem of resources from all involved parties, i.e. 'actors' (Greer et al., 2016). Service is explained as a process of applying actors' resources, performed for the creation and maximisation of utilitarian, hedonic, relational, and other benefits for themselves and others (Kuzgun & Asugman, 2015, Plé & Chumpitaz Cáceres, 2010).

Smart tourism should therefore be conceptualised as a mindset that enables a network of actors within the smart city ecosystem to share. The actors establish smart technology-enabled collaboration to maximise value for themselves and other actors (Boes et al., 2016). Service personalisation is an integral part of the value co-creation process. Enabled by the smart city ecosystem infrastructure, it is dependent on the network of the ecosystem actors and the resources they integrate into it.

SDL explains that the outcome of value formation relies both on the available resources and the practices of these resources' integration (Ramaswamy & Ozcan, 2018). Practice is a combination of explicitly articulated rules of doing things, knowledge of these rules, understanding the purpose of resource integration, and committing to it (Makkonen & Olkkonen, 2017; Vargo & Lusch, 2017; Plé, 2016). Practices allow actors to decide what resources should be integrated, in what amount and way. Successful value realisation depends on a common mindset and shared understanding of the applied practices. Given that service is a process, value can be co-created or co-destructed at any stage of resource integration (Vargo & Lusch, 2017). Considering relevant resources and their appropriate application in the service ecosystem can result in value co-creation. On the contrary, resource misuse, such as lack of appropriate resources, integration of irrelevant resources, or inappropriate practice in the application of relevant resources, is likely to hinder the improvement of the actors' wellbeing through service. Regardless of the purpose of an actor's participation in a service ecosystem, their wellbeing can either improve or decline as a result of resource integration (Plé & Chumpitaz Cáceres, 2010).

Figure 7.2 proposes a conceptual framework of co-creating and co-destructing personalised tourist experiences through smart tourism city infrastructure. Personalisation is a complex strategy that requires the processes of each layer to be properly executed. Each layer of personalisation sets an objective of creating a specific outcome, which enables the subsequent layer. Each layer requires specific resources and, therefore, engages multiple actors of a smart tourism city. Each actor has its own objectives of participating in value formation and its own practices of value realisation. As a result, each stage of the personalisation process can result in either a positive or negative outcome. Advanced tourist experiences can be achieved when all processes at each layer are realised in an appropriate way. Thus, the ability of the personalisation process to utilise resources of smart ecosystem to identify target customers, accurately recognises their immediate context through available data. It makes relevant inferences about their needs dynamically to match them with the predefined sets of differentiated services and creates the platform for co-creation of advanced tourist experiences (Assiouras et al., 2019).

In contrast, inappropriate data, such as obsolete information about tourist activities, may result in irrelevant or obsolete services. Mistakenly selected analytics, such as a model of human behaviour, built on irrelevant assumptions, may result in the wrong inference about tourist behaviour and related needs regardless of data relevance. Inappropriate business logic may result in service with irrelevant parameters being delivered to tourists. For example, a service provider may learn that the tourists from Mexico have consistently rated Mexican cuisine highly and may assume that these tourists would be delighted with a Mexican cuisine when travelling. Such as assumption can potentially prevent these tourists from experiencing authentic local food and acquiring unique and novel experiences (Antón et al., 2019). Accordingly, the tourist experience can be co- destructed when the outcome of at least one layer is not realised properly.

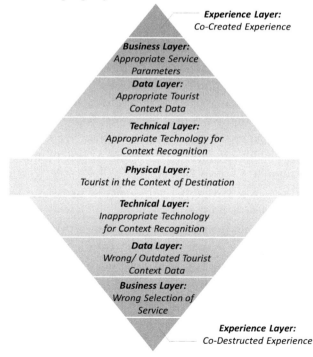

**Figure 7.2:** Co-creation and co-destruction of personalised tourist experiences through smart city infrastructure.

Whether intentionally or occasionally, each of the actors has a capacity to contribute to co-creation or co-destruction of value (Vargo & Lusch, 2017). Thus, misunderstanding the purpose of a personalisation strategy, commitment to another, more valuable collaboration, or unethical behaviour of at least one of the actors of a smart tourism city may prevent relevant service adaptation. Regardless of the relevance of the personalisation strategy developed by a travel business, successful personalisation depends on the performance of all engaged actors of a networked smart tourism city. Service ecosystems as a dynamic arrangement of resources (Storbacka et al., 2016) are empowered by smart tourism due to the capability of each actor to contribute to value co-creation and co-destruction. A successful strategy is determined by the ability of an ecosystem to fit into changing conditions (Vargo & Lusch, 2008). Therefore, the presence of the practices of appropriate value provision and communication to customers alone is insufficient to ensure a successful value co-creation strategy (Skålén et al., 2015). The ability of the service ecosystem to adapt to real-time changes is amongst the critical factors of successful value co-creation.

The strategy of co-creating advanced tourist experiences through personalisation requires a set of predefined resources and practices of their integration. This strategy faces a challenge to incorporate the complexity of smart ecosystems, and the presence of multiple actors, engaged in personalisation in real time, and to react to changes in dynamically changing tourist internal and external contexts (Buhalis & Sinarta, 2019). This restricts travel businesses from total control over the relevance of resource integration and the delivered outcome. Innovative practices are required to supplement the major strategy to enable systemic maintenance and agile adaptation to unplanned changes within an ecosystem (Vargo et al., 2015; Akaka et al., 2017).

The potential of smart tourism city infrastructures has been dramatically extended by the capabilities of AI (Luckey et al., 2020; Buhalis et al., 2019, Koo et al., 2019). Practitioners should explore opportunities to incorporate additional AI-enabled automation to monitor the presence of all relevant resources and the appropriateness of their integration within the personalisation strategy. This step may inform the personalisation system about the required changes to recover value after an occurred resource misuse, apply additional real-time adjustments of the marketing mix to deliver authentic, novel, pleasurable and memorable travel experiences or abort value realisation to prevent value co-destruction for tourists. Smart tourism supports the network approach for all stakeholders to optimise the value co-created dynamically (Buhalis, 2020).

## Conclusion

Personalisation is often named as a strategy that can support service providers in their challenge of providing tourists with advanced experiences. This chapter uses an interdisciplinary conceptual approach to propose a theoretical framework that explains the process of personalisation through smart tourism city infrastructure. It outlines the resulting opportunities for co-creating and co-destructing advanced tourist experience through personalisation within the smart tourism city ecosystem.

Smart cities have the potential for co-creating value by delivering novel, pleasurable, authentic and memorable tourist experiences when relevant resources are properly integrated at each layer of personalisation. The resources of smart city networks may have both positive and negative effects on the personalisation process and resulting tourist experience. Smart ecosystems also pose a threat of co-destructing tourist experience. This may occur at each stage of the personalisation process due to incorrect or obsolete data. This may lead to context incorrect inferences about tourist needs and preferences, or restriction by recognition algorithm, which lead to irrelevant assumptions about relevant elements of the marketing mix, which should be adapted to enable need satisfaction. The proposed framework can serve as a theoretical background for the systematic analysis of personalisation from a business perspective.

The practical implications of the proposed framework are related to the service design in smart tourism ecosystems. The proposed framework demonstrates that a flexible personalisation strategy with the practices of providing the planned process of service adaptation and monitoring this process, and reacting in real-time in case of inappropriate resource integration, can minimise the risk of co-destructing tourist experience. Instead of focusing solely on the end-service design, industry practitioners might follow the service design process for each layer of smart ecosystem-enabled personalisation to ensure that each layer performs according to the defined objectives.

This chapter takes a resource perspective and focuses on the business strategy of working in a smart city environment. Tourist experiences are individual and subjective occurrences, formed at the moment of interactions with travel services (Neuhofer et al., 2015). They represent personal perceptions on the relevance of applied resources and appropriateness of personal and other actors' 'resource integration'. Thus, tourists remain widely unaware of the exact ways smart cities can sense their data. However, they often develop concerns about smart ecosystems posing security and privacy threats for them (Camilleri & Neuhofer, 2017). Consequently, their experience can be co-created or co-destructed by their individual interpretation of smart ecosystems regardless of their parameters. Amongst other directions, future research could investigate the ways to improve tourists' understanding of the co-created or co-destructed experiences through smart city infrastructure to minimise the risks of co-destructed experiences.

# References

Akaka, M. A., Vargo, S. L. & Wieland, H. (2017). Extending the context of innovation: the co-creation and institutionalisation of technology and markets. *Innovating in Practice.* Springer. 43-57.

Antón, C., Camarero, C., Laguna, M., & Buhalis, D. (2019). Impacts of authenticity, degree of adaptation and cultural contrast on travellers' memorable gastronomy experiences. *Journal of Hospitality Marketing & Management,* 28(7), 743-764.

Ardito, L., Cerchione, R., Del Vecchio, P. & Raguseo, E. (2019). *Big data in smart tourism: challenges, issues and opportunities.* Taylor & Francis.

Assiouras, I., Skourtis, G., Giannopoulos, A., Buhalis, D. & Koniordos, M., (2019), Value co-creation effect on customer citizenship behavior, *Annals of Tourism Research,* 78, 102742. https://doi.org/10.1016/j.annals.2019.102742

Boes, K., Buhalis, D. & Inversini, A. (2016). Smart tourism destinations: ecosystems for tourism destination competitiveness. *International Journal of Tourism Cities,* 2, 108-124.

Buhalis, D. (2020). Technology in tourism - from information communication technologies to eTourism and smart tourism towards ambient intelligence tourism: a perspective article. *Tourism Review,* 75(1), 267-272.

Buhalis, D. & Wagner, R. (2013). E-destinations: Global best practice in tourism technologies and applications. In *Information and Communication Technologies in Tourism 2013.* Cham: Springer. pp. 119-130.

Buhalis, D. & Amaranggana, A. (2015). Smart tourism destinations enhancing tourism experience through personalisation of services. In: Tussyadiah, I. & Inversini, A. (eds.) *Information and Communication Technologies in Tourism 2015.* Cham: Springer. pp. 377-389.

Buhalis, D. & Foerste, M. (2015). SoCoMo marketing for travel and tourism: Empowering co-creation of value. *Journal of Destination Marketing & Management,* 4, 151-161.

Buhalis,D., Harwood, T., Bogicevic, V., Viglia, G., Beldona, S. & Hofacker, C. (2019). Technological disruptions in services: lessons from tourism and hospitality. *Journal of Service Management,* 30 (4), 484-506.

Buhalis, D. & Leung, R. (2018). Smart hospitality—Interconnectivity and interoperability towards an ecosystem. *International Journal of Hospitality Management,* 71, 41-50.

Buhalis, D. & Sinarta, Y. (2019). Real-time co-creation and nowness service: Lessons from tourism and hospitality. *Journal of Travel & Tourism Marketing*, 36, 563-582.

Buhalis, D. & Volchek, K. (2021). Bridging marketing theory and big data analytics: The taxonomy of marketing attribution. *International Journal of Information Management*, 56, 102253.

Camilleri, J. & Neuhofer, B. (2017). Value co-creation and co-destruction in the Airbnb sharing economy. *International Journal of Contemporary Hospitality Management*, 29, 2322-2340.

Chan, I.C.C., Law, R., Fong, L.H.N., & Zhong, L. (2021) Website design in tourism and hospitality: a multilevel review. *International Journal of Tourism Research*. 23, 805-815.

Choi, I. Y., Ryu, Y. U. & Kim, J. K. (2019). A recommender system based on personal constraints for smart tourism city. *Asia Pacific Journal of Tourism Research*, 1, 14.

Fiorini, L., Cavallo, F., Dario, P., Eavis, A. & Caleb-Solly, P. (2017). Unsupervised machine learning for developing personalised behaviour models using activity data. *Sensors*, 17, 1034.

Greer, C. R., Lusch, R. F. & Vargo, S. L. (2016). A service perspective. *Organizational Dynamics*, 1, 28- 38.

Gretzel, U. (2018). From smart destinations to smart tourism regions. *Investigaciones Regionales*, 42, 171-184.

Gretzel, U., Ham, J. & Koo, C. (2018). Creating the city destination of the future: The case of smart Seoul. *Managing Asian Destinations*. Springer. 199-214.

Gretzel, U., Reino, S., Kopera, S. & Koo, C. (2015a). Smart tourism challenges. *Journal of Tourism*, 16, 41-47.

Gretzel, U., Sigala, M., Xiang, Z. & Koo, C. (2015b). Smart tourism: foundations and developments. *Electronic Markets*, 25, 179-188.

Höpken, W., Fuchs, M., Zanker, M. & Beer, T. (2010). Context-based adaptation of mobile applications in tourism. *Information Technology and Tourism*, 12, 175-195.

Koo, C., Mendes-Filho, L. & Buhalis, D. (2019). Smart tourism and competitive advantage for stakeholders: Guest editorial. *Tourism Review*, 74, 1-4.

Kuzgun, E. & Asugman, G. (2015). Value in services – a service dominant logic perspective. *Procedia Social and Behavioral Sciences*, 207, 242-251.

Lamsfus, C., Alzua-Sorzabal, A., Wang, D. & Xiang, Z. (2015). Going mobile: defining context for on-the-go travelers. *Journal of Travel Research*, 54, 691-701.

Lei, S. I., Ye, S., Wang, D. & Law, R. (2020). Engaging customers in value co-creation through mobile instant messaging in the tourism and hospitality industry. *Journal of Hospitality & Tourism Research*, 44, 229-251.

## 7: Co-creating and co-destructing personalised experiences through smart tourism 121

Luckey, D., Fritz, H., Legatiuk, D., Dragos, K. & Smarsly, K. (2020). Artificial intelligence techniques for smart city applications. In: Toledo, S. & Eduardo, S. S., (eds.) *International Conference on Computing in Civil and Building Engineering*, Cham. Springer, 3-15.

Makkonen, H. & Olkkonen, R. (2017). Interactive value formation in inter-organizational relationships: Dynamic interchange between value co-creation, no-creation, and co-destruction. *Marketing Theory, 17,* 517-535.

Massimo, D. & Ricci, F. (2020). Next-POI recommendations for the smart destination era. In: Neidhardt, J. & Wörndl, W. (eds.) *Information and Communication Technologies in Tourism 2020.* Cham: Springer. 130-141.

Matos, A., Pinto, B., Barros, F., Martins, S., Martins, J. & Au-Yong-Oliveira,M. (2019). Smart cities and smart tourism: What future do they bring? *Proceedings of World Conference on Information Systems and Technologies,* 2019. Springer, 358-370.

Mehraliyev, F., Chan, I. C. C., Choi, Y., Koseoglu, M. A. & Law, R. (2020). A state-of-the-art review of smart tourism research. *Journal of Travel & Tourism Marketing, 37,* 78-91.

Neuhofer, B., Buhalis, D. & Ladkin, A. (2015). Smart technologies for personalised experiences: a case study in the hospitality domain. *Electronic Markets,* 25, 243-254.

Otebolaku, A. M. & Andrade, M. T. (2016). User context recognition using smartphone sensors and classification models. *Journal of Network and Computer Applications,* 66, 33-51.

Pearce, P. L. (2011). *Tourist Behaviour and the Contemporary World,* Bristol Channel View Publications.

Piccoli, G., Lui, T.-W. & Grün, B. (2017). The impact of IT-enabled customer service systems on service personalisation, customer service perceptions, and hotel performance. *Tourism Management, 59,* 349-362.

Pillmayer, M., Scherle, N. & Volchek, K. (2021). Destination management in times of crisis - potentials of open innovation approach in the context of COVID-19? In: Wörndl, W., Koo, C. & Stienmetz, J. L., (eds.) *Information and Communication Technologies in Tourism 2021* Cham. Springer, 517-529.

Plé, L. (2016). Studying customers' resource integration by service employees in interactional value co-creation. *Journal of Services Marketing, 30,* 152-164.

Plé, L. & Chumpitaz Cáceres, R. (2010). Not always co-creation: introducing interactional co-destruction of value in service-dominant logic. *Journal of Services Marketing, 24,* 430-437.

Porter, M. E. (1998). *On Competition,* Boston, MA: Harvard Business School, 1998.

Pung, J. M., Gnoth, J. & Del Chiappa, G. (2020). Tourist transformation: Towards a conceptual model. *Annals of Tourism Research,* 81, 102885.

Ramaswamy, V. & Ozcan, K. (2018). What is co-creation? An interactional creation framework and its implications for value creation. *Journal of Business Research,* 84, 196-205.

Ricci, F., Rokach, L. & Shapira, B. (2015). Recommender systems: introduction and challenges. *Recommender Systems Handbook.* Boston, MA: Springer. 1-34.

Salonen, V. & Karjaluoto, H. (2016). Web personalisation: The state of the art and future avenues for research and practice. *Telematics and Informatics, 33,* 1088-1104.

Sigala, M. (2012). Mass customisation models for travel and tourism information e-services: Interrelationships between systems design and customer value. In *Advancing the Service Sector with Evolving Technologies: Techniques and Principles* (pp. 135-157). IGI Global.

Skålén, P., Gummerus, J., Koskull, C. & Magnusson, P. (2015). Exploring value propositions and service innovation: a service-dominant logic study. *Official Publication of the Academy of Marketing Science, 43,* 137-158.

Skavronskaya, L., Moyle, B. & Scott, N. (2020). The experience of novelty and the novelty of experience. *Frontiers in Psychology, 11,* 322.

Smith, A. M. (2013). The value co-destruction process: a customer resource perspective. *European Journal of Marketing, 47,* 1889-1909.

Storbacka, K., Brodie, R. J., Böhmann, T., Maglio, P. P. & Nenonen, S. (2016). Actor engagement as a microfoundation for value co-creation. *Journal of Business Research, 69,* 3008-3017.

Stylos, N., Zwiegelaar, J. & Buhalis, D. (2021), Big data empowered agility for dynamic, volatile, and time-sensitive service industries: the case of tourism sector. *International Journal of Contemporary Hospitality Management, 33(3),* 1015-1036. https://doi.org/10.1108/IJCHM-07-2020-0644

Tussyadiah, I. (2020). A review of research into automation in tourism: Launching the Annals of Tourism Research curated collection on artificial intelligence and robotics in tourism. *Annals of Tourism Research, 81,* 102883.

Ullah, Z., Al-Turjman, F., Mostarda, L. & Gagliardi, R. (2020). Applications of artificial intelligence and machine learning in smart cities. *Computer Communications, 154,* 313-323.

Vargo, S. L. & Lusch, R. F. (2008). Service-dominant logic: continuing the evolution. *Journal of the Academy of Marketing Science, 36,* 1-10.

Vargo, S. L. & Lusch, R. F. (2017). Service-dominant logic 2025. *International Journal of Research in Marketing, 34,* 46-67.

Vargo, S. L., Wieland, H. & Akaka, M. A. (2015). Innovation through institutionalisation: A service ecosystems perspective. *Industrial Marketing Management, 44,* 63-72.

Volchek, K., Law, R., Buhalis, D. & Song, H. (2019). The good, the bad, and the ugly: Tourist perceptions on interactions with personalised content. *e-Review of Tourism Research, 16,* 62- 72.

Volchek, K., Yu, J., Neuhofer, B., Egger, R. & Rainoldi, M. (2021) Co-creating personalised experiences in the context of the personalisation-privacy paradox. In: Wörndl, W., Koo, C. & Stienmetz, J. L., eds. *Information and Communication Technologies in Tourism 2021* Cham. Springer, 95-108.

Wise, N. & Heidari, H. (2019). Developing smart tourism destinations with the Internet of Things. *In:* Sigala, M., Rahimi, R. & Thelwall, M. (eds.) *Big Data and Innovation in Tourism, Travel, and Hospitality: Managerial Approaches, Techniques, and Applications.* Singapore: Springer. 21-29.

Xiang, Z. & Fesenmaier, D. R. (2017). Big data analytics, tourism design and smart tourism. In Xiang, Z. & Fesenmaier, D. R. (eds.) *Analytics in Smart Tourism Design.* Springer. pp. 299-307.

Xie, K., Wu, Y., Xiao, J. & Hu, Q. (2016). Value co-creation between firms and customers: The role of big data-based cooperative assets. *Information & Management, 53,* 1034-1048.

Zanker, M., Rook, L. & Jannach, D. (2019). Measuring the impact of online personalisation: Past, present and future. *International Journal of Human-Computer Studies, 131,* 160-168.

# Part III:
# Smart Cities and Smart Tourism Destinations

# 8 Smart city or smart tourism destination?
## The formation of smart Ljubljana in Slovenia

*Abbie-Gayle Johnson and Jillian M. Rickly*

## Introduction

A city comes to be known as 'smart' through the deployment of smart initiatives (Komninos et al., 2019). Smart initiatives contribute to the management of urban challenges and are present in varying forms, namely social media platforms, wireless internet, mobile applications, booking platforms, information beacons and so on (Femenia-Serra et al., 2018; Roopchund, 2020). The efficiency of these solutions is made possible through optimisation techniques that increasingly employ machine learning, deep learning and artificial intelligence algorithms (Buhalis et al., 2019; Fox, 2017; Estrada et al., 2019). In some places, smart initiatives have been designed specifically in response to tourism management needs and for enhancing visitor experiences, thus extending the nomenclature to 'smart tourism destinations' (Cavalheiro et al., 2020). Importantly, both smart cities and smart destinations emphasise the core principle of interoperable systems that connect and generate value for stakeholders (Buhalis, 2020). Smart cities are also capitalising on sharing economy (Taheri et al., 2022; Buhalis et al., 2020).

Little is known of the processes that drive smart initiatives (Mehraliyev et al., 2020). While some have shed light on the core resources and conditions necessary for achieving smartness (Lee et al., 2014; Boes et al., 2016; Shafiee et al., 2019), fewer have elaborated the stages of smart development through which these resources and conditions are organised towards their practical design and implementation. For example, working in the context of smart cities in Korea, Lee et al. (2013) developed a three-stage development model: preliminary activity, developing actions and follow-up stage of implementation. In the case of smart tourism destinations in China, Zhu et al. (2014) provided two stages of smart development – designing and operating – which involve government and organisations such as technology and tourism enterprises. However, Gretzel et al. (2015) suggest that smart tourism should be conceived as an ecosystem in which various technological components and entities exist with diverse roles and identities. The experience value co-creation process on destination online platforms in the pre-travel stage significantly affects the destination emotional experience (Zhang et al., 2018).

This chapter moves this conversation further by focusing on the role of collaboration in bringing together these diverse stakeholders and roles. Stakeholder collaboration is essential to smart cities. Janssen et al. (2019) argue that lack of stakeholder collaboration can inhibit interoperability and robustness, thereby hindering smart city developments. Indeed, the optimisation of smart networks are far from 'neutral', 'politically benign and commonsensical' (Kitchin, 2014: 8). Instead, they rely on multiple, diverse stakeholders who construct and dictate the efficiency of operations (see also Baggio et al., 2020). Yet, as Zuzul (2019) observes, the smart city collaboration process is still not clearly understood and, as a result, necessitates further insights from varying contexts.

Collaboration is central to tourism destination management and has historically been integrated into destination process frameworks (Zhang et al., 2018). Gray (1985) formulated a destination management model with three stages: problem-setting, direction-setting, and structuring. Selin and Chavez (1995) built on Gray's model to emphasise partnership, thereby adding the stages of structuring and outcomes. While several other studies examine the development of collaborations (Waddock, 1989; Caffyn, 2000), it is Wang and Fesenmaier (2007) who present the most detailed framework for examining the formation of destination collaboration. Collaborative frameworks are linear and focused on internal processes. Bramwell and Cox (2009) suggest applying path dependence theory to incorporate the historical contexts that can influence collaborative stages. Considering the importance of the interoperability of diverse stakeholders and technological components (Buhalis et al., 2019), there is a need to understand better the social, political, and technical processes that drive 'smartness' (see Zuzul, 2019).

This chapter investigates the processes by which Europe's Capital of Smart Tourism (2019 and 2020) – Ljubljana, Slovenia – has developed and instituted its smart initiatives. By doing so, the chapter bridges the academic literature on smart cities and smart tourism and extends our understanding of the social, political, and technological processes that drive 'smartness' at the destination level. Using Ljubljana as a case study, this chapter employs Wang and Fesenmaier's (2007) destination collaboration process framework alongside path dependence theory to trace the city's development of smart tourism initiatives. While the technological aspects of smart cities and smart tourism destinations have received considerable attention in the literature (Mora et al., 2019; Bastidas-Manzano et al., 2020), focussing on the human dimension and collaboration specifically enriches our understanding across both smart cities and smart tourism literature.

# Literature review

## Understanding smart cities and smart tourism destinations

The concept of smart cities remains debated and somewhat abstract within both practice and academic literature (Kumar, 2017; Bibri, 2019). Within academic research, smart cities are conceptualised as being *"related to solutions that optimise urban systems and user behaviour through smart devices, ICT-based automation, sensors and instrumentation"* (Komninos, 2014: 20–21). Governing bodies such as the European Union note that a smart city is *"a place where traditional networks and services are made more efficient with the use of digital and telecommunication technologies for the benefit of its inhabitants and business"* (EU, 2020: n.p.). In light of the varying definitions, Bibri (2019) proposes a contextual conceptualisation. The varied meanings of smart cities have resulted in diverse representations and understandings of how these places should develop (Zuzul, 2019).

Some authors have formulated smart city development models based on a stage model approach (Lee et al., 2013; Siokas et al., 2021). Kumar et al. provide a smart city transformation framework in which a city is said to undergo four stages: planning phase, creation of physical infrastructure, formation of information and communication technologies (ICT) infrastructure and deployment of smart solutions. Noori et al. (2020) create a three-stage model: input resources, throughputs, and outputs; however, the type of stakeholder engagement is unclear. The city government drives most smart city developments in Europe to provide a better standard of living for local citizens (Perboli & Rosano, 2020).

Despite the diversity in models, they focus heavily on the technological and urban aspects of smart cities. For instance, Lee et al. (2013) provided a smart city process emphasising smart technology. As a result, the participants involved in these studies are usually the urban planners and technology experts, representing solely the developers of infrastructure to improve quality of life (see Lee et al., 2013). However, thinking more broadly, Giffinger et al. (2007) propose that a smart city has six characteristics, namely: smart economy, smart people, smart governance, smart mobility, smart environment, and smart living.

Considering the role of tourism, Kumar (2017) recognises the smart economy as a place with businesses that tourists are interested in visiting. Tourism businesses are therefore identified as a component in the smart economy. Furthermore, Kumar et al. (2020) highlight smart tourism as one of the outputs of the smart city development process planned and implemented by government entities. Tourism stakeholders are represented then as beneficiaries rather than engaged stakeholders. While smart cities incorporate tourism, a separate research area explores smart tourism in cities, further discussed.

A few definitions have been proposed for a smart tourism destination (Buhalis, 2015, 2020; Ivars-Baidal et al., 2019). For instance, Buhalis (2015: n.p.) builds from smart cities:

*"a smart tourism destination successfully implements smartness which is fostered by open innovation, supported by investments in human and social capital, and sustained by participatory governance to develop the collective competitiveness of tourism destinations to enhance social, economic and environmental prosperity for all stakeholders"*

Buhalis' (2015) definition mentions some of the critical components of smart destination development: innovation, human and social capital. According to Boes et al. (2016), the core components of smartness are ICT, innovation, leadership, human and social capital. Moving beyond resources, Zhu et al. (2014) formulates a smart destination development model based on two stages: designing and operating. However, like smart cities models, Zhu et al. (2014) provide a simplistic account of smart development. These conceptual models (Lee et al., 2013; Zhu et al., 2014; Letaifa, 2015) have a one-directional flow and do not represent a collective representation of stakeholders and initiatives. Although previous studies have provided valuable insights, Zuzul (2019) concludes that there is a need for greater in-depth accounts of smart development that reflect a complex reality since there still exists process ambiguity.

## Tourism destination collaboration

The process of tourism destination collaboration has been conceptualised mainly using two approaches: path dependence and stages. Path dependence, the less commonly used theoretical approach, is an evolutionary economic perspective that acknowledges the importance of connected and disconnected historical events in explaining the adoption of new processes, mainly when there exist more efficient, alternative pathways (David, 1985; Puffert, 2002). According to path dependence, *"history matters […] the respective events represent initial conditions that, by triggering a self-reinforcing process, have an enduring impact upon the course of the path's future trajectory"* (Sydow et al., 2012: 157). This has been applied to tourism collaboration research, illustrating how temporal continuities influence activities within a collaboration (Bramwell & Cox, 2009). Applying path dependence, Bramwell and Cox (2009) find that establishing a steering group for a tourism collaboration in the United Kingdom was a historical trend in other countries. Furthermore, the inclusion of multiple stakeholders in the process also stemmed from a past culture of consultation.

Unlike the path dependence approach, which highlights activities as temporal continuities, the stage approach is more prominently applied in tourism collaboration studies, as it focuses on internal, sequential processes (Bramwell & Cox, 2009). Stage processes have also been used to examine smart development (see Lee et al., 2013; Letaifa, 2015; Kumar et al., 2020; Siokas et al., 2021). This chapter applies the Wang and Fesenmaier's (2007) five-stage process of collaboration formation, which builds upon major theories necessary for understanding destination collaboration (Menon et al., 2017). The five stages include assembling, ordering, implementation, evaluation, and transformation (see Figure 8.1) and are yet to be extended to the smart tourism context.

Wang and Fesenmaier's (2007) process was designed based on responses garnered through interviews with tourism representatives in Indiana (USA), where the success of the destination has been partly due to its collaborative marketing initiatives. Compared to smart city models, Wang and Fesenmaier's model provides greater detail of each stage and the final stage of transformation. The steps are also connected, though lacking indications. The model is also the only one crafted for destination collaborations, as the others previously mentioned were mainly based on partnerships and community-based collaborations. One of the model's limitations is that macro-environmental factors, which were not explicitly identified, are only mentioned as being responsible for setting the preconditions for initiating a collaboration. Environmental conditions are connected to the reason for the

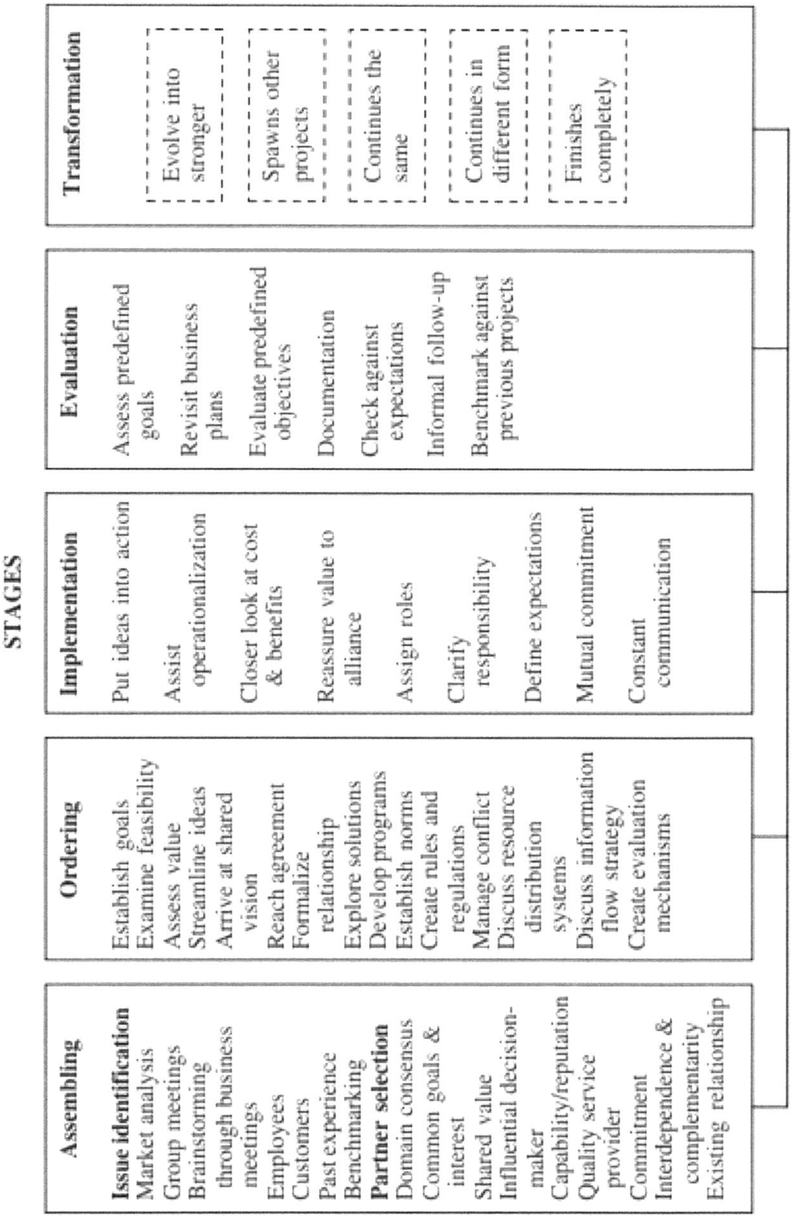

STAGES

| Assembling | Ordering | Implementation | Evaluation | Transformation |
|---|---|---|---|---|
| **Issue identification**<br>Market analysis<br>Group meetings<br>Brainstorming through business meetings<br>Employees<br>Customers<br>Past experience<br>Benchmarking<br>**Partner selection**<br>Domain consensus<br>Common goals & interest<br>Shared value<br>Influential decision-maker<br>Capability/reputation<br>Quality service provider<br>Commitment<br>Interdependence & complementarity<br>Existing relationship | Establish goals<br>Examine feasibility<br>Assess value<br>Streamline ideas<br>Arrive at shared vision<br>Reach agreement<br>Formalize relationship<br>Explore solutions<br>Develop programs<br>Establish norms<br>Create rules and regulations<br>Manage conflict<br>Discuss resource distribution systems<br>Discuss information flow strategy<br>Create evaluation mechanisms | Put ideas into action<br>Assist operationalization<br>Closer look at cost & benefits<br>Reassure value to alliance<br>Assign roles<br>Clarify responsibility<br>Define expectations<br>Mutual commitment<br>Constant communication | Assess predefined goals<br>Revisit business plans<br>Evaluate predefined objectives<br>Documentation<br>Check against expectations<br>Informal follow-up<br>Benchmark against previous projects | Evolve into stronger<br>Spawns other projects<br>Continues the same<br>Continues in different form<br>Finishes completely |

**Figure 8.1:** Stages of collaboration formation process (Wang & Fesenmaier, 2007: 867).

**130** Smart Cities and Tourism

formation of collaborations rather than the rationale for unfolding specific activities within the process. By incorporating a path dependence perspective, this chapter examines the historical conditions contingent on how the process unfolds while also addressing Zuzul's (2019) call for greater attention to collaboration in smart destinations.

## Methodology

This chapter applies a case study research design, as it provides results from a specific location that can be used to generate in-depth, novel findings (Easton, 1995). A qualitative enquiry was conducted within the smart tourism destination of Ljubljana, Slovenia. The city was awarded the European Capital of Smart Tourism in 2019 and 2020. Ljubljana has over 45 smart initiatives, although less than half of them were recognised in its bid to become a smart tourism destination. Reviewing the list of initiatives presented for the European Capital of Smart Tourism award, most benefit both locals and visitors. Only three initiatives could be identified as being specifically for visitors: the electric train, Taste Ljubljana tour and the destination management organisation's (DMO's) website. The other initiatives, which included wi-fi, mobile applications, bicycle, and car-sharing systems, could be used by locals and visitors and have also been referenced by other smart city studies as examples of initiatives (see Araral, 2020).

Examining the development process of smart initiatives in Ljubljana, interestingly, presents a different context than those previously studied. For instance, Yigitcanlar et al. (2019) examine Songdo, Masdar, Amsterdam, San Francisco and Brisbane; Noori et al. (2020) explore Amsterdam, Barcelona, Dubai and Abu Dhabi; Lee et al. (2014) investigate Seoul and San Francisco and Lee et al. (2013) study Songdo. These are internationally popular and well-established destinations compared to Slovenia, which gained its independence in 1991 from Yugoslavia. Like Ljubljana, Songdo and Seoul represent post-communist/colonial destinations. However, studies of the latter smart developments often concentrate on the technological aspect rather than incorporating the historical context (see Lee et al., 2013; Lee et al., 2014), which this analysis will demonstrate as significant macro-environmental factors in smart collaboration.

Data sources for this case study included documents, observation and 24 semi-structured interviews with supplier stakeholders representing 31 businesses involved in Ljubljana's tourism industry. NVivo, a qualitative data analysis software, was used to access, organise, and analyse data. During the transcription process, the individuals were anonymised (Gibbs, 2010). Thematic analysis was applied to capture the stages of development of the city's smart tourism initiatives. This was guided by pre-determined codes based on the different stages from Wang and Fesenmaier's (2007) five-stage process of collaboration formation.

# Analysis and findings: The formation process of smart Ljubljana

The formation process of smart Ljubljana points to the following insights that have not been previously discussed in the smart cities or collaboration literature. Previous conditions affect how stages develop, the cyclical nature of the stages, the simultaneous nature and omission of stages and the varying levels of interactions between stakeholders. These insights highlight the complexity involved in forming a smart destination.

## The stages of smart development

The use of Wang and Fesenmaier's (2007) stages of destination collaboration aids in providing a sequential explanation of Ljubljana's smart development but required adaptation to account for the findings. The original model (Figure 8.1) was extended to demonstrate the interconnectedness and cyclical nature of smart development and the needed resources and stakeholders (Figure 8.2). Path dependence theory enhanced the model and illustrated the importance of historical context in shaping occurrences within smart development, such as the omission of formalisation and rules of engagement.

### Assembling stage

The first stage, the assembling stage, involves gathering individuals and ideas for creating a vision, which resembles the starting phase of most smart city models (Wang & Fesenmaier, 2007; Letaifa, 2015; Kumar et al., 2020). While different visions were identified that guided smart development, they were not directly crafted within smart collaborations or for the development of Ljubljana's smart destination. The destination did not begin by constructing a smart city as seen in other locations (see Zuzul, 2019). Instead, many different initiatives contributed to it eventually becoming a smart city. This is similar to Masdar, which started with building an eco-centred project (Noori et al., 2020).

Ljubljana's first focus on smart was evident through its introduction of smart mobility solutions such as the smart transportation cards planned for 2017. These initiatives were part of the city's vision of pursuing sustainability. In Slovenia, focus on sustainability can be traced to 1996 when the destination launched 'The Green Piece of Europe', its first official promotional campaign to highlight the environment (Hall, 2000).

## 132  Smart Cities and Tourism

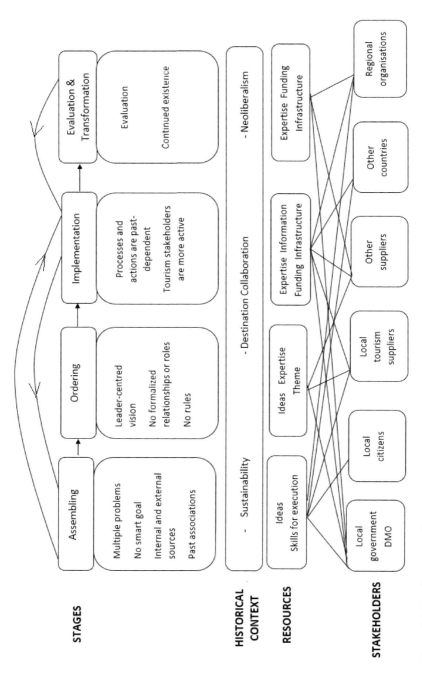

**Figure 8.2:** The formation of a smart destination

Since then, the destination has continued shaping its brand identity through a sustainability lens. This is evident in branding campaigns such as 'I Feel Slovenia' in 2006 and activities that led to numerous awards, such as Ljubljana being European Green Capital in 2016.

Various groups have been working on these initiatives for the implementation of sustainability strategies over the years. However, several distinct groups have been identified in Ljubljana's smart development: DMO with tourism suppliers and municipality representatives with private stakeholders and government partners, such as the Ministry of Economic Development and Technology; the Ministry of Defence; and Ministry of Public Administration. The joint deliberations mainly took place between the DMO and municipality lead, rather than the entire group of stakeholders. Tourism industry practitioners were invited to participate via meetings, emails and telephone calls. While meetings were designed to encourage dialogue, one stakeholder lamented that it was a less accommodating space for entertaining supplier feedback, similarly seen in smart cities participation (Engelbert et al., 2019). Meanwhile, at the time of taking office, the mayor requested ideas from the municipality. Locals were encouraged to submit their feedback, which is how the wheelchair application, considered a smart idea, was incorporated.

In Ljubljana, ideas were not only generated from organisations within the city as found in other smart cities (see Zuzul, 2019) but also externally. Due to the close relationship that the city has with Vienna, government representatives have regularly interacted and consulted with each other on smart-related matters. Ljubljana's municipality also consulted external organisations such as the European Union (EU). Representatives from the Ljubljana municipality reviewed various smart city bids by the EU and then submitted their application, which is the case for many European smart cities (Perboli & Rosano, 2020). This chapter supports Zhu's *et al.* (2014) view that government and tourism suppliers should participate in smart tourism design and development. However, upon further examination, the focus on stages of development reveals that the plan was influenced less by the local community and more by top-down leadership and influencers further afield who were outside of the city.

## Ordering stage

The smart initiative ideas were further examined and developed alongside plans, representing Wang and Fesenmaier's (2007) ordering stage. Unlike the assembling stage, where participation included residents, suppliers and municipality, the ordering stage in Ljubljana adopted more of a top-down approach, similar to smart destinations such as China (Zhu et al., 2014) and

## 134    Smart Cities and Tourism

Barcelona (Boes et al., 2016). For bids submitted to the EU, screening was conducted by EU representatives. If successful, the municipal representative responsible for smart programmes was alerted and the destination was provided with the financial, technical resources and expertise. These EU initiatives were not deliberated on within collaboration. Hence, this stage is not necessary for explaining those specific initiatives as they proceeded to the implementation phase.

According to Wang and Fesenmaier (2007), strategies, rules and roles are developed during the ordering stage to guide the behaviour of stakeholders within the group and throughout the initiatives. As there was also no smart strategy in Ljubljana, development drew upon existing tourism plans and the city's Vision 2025. Ideas and details needed to be aligned with the vision and the theme of sustainability, which illustrates the role of path dependence. The sustainability path gave rise to infrastructure before the term 'smart' appeared in tourism development plans. This allowed integration, which is unlike some smart city cases where the infrastructure was newly developed for smartness (see Zuzul, 2019). For instance, the smart space that accommodates Ljubljana's electric vehicles and sharing systems was formed in 2007, which was ten years before the term smart appeared in tourism plans. Much of the planning, idea development and execution of activities were associated with the municipality representatives rather than tourism stakeholders, making Ljubljana more aligned with smart cities than smart destinations.

There were no rules or processes to guide tourism suppliers' engagement in the initiatives. Participants' feedback revealed that activities followed the same path of occurrences within other tourism destination collaborations. For instance, marketing collaborations such as World Travel Market and ITB did not require the establishment of rules for participation. During these initiatives, tourism suppliers took on a more laissez-faire approach for involvement while the DMO led, facilitated plans and engagement during the early stages. The same was being witnessed in Ljubljana's smart development and contributed to the top-down orientation. Some stakeholders regarded smart initiatives as another collaborative destination initiative, closely aligning with Ivars-Baidal et al.'s (2019) interpretation of intelligence being a destination management approach.

### Implementation stage

Wang and Fesenmaier (2007) recognise the implementation stage as the point at which ideas are put into action. Tourism stakeholders were more evident during the promotion of smart initiatives and the delivery of smart experiences. In Ljubljana, smart platforms depended on the supply of information provided by the tourism stakeholders. Data were gathered through site visitations and email requests. The DMO promoted Ljubljana as a smart destination. This could have been expected, as it is mainly responsible for the management and marketing of destination activities (Volgger & Pechlaner, 2014). This is unlike smart cities, where promotion usually resides with real estate and technology developers (Zuzul, 2019).

Promotion of smart initiatives occurred online via websites and social media pages for the DMO, and offline in the visitor offices, brochures and tradeshows. The organisation did not create new marketing campaigns but instead utilised already established promotional programmes for Ljubljana. Tourism suppliers also promoted, sold the products and provided the experience within their establishments, which is in keeping with Gretzel et al.'s (2015) stance that suppliers have dynamic roles. Suppliers were not just beneficiaries of smart initiatives, as Kumar et al.'s (2020) smart city model suggest, but were also active stakeholders in Ljubljana.

The municipality office was instrumental in endorsing smart cities conferences where knowledge sharing was encouraged. Although municipality representatives were evident in photos such as those taken at the European Capital of Smart Tourism presentation, they were representatives rather than spokespersons for the city. The mayor was seen as being vocal in promoting these initiatives. Promotion by public state officials reflected a path dependence trend found globally. City officials pay less attention to implementing smart city plans to benefit their citizens but instead embrace a market mentality, which focuses on competitive market practices associated with neoliberalism (Engelbert et al., 2019). In the following quote, one participant made mention of the city's business logic while explicitly noting the mayor's role:

*'Ohh, there was long time stagnation until the new, which is still current mayor who is a businessman and kind of runs the city more like a private enterprise.'* (Participant 9)

The promotional narratives of the mayor, though different from the DMO, promoted the same initiatives. For instance, in an interview with a smart cities' expert, the mayor explained that a smart day entailed residents utilising electric vehicles and bicycle sharing, which led to the city's designation as a smart tourism destination. The narratives were tailored to suit either the local citizens or tourists, depending on the marketing medium. Smart city Ljubljana, therefore, appears to be the same as smart destination Ljubljana. Nonetheless, there was an emphasis on promotion, which was further seen when the destination was recognised for the second time as a European Capital of Smart Tourism. Mention was made of an initiative that was not yet implemented in the destination. When questioned about Ljubljana's status as a smart destination, Participant 5 responded that:

*'Ahhm, but yes, Slovenia will always try to follow the initiatives and jump on the wagons cause we know that we are lagging. So we will be very active in kind of, formally, officially adopting new things, but will be much slower with the implementation of those.'* (Participant 5)

After implementing numerous smart initiatives aligned with sustainability, the focus of smartness in Ljubljana had changed to digitisation, having been awarded for this in October 2019 in the European Capital of Smart Tourism programme. Based on Wang and Fesenmaier's (2007) model, the focus would have been initially set during the assembling stage. However, this arose during the promotion of other smart initiatives such as Urbana Card and Taste Ljubljana. This highlights the cyclical nature of the process. Most smart cities concentrate on digitisation (Angelidou, 2015; Yigitcanlar et al., 2019), but this was not the case in Ljubljana. The destination was still tied to its long-held path of sustainability rather than embracing digitisation through advanced technological initiatives such as big data platforms (Noori *et al.*, 2020). The sustainability context has determined the type of initiatives that the destination was able to embrace. Indeed, the notion that the past conditions the direction of new pathways is evident here (David, 1985; Sydow et al., 2012).

## Evaluation and transformation stage

Once developed and promoted, initiatives are then evaluated resulting in one of the following actions: continued existence, further development, an extension of the initiative or termination. This stage is not evident in previous smart city models (see Lee et al., 2013; Letaifa, 2015; Siokas et al., 2021). Regarding continued existence, the wheelchair application fell within this category. The application was still being promoted to tourists while garnering further interests from tourism suppliers, which led to an increase in the number of suppliers on the platform. Taste Ljubljana was one of the initiatives that was further developed. The DMO reviewed it and plans were put in place to establish it as a more extensive programme. It still focused on the culinary aspect of Ljubljana but included local events that would be developed throughout the year. Then, some initiatives were also extended to other surrounding areas, resulting in the creation of smart communities and towns. While all initiatives continued to (re)develop in Ljubljana, some stakeholders noted that they can be terminated due to lack of the resources needed for sustenance, namely availability of finance, technical skills and knowledge.

Activities that were expected during the early stages were observed during the later stages of collaboration. For instance, the formalisation of roles and duties that should have occurred during ordering manifested after implementation. One of the participants was officially given the title to lead smart city initiatives in 2018. According to the Wang and Fesenmaier's (2007) model, this should have happened at the start of implementation or during the planning stage of smart cities (see Lee et al., 2013). This further illustrates the cyclical nature of smart development and may explain why not all expected collaborative activities were established during the early stages.

## Conclusion

This chapter advances understanding of smart cities formation while addressing the lack of smart tourism destination models. Extending the limited research on the evolution of smart cities that are based on one-directional and linear models (see Lee et al., 2013; Kumar et al., 2020; Noori et al., 2020; Siokas et al., 2021), this study concludes that the collaborative process is in fact complex, surfacing in cyclical and historically contingent pathways. Although findings illustrate that a smart city and smart tourism destination can undergo a similar collaborative process, applying Wang and Fesenmaier's (2007) stages of destination collaboration extends the understanding of smart formation through the evaluation and transformation stage. Specific activities, not previously discussed in the smart cities' literature, are also included; for instance, the practice of promotion within the implementation stage. It was also found that during implementation, smart city Ljubljana and smart destination Ljubljana seem to be identical and only differed based on the narratives used by stakeholders.

Path dependence theory also serves as a meaningful theoretical approach, as it enhanced the stage approach by focusing on external processes that affect different stages of collaborations. It illustrates that some of the internal collaborative activities are a result of historical trends. For instance, smart development in Ljubljana is past dependent, emerging from the destination's concentration on sustainability, with mechanisms such as infrastructure previously in place and not requiring focus as seen in smart city development. Though previous smart city formation models have not captured the historical context, it helps to illustrate the rationale for the adoption of smart and Ljubljana's vision not being as technologically advanced as other destinations. This also supports a context-specific understanding of smart cities (Bibri, 2019).

This chapter provides an alternate perspective to the straightforward processes proposed in smart research. Key stakeholders involved in smart development must be mindful of its complex and cyclical process. It is not well-established with a clear focus and networks as seen in traditional destination collaborations. Furthermore, the process is not time-bound, which

## 138 Smart Cities and Tourism

is prudent to note for destination practitioners who craft tourism development plans for short-term periods such as four years, as is the case of Ljubljana. This chapter provides guidance and a deeper look at occurrences in a well-recognised and rewarded smart context, which can prove useful to many industry practitioners who aspire to be like smart Ljubljana and create their own smart destination. Practitioners are further equipped with novel insights for tackling destination challenges through smart now and going forward. While this study provides greater insights, future research is recommended to explore the day-to-day stakeholder interactions and monitor the changes within smart development.

# References

Angelidou, M. (2015). Smart cities: A conjuncture of four forces. *Cities*, 47, 95-106.

Araral, E. (2020). Why do cities adopt smart technologies? Contingency theory and evidence from the United States, *Cities*, 106.

Baggio, R., Micera, R. & Del Chiappa, G. (2020). Smart tourism destinations: a critical reflection, *Journal of Hospitality and Tourism Technology*, 11(3).

Bastidas-Manzano, A., Fernandez, J. & Casado-Aranda, L. (2020). The past, present and future of smart tourism destinations: a bibliometric analysis, *Journal of Hospitality & Tourism Research*, 1-24.

Bibri, S. (2019). On the sustainability of smart and smarter cities in the era of big data: an interdisciplinary and transdisciplinary literature review, *Journal of Big Data*, 6 (2019), 1-64.

Boes, K., Buhalis, D. & Inversini, A. (2016). Smart tourism destinations: ecosystems for tourism destination competitiveness. *International Journal of Tourism Cities*, 2 (2), 108–124.

Bramwell, B. & Cox, V. (2009). Stage and path dependence approaches to the evolution of a national park tourism partnership. *Journal of Sustainable Tourism*, 17 (2), 191- 206.

Buhalis, D. (2020). Technology in tourism-from information communication technologies to eTourism and smart tourism towards ambient intelligence tourism: a perspective article. *Tourism Review*, 75 (1), 267-272.

Buhalis, D. (2015).Working definitions of smartness and smart tourism destination. Buhalis Blog http://t.co/xrLRpGipvu, 10 February 2015.

Buhalis, D., Harwood, T., Bogicevic, V., Viglia, G., Beldona, S. & Hofacker, C. (2019). Technological disruptions in services: lessons from tourism and hospitality.*Journal of Service Management*, 30 (4), 484-506.

Buhalis, D., Andreu, L., & Gnoth, J. (2020). The dark side of the sharing economy: balancing value co-creation and value co-destruction. *Psychology & Marketing*, 37(5), 689-704.

Caffyn, A. (2000). Is there a tourism partnership life cycle?, in B. Bramwell and B. Lane (eds.), *Tourism Collaboration and Partnerships – Politics, Practice and Sustainability*, New Delhi: Viva Books, pp. 333–341.

Cavalheiro, M., Joia, L. & Cavalheiro, G. (2020). Towards a smart tourism destination development model: promoting environmental, economic, sociocultural and political values. *Tourism Planning & Development*, 17(3), 237-259.

David, P. (1985). Clio and the economics of QWERTY'.*American Economic Review*, 75 (2), 332- 337.

Easton, G. (1995). Methodology and industrial networks, in K. Moller and D.T. Wilson (eds.), *Business Marketing: An Interaction and Network Perspective*, Boston: Kluwer, pp. 411-492.

Engelbert, J., Zoonen, L. & Hirzalla, F. (2019). Excluding citizens from the European smart city: The discourse practices of pursuing and granting smartness.*Technological Forecasting & Social Change*, 142 (2019), 347- 353.

Estrada, E., Maciel, R., Negron A., Lopez, G., Larios, V. & Ochoa, A. (2019). Framework to support the data science of smart city models for decision-making oriented to the efficient dispatch of service petitions. *IET Software*, 14 (2), 159-164.

EU (2020). Smart cities, European Commission, https://ec.europa.eu/info/eu-regional-and-urban-development/topics/cities-and-urban-development/city-initiatives/smart-cities_en, 2 December 2020.

Femenia-Serra, F., Perles-Ribes, J. & Ivars-Baidal, J. (2018). Smart destinations and tech-savvy millennial tourists: hype versus reality.*Tourism Review*, 74 (1), 63- 81.

Fox, L. (2017). How Expedia is using deep learning to improve the hotel booking process, Phocuswire, https://www.phocuswire.com/Expedia-Partner-Solutions-machine-learning, 2 December 2020.

Gibbs, G. (2010). *Analysing Qualitative Data*, London: SAGE Publications.

Giffinger, R., Fertner, C., Kramar, H., Kalasek, R., Pichler-Milanovic, N. & Meijers, E. (2007). Smart Cities - Ranking of European medium-sized cities, Centre of Regional Science at the Vienna University of Technology. http://www.smart-cities.eu/download/smart_cities_final_report.pdf.

Gray, B. (1985). Conditions facilitating interorganizational collaboration, *Human Relations*, 38 (10), 911-936.

Gretzel, U., Werthner, H., Koo., C. & Lamsfus, C. (2015). Conceptual foundations for understanding smart tourism ecosystems.*Computers in Human Behavior*, 50, 558–563.

Hall, D. (2000). Sustainable tourism development and transformation in Central and Eastern Europe. *Journal of Sustainable Tourism*, 8 (6), 441- 457.

Ivars-Baidal, J. A., Celdrán-Bernabeu, M. A., Mazón, J. N., & Perles-Ivars, Á. F. (2019). Smart destinations and the evolution of ICTs: a new scenario for destination management?. *Current Issues in Tourism*, 22(13), 1581-1600.

## 140 Smart Cities and Tourism

Janssen, M., Luthra, S., Mangla, S., Rana, N. & Dwivedi, Y. (2019). Challenges for adopting and implementing IoT in smart cities - an integrated MICMAC-ISM approach.*Internet Research*, 29 (6), 1589- 1616.

Kitchin, R. (2014). The real-time city? Big data and smart urbanism.*Geojournal*, 79 (1), 1-14.

Komninos, N., Kakderi, C., Panori, A. & Tsarchopoulos, P. (2019). Smart city planning from an evolutionary perspective.*Journal of Urban Technology*, 26 (2), 3- 20.

Kumar, T. (2017). *Smart Economy in Smart Cities*. Singapore: Springer.

Lee, J., Phaal, R. & Lee, S. (2013). An integrated service-device-technology roadmap for smart city development.*Technological Forecasting & Social Change*, 80 (2013), 286-306.

Lee, J., Hancock, M. & Hu, M. (2014). Towards an effective framework for building smart cities: Lessons from Seoul and San Francisco.*Technological Forecasting & Social Change*, 89, 80-99.

Letaifa, S. (2015). How to strategize smart cities: Revealing the SMART model. *Journal of Business Research*, 68, 1414- 1419.

Mehraliyev, F., Chan, I., Choi, Y., Koseoglu, M. & Law, R. (2020). A state-of-the-art review of smart tourism research. *Journal of Travel & Tourism Marketing*, 37 (1), 78- 91.

Menon, S., Edward, M. & George, B. (2017). Inter-stakeholder collaboration in event management: a case study of Kerala Travel Mart. *International Journal of Leisure and Tourism Marketing*, 5 (4).

Mora, L., Deakin, M. & Reid, A. (2019). Strategic principles for smart city development: a multiple case study analysis of European best practices. *Technological Forecasting and Social Change*, 142, 70-97.

Noori, N., Hoppe, T., & de Jong, M. (2020). Classifying pathways for Smart City development: comparing design, governance and implementation in Amsterdam, Barcelona, Dubai, and Abu Dhabi. *Sustainability*, 12(10), 4030.

Perboli, G. & Rosano, M. (2020). A taxonomic analysis of smart city projects in North America and Europe. *Sustainability*, 12, 7831.

Puffert, D. (2002). Path dependence in spatial networks: the standardization of railway track gauge. *Explorations in Economic History*, 39 (3), 282-314.

Roopchund, R. (2020). Mauritius as a smart tourism destination: technology for enhancing tourism experience. In Pati, B. Panigrahi, C. R., Buyya, R. & Li, K.C. (eds.) *Advanced Computing and Intelligent Engineering*, Springer.

Selin, S. & Chavez, D. (1995). Developing an evolutionary tourism partnership model. *Annals of Tourism Research*, 22 (4), 844-856.

Shafiee, S., Ghatari, A., Hasanzadeh, A. & Jahanyan, S. (2019). Developing a model for sustainable smart tourism destinations; a systematic review. *Tourism Management Perspectives*, 21, 287-300.

Siokas, G., Tsakanikas, A. & Siokas, E. (2021). Implementing smart city strategies in Greece: Appetite for success. *Cities*, 108.

Sydow, J., Windeler, A., Muller-Seitz, G. & Lange, K. (2012). Path constitution analysis: a methodology for understanding path dependence and path creation. *Business Research*, 5, 155-176.

Taheri, B., Rahimi, R. & Buhalis, D. (2022) *The Sharing Economy and the Tourism Industry*. Oxford: Goodfellow http://dx.doi.org/10.23912/9781915097064-4970

Volgger, M. & Pechlaner, H. (2014). Requirements for destination management organizations in destination governance: understanding DMO success. *Tourism Management*, 41, 64- 75.

Waddock, S. (1989). Understanding social partnerships: an evolutionary model of partnership organizations. *Administration & Society*, 21 (1), 78-100.

Wang, Y. & Fesenmaier, D. (2007). Collaborative destination marketing: a case study of Elkhart county, Indiana. *Tourism Management*, 28, 863- 875.

Yigitcanlar, T., Han, H., Kamruzzaman, Md., Ioppolo, G. & Sabatini- Marques, J. (2019). The making of smart cities: are Songdo, Masdar, Amsterdam, San Francisco and Brisbane the best we could build?. *Land Use Policy*, 88.

Zhang, H., Gordon, S., Buhalis, D. & Ding, X. (2018). Experience value co-creation on destination online platforms. *Journal of Travel Research*, 57 (8), 1093-1107.

Zhu, W., Zhang, L. & Li, N. (2014).Challenges, function changing of government and enterprises in Chinese smart tourism. Paper presented at *ENTER 2014 Conference on Information and Communication Technologies*, 21-25 January, Dublin.

Zuzul, T. (2019). Matter battles: cognitive representations, boundary objects, and the failure of collaboration in two smart cities. *Academy of Management Journal*, 62 (3), 739-784.

# 9 Tourism destination metagovernance and smart governance in Milan, Italy

*Alberto Amore, Pavlos Arvanitis, Francesca d'Angella and Manuela De Carlo*

## Introduction

The governance of smart cities and smart urban destinations is a relevant yet oftentimes overlooked dimension of the 21st Century city (Andreani et al., 2019; Appio et al., 2019; Buonincontri & Micera, 2016). Since the pioneering work of Buhalis (2000), research on smart destinations has shifted over the years (Jovicic, 2019), leading to a reframing of the political and governance dimensions in tourism policy and planning (Amore & Hall, 2016). This has implications for research in smart cities and smart destinations, the latter being defined as a destination that *"successfully implements smartness which is fostered by open innovation, supported by investments in human and social capital and sustained by participatory governance"* (Buhalis, 2015, n.p.). Sound urban tourism governance should lead to *"greater net benefits for the host community … and improved functioning of the total, interdependent industry within the urban environment"* (Edwards et al., 2009: 102). In such context, Information and Communication Technologies (ICT) act *"as an operant and operand"* (Boes et al., 2016: 118) in the support and implementation of long-term strategies that reflect the instances of the many destination-relevant stakeholders (Buhalis, 2020; Sigalat-Signes et al., 2020).

Tourism destination marketing and management organizations (DMMOs) have the potentiality to be key enablers of effective destination governance (e.g., Amore & Hall, 2017; Pike & Page, 2014; Luthe & Wyss, 2016). Pechlaner et al. (2012) and Pechlaner and Volgger (2013) highlight that DMMOs are spatially embedded organizations combining elements of territorial (political) and corporate (business) governance. DMMOs are the reflection of the changing policy environment at the macro-and-meso level over the years (Hall & Veer, 2016). This is particularly observed in a review of destination management organization archetypes in European cities (Boes et al., 2016; D'Angella et al., 2010; Sigalat-Signes et al., 2020). Numerous cities around the world are shifting towards modes of smart governance to anticipate and address foreseeable challenges (Carmero & Alba, 2019; Cowley & Caprotti, 2019). ICT is widely acknowledged as a means to foster multi-actor, multi-sector and multi-level responses to overcome ecological, logistic, economic, and social challenges of cities (Manville et al., 2014; Paskaleva, 2009). Scholars and practitioners argue that implementing smart governance exceed the scope and capabilities of the current institutional arrangements and governance structures (Bolívar, 2016; Caragliu et al., 2011; Desdemoustier et al., 2019; Gil-Garcia et al., 2015). Regardless of the context and the extent of technological innovation involved, the absence of suitable government arrangements seems to be the most prominent obstacles to the smart governance transformation (Nillsen, 2019; Praharaj et al., 2017).

Further research is needed to understand *"the processes of information knowledge transfer, sharing and conversion in smart tourism destinations"* (Del Chiappa & Baggio, 2015:145). This applies, in particular, to longitudinal studies on destination governance and planning and the evolution of organizational structure and scope of DMMOs over time. This chapter, therefore, provides empirical evidence from Milan, Italy, through a longitudinal analysis of destination metagovernance and smart governance processes between 2004 and 2019. From a destination metagovernance perspective, the genesis of Milan as tourist destination saw a shift from a networked hierarchy (De Carlo & D'Angella, 2011) to a more collaborative and adaptive mode of smart metagovernance. The insights from Milan provide a timely reflection on the nexus between new technologies, governance archetypes and metagovernance responses and how these contribute to the development of the city into a culturally vibrant and smart destination.

## Smart city governance

According to Desdemoustier et al. (2019), the notion of smart city is fuzzy and often improperly used. Smart cities encompass different features and characteristics, including enhanced quality of life, economic competitiveness, transport and mobilities, energy efficiency, public and social services, and citizen participation (Appio et al., 2019; Desdemoustier et al., 2019). A good extent of the literature on smart cities tends to focus on the role of technology as driver for efficiency, planning and resource co-ordination (Marsal-Llacuna et al., 2015; Meijer & Bolívar, 2016). However, recent advancements in the field have shifted the focus from technocratic to human-centred understandings of smart cities (Andreani et al., 2019; Angelidou, 2015; Caragliu et al., 2011). As Desdemoustier et al. (2019) observe, the integration of notions related to human and social capital allows for an enhanced conceptualisation of smart city governance in which technology acts as a medium to reach certain ends, rather than an end. This echoes Andreani et al. (2019: 24) argument that *"a city can be truly 'smart' only if it uses technology to empower citizens and enhance democratic debates about the kind of city it wants to be"*. Moving beyond the technocratic approach to smart cities enables stakeholders and urban communities to unleash the potential of creative collaboration and co-creation (Desdemoustier et al., 2019; Kummitha & Crutzen, 2017), and for cities to improve the quality of life of their citizens (Appio et al., 2019).

Governance is central to the success of smart cities. Accountability, collaboration, cooperation, leadership, partnership, and transparency are among the essential features of smart city governance (Desdemoustier et al., 2019). According to Nillsen (2019) and Meijer and Bolívar (2016), smart city governance fosters pro-active and innovative governance structures which, in turn, benefit the socio-economic and ecological performance of the city. Through ICT, smart governance can monitor and reflect on the dynamics and decision-making processes among stakeholders (Desdemoustier et al., 2019) as well as on the roles of different actors in the urban strategy (Nilssen, 2019; Sørensen & Torfing, 2011). This echoes the European Commission's (2014: 6) definition of smart city governance as the *"place where traditional networks and services are made efficient using digital and telecommunication technologies, for the benefit of inhabitants and businesses"*. The result is a step forward from traditional top-down governance (Engelbert et al., 2019), whose limitations and excessive bureaucratism have been widely acknowledged and reiterated in both planning theory and urban studies (Jessop, 2011). Thus, metagovernance best encapsulates such a transition towards a *"mixture of hierarchies, networks and markets"* (Meuleman, 2008: 73) in cities. As Jessop (2011: 119) notes, *"metagovernance comprises a complex array of more or less reflexive social practices concerned with the governance of social relations characterized by complex, reciprocal interdependence"*. Adaptability and reflexivity are central to the notion of metagovernance (Meuleman, 2008) and collaborative planning as a structured and ongoing leaning process.

## Smart tourism destination governance

Research by Del Chiappa and Baggio (2015) shows how smart tourism destination environments are more efficient and effective in multi-stakeholder knowledge creation and sharing. The emphasis on network marketing and integrated tourism information is a common denominator in smart tourism and smart destination (Shafiee et al., 2019). Interoperability of network players support the development of the tourism ecosystem (Buhalis, 2020). Particularly in cites, the accent on sustainability is intertwined with smart tourism destinations (Gonzalez-Reverte, 2019). Other aspects of smart destination are related to the use of big data and social media (Buhalis & Foerste, 2015; Camero & Alba, 2019) which has changed the way urban destinations in particular are managed and marketed. As Ardito et al. (2019) state, big data provide an opportunity for destinations to become smart and, in turn, empower co-creation (Buhalis & Foerste, 2015).

Smart destination governance can be conceived as an umbrella concept encompassing essential traits of urban planning practices, including participation, adaptability, sustainability, innovation, and competitiveness (Boes et al., 2016; Jovicic, 2019). Modes of smart destination governance require *"dynamically interconnecting stakeholders through a technological platform on which information relating to tourism activities could be exchange instantly"* (Buhalis & Amaranggana, 2013: 557). In principle, smart destination governance advocates the inclusion of a heterogeneous array of relevant stakeholders, including government bodies, businesses, active citizenry, and city users (Ruhlandt, 2018; Boes et al., 2016). Smart destination governance acts as an effective node of decision-making, policy, and planning implementation as long as there are established social capital and connectivity at the destination level (Buhalis & Amaranggana, 2013; Shafiee et al., 2019). Like smart city governance, smart destination governance is the result of ITC-enhanced and dynamic cooperation between relevant stakeholders that, ultimately, contributes to add value to the destination (Buhalis, 2022; Baggio & Del Chiappa, 2014; Neuhofer et al., 2012; Sigala, 2018). The support of the public sector is key in smart destination governance. Shalfiee et al. (2019: 296) observe, *"governments and other agencies have begun to incorporate smartness in new policies and strategies to enhance dynamic development and economic growth"*. Overall, scholars and practitioners convene that effective smart destination governance fosters destination competitiveness (Shafiee et al., 2019) and facilitates DDMO's strategic goals (Buhalis, 2020, Gretzel et al., 2015; Lamsfus et al., 2015).

## Smart destination metagovernance: A way forward?

Research has advocated to a shift towards metagovernance theory to better understand the *"actual political practices"* of structurationist decision-making in tourism (Amore & Hall, 2016:116). According to Jenkins, Hall, and Mkono (2014:549), *"there is a wide range of tourism metagovernance practice in operation"* which has been overlooked in the literature. To overcome this gap,

# 146 Smart Cities and Tourism

advancements in the field contributed to the conceptualization of destination metagovernance (Amore & Hall, 2016). In this aspect, *"DMOs have an important role to play as vehicles of metagovernance"* (Spyriadis, et al., 2011: 198) in the coordination, integration and implementation of multi-level and cross-level policies. Metagovernance encompasses a series of different archetypes of coordinated governance to achieve long-term outcomes as well as short-term policy responses (Hall, 2011; Jessop, 2011; Meuleman, 2008, 2019). Destination metagovernance reiterates the importance of building consensus and enhancing stakeholder participation to overcome structural failures in prevailing modes of governance (Costa, 2013; Spyriadis et al., 2011). Destination metagovernance emphasizes the creation, development, and implementation of effective metagovernance mechanisms to communicate and plan within the destination's stakeholders (Amore & Hall, 2016; Spyriadis et al., 2011).

Particularly in urban tourism destinations, DMMOs' spheres of action go beyond the traditional mission of destination management, including transport and viability, green economy and sustainability, urban liveability, cultural development, social wellbeing, and internationalization (Bell & Park, 2006; Pike & Page, 2014; Sørensen & Torfing, 2017). Within tourism destinations the challenges of applying smart governance are even greater given the nature of tourism itself, the fragmented array of relevant stakeholders involved and the need to cooperate and align their efforts to produce the desired outcome (Franzoni, 2015; Laws et al., 2011). The challenge lies in the definition of stakeholders' roles and influences in a balance between individual objectives and destination-wide goals. Stakeholders need to get involved in a coordinated way to co-design and co-produce the products and services offered at the destination (Franzoni, 2015; Klijn et al., 2010). Smart urban governance is a step forward from the narrow pro-tourism growth narrative as it seeks to take into consideration the opinions of numerous relevant stakeholders (Sigalat-Signes et al., 2020; Buhalis, 2022).

## Smart tourism destination best case example: Milan

The case study of Milan, Italy, was chosen to examine the urban and destination governance dynamics and the genesis of smart tourism metagovernance from a longitudinal perspective (2005-2019). Prior to 2005, the appeal of Milan as an urban destination was almost exclusively tied to conferences and exhibitions held at *Fiera Milano*. Tourism in Milan was highly seasonal, particularly during hallmark weekly business events between February and May and there was no deliberate tourism development strategy for the city as a whole. In this context, the Municipality (*Comune di Milano*) was the sole government stakeholder acting as enabler of tourism initiatives in the city, without any structured form of collaboration with other tourism-relevant stakeholders (De Carlo & d'Angella, 2011).

In 2015, the hosting of the BIE 2015 Expo *Feeding the Planet, Energy for Life* represented a turning point for the city as a whole and the governance of the destination in particular. Since then, the appeal and popularity of Milan as a destination as steadily increased: in 2019, Milan was the second Italian destination for visitors after Rome (ISTAT, 2019) and has established a DMMO (*Milano & Partners*) to enhance the city's attractiveness and branding through "*partnerships and collaborations with local businesses, global brands, universities, cultural institutions, and other public entities*" (Yes Milano, 2020: n.p.). The DMMO proactively promotes forms of public-private collaboration as well as systems for collecting and sharing information to support purposeful strategies for city development. The development of both low-cost and full services airlines routes into the three Milan international airports, namely Malpensa, Linate and nearby Bergamo airport, as well as the rapid growth of accommodation mainly through sharing economy (Buhalis et al., 2020) made Milan more accessible internationally. Over the years, the city has gained a strong leisure component in the mix of visitors, improved its positioning in major international rankings and significantly reduced seasonality thanks to a vibrant calendar of events.

## Smart Milan tourism destination metagovernance

A longitudinal reflection builds from extensive research in Milan between the *Comune di Milano*, the *Camera di Commercio di Milano*, *Regione Lombardia* and IULM University, Milan. The findings are discussed in light of the literature on smart city governance and smart destination governance to illustrate the phases of destination governance within the wider process of smart governance in Milan.

The shift towards smart destination metagovernance in Milan can be articulated in three main phases (Table 9.1). Each phase has distinctive characteristics related to: (I) the type of approach to tourism, (II) the degree of maturity of the metagovernance processes based on the type of stakeholders involved, the relationships between stakeholders and the actions achieved and; (II) the role of technology. The three phases illustrate the key governance progresses and metagovernance evolutions that led the city of Milan from a situation of total absence of networked governance structures and processes to the establishment of a preliminary form of smart destination metagovernance. The latter encompasses collaborative, organisational, and technological dimensions that have been identified as quintessential in smart city governance (Nillsen, 2019). The third phase (2013-2019) is a combination of government action, bu siness initiatives and knowledge exchanges that paved the way for the development of Milan as a smart destination. In this phase, ICT enhances the inclusivity between different actors (Engelbert et al., 2019). Undoubtedly, a series of triggers at the urban level contributed to the rise and affirmation of smart tourism metagovernance governance, including the hosting of hallmark events (e.g., 2015 BIE Expo; Milan Fashion Week) and the successful bidding for the forthcoming 2026 Winter Olympics Games. The salient features of the three stages of metagovernance development are further discussed below.

The evolution towards smart destination metagovernance in the case study of Milan underpins the insights from other studies in the field (Del Chiappa & Baggio, 2015; Shalfiee et al., 2019). The absence of formal structures and processes of destination governance shows a relevant divide in comparison to principles and evidence of smart city infrastructure (Appio et al., 2019). The unconcern among government authorities on the importance of tourism in the economy and competitiveness of the city can also be found in the genesis of other urban destinations (Sigalat-Signes et al., 2020). This phase is characterised by short-lived initiatives among a sporadic range of tourism stakeholders from the private sector. For example, the Milan congress centre (MiCo) organized integrated offers of hospitality and entertainment services specific to the MICE industry. However, there were no stable forms of collaboration between these stakeholders, nor was there a shared vision of the tourist development. Instead, initiatives were piecemeal and opportunistic, without a defined holistic vision of the city as a destination. This fragmentation represented itself a governance failure (Jessop, 2011) that is also acknowledged in smart-less cities (Cowley & Caprotti, 2019). In this initial phase, ICT was not regarded as relevant in the processes of sharing information and knowledge among the stakeholders or to support the development of tourist offers and interaction with visitors. Milan lagged behind other cities in Italy (e.g., Turin) and abroad (e.g., Gandia) in the use of networks and IT platforms 2.0 for the promotion of relevant tourism and leisure services in the city.

The second phase encompasses the period between 2005 and 2013. In this phase, the city of Milan began to regard tourism as a driver for economic development. The transition to this phase is fostered by the hosting of weekly events (e.g., Fashion Week) rather than by integrated destination

Table 9.1: Metagovernance and Smart Governance in Milan (2005 -2019)

| Phase 1: spontaneous development with leading firms (Before 2005) | |
| --- | --- |
| **Period (years)** | Before 2005 |
| **I. Approach to tourism** | Tourism as a secondary component of the local economy |
| **II. Maturity of metagovernance processes** | Market-driven |
| Key stakeholders | Fiera Milano (Trade Fair), MiCo Congress center, SEA Group (Milan's Airports management), Milan's Chamber of Commerce; |
| Type of relations | Sporadic networking among private actors |
| Key actions | |
| **III. Role of technology** | Absent |
| Technological platforms | None |

| Phase 2: tourism planning by public bodies | |
| --- | --- |
| **Period (years)** | 2005-2012 |
| **I. Approach to tourism** | Tourism as a driver of urban attractiveness |
| **II. Maturity of metagovernance processes** | Public-driven |
| Key stakeholders | 2006: *Central Direction Tourism, Territorial Marketing and Identity* of the Municipality<br>2008: *Expo 2015 S.p.A.*<br>2008: Local public tourism system *"Città di Milano"* by Municipality<br>2009: and Local public tourism system *"Luoghi da vivere"* by Province and Region |

| | |
|---|---|
| Type of relations | Permanent formal and informal collaboration (public driven) |
| Key actions | Expo Milano thematic working groups<br>Two observatories: "territorial marketing observatory" + "tourism observatory of the Milanese urban region"<br>2010: AmaMI (Milano tourism card) |
| **III. Role of technology** | Co-ordination and data sharing |
| Technological platforms | E015 platform, urban tourism website |

| **Phase 3: smart metagovernance and DMOs** | |
|---|---|
| **Period (years)** | 2013–2019 |
| **I. Approach to tourism** | Tourism as a key component of a wider visitor economy |
| **II. Maturity of metagovernance processes** | Hierarchical supervision of networks and markets |
| Key stakeholders | 2013: Explora (DMO Lombardy Region)<br>2015: MiCo DMC<br>2019: Milano & Partners (DMMO Milan) |
| Type of relations | Institutionalized public-private collaboration |
| Key actions | Cultural Weeks; Tourism permanent observatories (AssoLombarda); Smart City Plan; specific tourism smart initiatives (map of phone calls and credit cards by SEA + Municipality); |
| **III. Role of technology** | B2B and P2B co-creation |
| Technological platforms | E015 platform, municipality open data, e-mobility services, smart tag info monuments, urban & regional tourism websites, tourism booking and ecommerce |

planning. This is not unusual if we compare the origins and proliferation of smart destinations in other cities (Shafiee et al., 2019). The designation of Milan as host city of the 2015 BIE Expo represents a turning point in the transition towards a new phase in destination metagovernance, with stakeholders urging to coalesce and collaborate (Buonincontri & Micera, 2016; Shafiee et al., 2019). This second phase occurred without the presence of a dedicated DMMO: instead, destination metagovernance processes were carried out by the initiative of government bodies responsible for managing the territory such as the *Comune di Milano* the Milanese province entity, the Milan greater metropolitan authority and the *Regione Lombardia*. This feature is also observed in research focusing on smart government and co-production of public services in cities (Ismagilova et al., 2019).

In 2006, the *Comune di Milano* tasked the Central Board of Advisors for Tourism, Territorial Marketing to draw the first 3-year tourism development plan. Between 2008 and 2009, two local public systems were set up for the coordination of infrastructures and tourist offers at urban and regional levels (*Luoghi da vivere* and *Citta di Milano*). Undeniably, the hosting of the 2015 BIE Expo significantly contributed to the establishment of a dedicated public joint company (Expo 2015 S.p.A) between different local and regional government bodies. At the same time, there is the development of complementary formal coordination structures and the establishment of entities for the development and sharing of information for the city of Milan. These entities are mostly in the form of partnerships and cross-institutional collaborations, a feature that is central to the success of smart city governance (Desdemoustier et al., 2019). It is during this phase that Milan launches the first permanent integrated destination marking system along with the AmaMI tourist card. The scheme is similar to other ICT initiatives to closely monitor and network the wide tourist supply of destinations (Camero & Alba, 2019; Sigalat-Signes et al., 2020).

The final phase of the metagovernance development in Milan is exemplified by the setting up of new entities to build from the 2015 BIE Expo legacy and a shift towards smart destination metagovernance. Two additional entities are established to support planning, and monitoring of tourism in Milan. In 2013, the *Regione Lombardia* and the *Camera di Commercio di Milano* establish a dedicated territorial marketing unit (Explora) to promote the city of Milan and its region to national and international tourism markets. In 2015, as a substitute, MICE stakeholders operating in the area establish a MiCo DMC to promote Milan as international business destination. In 2019, we see the establishment of a new DMMO (*Milano & Partners*): in this revised destination metagovernance, the Milan Municipality, the local Chamber of Commerce widened the reach of the partnership to include local businesses, global brands, universities, and cultural institutions. Despite its nature as a public company, *Milano & Partners* has been strongly supported by the local businesses who bought into the new destination metagovernance steering mode for the future development of Milan as a destination. The new DMO not only aims at marketing Milan to larger share of international visitors but also acts as a metropolitan development agency for the attraction of human capital and foreign direct investments to the city. Their mission is to make Milano the greatest, most welcoming city in the world. Unfortunately, the COVID crisis in 2020 naturally derailed much of this activity and the organisation is focusing on resilience.

Apart from the changing stakeholder base and purpose, the main collaborative key-actions of metagovernance resulting from the activity of these new bodies are related to the areas of events management, product development, the measurement of the destination's performance and the writing of strategic documents for the future development of the city. Particularly with events management and product development, they adopt a bottom-up approach between private stakeholders that reflects and adapts to the destination market dynamics. Conversely, destination performance and drafting of strategic documents are achieved through top-down, public-driven approaches that resemble the principles of new public management.

In all this governance phase, technology has provided valuable help and a stimulus for accelerating the process. The main technological platform for the data connection is called E015. It is a digital ecosystem promoted by the Lombardy Region together with tourism associations and the Milan Chamber of Commerce. It consists of the combination of data, functionality, processes, apps, and services. The sharing of functionality and information in E015 takes place through the publication of a communication interface (API) written according to common guidelines. The setup of this platform is part of the decision of the municipality to make Milan a smart city. Indeed, since 2014, the city has defined its own 'smart city planning' in order to combine economic development and social inclusion, innovation, and training, research, and participation.

Being a smart city entails much more than creating digital infrastructures, collecting data and indicators solely to 'measure the city'. It can be a lever to improve both the internal and the external destination environment. At an internal level, being smart enhances the coordination and synergies between the various local actors. At an external level, it is a powerful factor to improve the overall attractiveness of a city. Urban areas compete in the global scenario to attract tourists, talents, investments, and multinationals, based on their ability to evolve in order to: 1) meet the new needs of businesses; 2) create new contexts in which talents thrive; and 3) respond to the new demands of tourists. In addition, data is needed to propose services, to rethink the narrative of the city, to establish and strengthen its international positioning, to develop coherent models of territorial development and to monitor their impact and evolution over time.

Milan offers a very broad vision of smartness, in which being a smart city is also considered a communication and marketing lever, useful for building the narrative of Milan as an attractive global city. With regards to 'tourism and culture', a smart approach to technology has led to the establishment of e-mobility services, smart tags to access to information of local monuments, urban and regional tourism websites, tourism booking and ecommerce platforms and tourism apps.

## Conclusions

The city approach towards tourism has substantially changed over the period observed. Tourism represents a key component of a wider visitor economy that encompasses a long list of city users such as tourists, residents, students, businessmen, researchers, event attendees, among others. This is line with benchmark European cities that formulate tourism destination strategies as part of wider urban development policies. From a destination metagovernance perspective, the city assisted the shift from extemporaneous market-driven collaborations between private stakeholders to a greater involvement of government authorities in the steering of relevant stakeholders in the agenda setting for the development of the city as a destination. This reflects elements of the new public management and reflexive metagovernance highlighted in the literature (Amore & Hall, 2016; Meuleman, 2008).

Building from the experiences and projects over the years, relevant institutional stakeholders adapted the nature and scope of their collaborations to deal with the COVID crisis and to build resilience. This has led to a new phase in which Milano & Partners acts as the dedicated DMMO for the city of Milan. This trend can be found in cities across Europe (e.g., London, Lyon, and Manchester) as well as in the academic literature (Amore & Hall, 2017). Milan is applying the forms of smart metagovernance which is in line with what observed in the literature (e.g., Buhalis, 2022, 2020, Buhalis & Amaranggana, 2013; Ruhlandt, 2018). This is evident in the third phase observed in the Milan case study, with the establishment of network of stakeholders who collaborate freely and only when necessary. This approach incorporates the advantages of expediting decision-making processes as well as enabling the formation of flexible working groups whenever needed with the most suitable stakeholders (Buonincontri & Micera, 2016; Desdemoustier et al., 2019; Sigalat-Signes et al., 2020).

Hence, this chapter provided a reflection on key governance and metagovernance episodes of Milan as a destination from a longitudinal perspective. It highlights the dynamic nature that ultimately contributed to enhancing the competitiveness and the smartness of Milan as a city and a destination in particular. This chapter also highlights the role of technology in fostering reflexive and adaptive modes of destination metagovernance and how relational resources and knowledge sharing are currently at the heart of the new Milano & Partners. Further research should look specifically at this DMMO, at the consulting processes and decision-making stages in the years to come, particularly in rebuilding tourism sustainably in the post COVID era.

# References

Amore, A., & Hall, C. M. (2016). From governance to meta-governance in tourism? Re-incorporating politics, interests, and values in the analysis of tourism governance. *Tourism Recreation Research*, 41(2), 109-122.

Amore, A., & Hall, C. M. (2017). National and urban public policy agenda in tourism. Towards the emergence of a hyperneoliberal script? *International Journal of Tourism Policy*, 7(1), 4-22.

Andreani, S., Kalchschmidt, M., Pinto, R., & Sayegh, A. (2019). Reframing technologically enhanced urban scenarios: A design research model towards human centered smart cities. *Technological Forecasting and Social Change*, 142, 15-25.

Angelidou, M. (2015). Smart cities: A conjuncture of four forces. *Cities*, 47, 95-106.

Ardito, L., Cerchione, R., Vecchio Del, P. & Raguseo, E. (2019). Big data in smart tourism: Challenges, issues and opportunities. *Current Issues in Tourism*, 22(15), 1805-1809.

Appio, F. P., Lima, M., & Paroutis, S. (2019). Understanding smart cities: Innovation ecosystems, technological advancements, and societal challenges. *Technological Forecasting and Social Change*, 142, 1-14.

Baggio, R., & Del Chiappa, G. (2014). Real and virtual relationships in tourism digital ecosystems. *Information Technology & Tourism*, 14(1), 3-19.

Bell, S., & Park, A. (2006). The problematic metagovernance of networks: Water reform in New South Wales. *Journal of Public Policy*, 26(1), 63-83.

Boes, K., Buhalis, D., & Inversini, A. (2016). Smart tourism destinations: Ecosystems for tourism destination competitiveness. *International Journal of Tourism Cities*, 2(2), 108-124.

Bolívar, M. P. R. (2016). Mapping dimensions of governance in smart cities. In Y. Kim, & M. Liu (Eds.), *Proceedings of the 17th International Digital Government Research Conference on Digital Government Research/*. Retrieved from http://dx.doi.org/10.1145/2912160.2912176 (accessed 10 May 2021).

Buhalis, D. (2000). Marketing the competitive destination of the future. *Tourism management,* 21(1), 97-116.

Buhalis, D. (2015). *Working definitions of smartness and smart tourism destination.* Retrieved from: http://buhalis.blogspot.co.uk/2014/12/working-definitions-of-smartness-and.html (accessed 10 May 2021).

Buhalis, D. (2020). Technology in tourism - from information communication technologies to eTourism and smart tourism towards ambient intelligence tourism: A perspective article. *Tourism Review,* 75(1), 267-272.

Buhalis, D., (2022), Tourism management and marketing in transformation: Introduction and Editor's statement, in Buhalis, D., (ed) *Encyclopedia of Tourism Management and Marketing*, Cheltenham, UK: Edward Elgar.

Buhalis, D., & Amaranggana, A. (2013). Smart tourism destinations. In U. Gretzel, R. Law, & M. Fuchs (Eds.), *Information and Communication Technologies in Tourism* (pp. 553-564). Amsterdam: Springer.

Buhalis, D., & Foerste, M. (2015). SoCoMo marketing or travel and tourism: Empowering co-creation of value. *Journal of Destination Marketing & Management,* 4, 151-161.

Buhalis, D., Andreu, L. & Gnoth, J., (2020), The dark side of the sharing economy: Balancing value co-creation and value co-destruction. *Psychology and Marketing.* 37(5), 689–704. https://doi.org/10.1002/mar.21344

Buonincontri, P., & Micera, R. (2016). The experience co-creation in smart tourism destinations: A multiple case analysis of European destinations. *Information Technology & Tourism,* 16(3), 285-315.

Camero, A., & Alba, E. (2019) Smart City and information technology: A Review. *Cities,* 93, 84-94.

Caragliu, A., Del Bo, C., & Nijkamp, P. (2011). Smart cities in Europe. *Journal of Urban Technology,* 18(2), 65-82.

Costa, N. (2013). The applied sociology of tourism. The up skills of the facilitator in the Italian hospitality industry. *Advances in Applied Sociology,* 3(1), 1-12.

Cowley, R., & Caprotti, F. (2019). Smart city as anti-planning in the UK. *Environment and Planning D: Society and Space,* 37(3), 428-448.

D'Angella, F., De Carlo, M., & Sainaghi, R. (2010). Archetypes of destination governance: A comparison of international destinations. *Tourism Review,* 65(4), 61-73.

De Carlo, M., & D'Angella, F. (2011). Repositioning cities and events: Milan. In N. Morgan, A. Pritchard, & R. Pride (Eds.), *Destination Brands. Managing Place Reputation* (3rd ed., pp. 225-238). Abingdon: Routledge.

Del Chiappa, G., & Baggio, R. (2015). Knowledge transfer in smart tourism destinations: Analyzing the effects of a network structure. *Journal of Destination Marketing & Management,* 4(3), 145-150.

Desdemoustier, J., Crutzen, N., & Giffinger, R. (2019). Municipalities' understanding of the Smart City concept: An exploratory analysis in Belgium. *Technological Forecasting and Social Change,* 142, 129-141.

Edwards, D., Griffin, T., & Hayllar, B. (2009). Urban tourism precincts: An overview of key themes and issues. In B. Hayllar, T. Griffin, & D. Edwards (Eds.), *City Spaces-Tourist Places: Urban Tourism Precincts* (pp. 95-106). Amsterdam: Butterworth-Heinemann.

Engelbert, J., van Zoonen, L., & Hirzalla, F. (2019). Excluding citizens from the European smart city: The discourse practices of pursuing and granting smartness. *Technological Forecasting and Social Change,* 142, 347-353.

European Commission (2014). *A Digital Agenda for Europe.* Luxembourg: Publications Office of the European Union.

Franzoni, S. (2015) Destination governance for sustainable tourism. *Journal of Tourism and Hospitality Management,* 3(11-12), 215-223.

Gil-Garcia, J. R., Pardo, T. A., & Nam, T. (2015). What makes a city smart? Identifying core components and proposing an integrative and comprehensive conceptualization. *Information Polity,* 20(1), 61–87.

Gonzales-Reverte, F. (2019). Building sustainable smart destinations: An approach based on the development of Spanish smart tourism plans. *Sustainability,* 11, 6874

Gretzel, U., Werthner, H., Koo, C., & Lamsfus, C. (2015). Conceptual foundations for understanding smart tourism ecosystems. *Computers in Human Behavior,* 50, 558-563.

Hall, C. M. (2011). A typology of governance and its implications for tourism policy analysis. *Journal of Sustainable Tourism,* 19(4-5), 437-457.

Hall, C. M., & Veer, E. (2016). The DMO is dead. Long live the DMO (or, why DMO managers don't care about post-structuralism). *Tourism Recreation Research,* 41(3), 354-357.

ISTAT (2019). *Movimento Turistico in Italia – Anno 2018.* Retrieved from https://www.istat.it/it/files/2019/11/Movimento-turistico-in-Italia-2018.pdf (accessed 1 May 2020).

Ismagilova, E., Hughes, L., Dwivedi, Y. K., & Raman, K. R. (2019). Smart cities: Advances in research—An information systems perspective. *International Journal of Information Management,* 47, 88-100.

Jenkins, J. M., Hall, C. M., & Mkono, M. (2014). Tourism and public policy: Contemporary debates and future directions. In A. A. Lew, C. M. Hall, & A. M. Williams (Eds.), *The Wiley Blackwell Companion to Tourism* (pp. 542-555). Hoboken, NJ: John Wiley & Sons.

Jessop, B. (2011). Metagovernance. In M. Bevir (Ed.), *The SAGE Handbook of Governance* (pp. 106-123). London: SAGE.

Jovicic, D. Z. (2019). From the traditional understanding of tourism destination to the smart tourism destination. *Current Issues in Tourism,* 22(3), 276-282.

Klijn, E. H., Steijn, B., & Edelenbos, J. (2010). The impact of network management on outcomes in governance networks. *Public Administration,* 88(4), 1063-1082.

Kummitha, R. K. R., & Crutzen, N. (2017). How do we understand smart cities? An evolutionary perspective. *Cities,* 67, 43-52.

Lamsfus, C., Martín, D., Alzua-Sorzabal, A., & Torres-Manzanera, E. (2015). Smart tourism destinations: An extended conception of smart cities focusing on human mobility. In I. Tussyadiah, & A. Inversini (Eds,), *Information and Communication Technologies in Tourism* (pp. 363-375). Amsterdam: Springer.

Laws, E., Argusa, J., Richins, H., & Scott, N. (2011). Tourist destination governance: practice, theory and issues. In E. Laws, H. Richins, J. Argusa, & N. Scott (Eds.), *Tourist Destination Governance: Practice, Theory and Issues* (pp. 1-16). Wallingford: CABI.

Luthe, T., & Wyss, R. (2016). Resilience to climate change in a cross-scale tourism governance context: a combined quantitative-qualitative network analysis. *Ecology and Society,* 21(1), 27-44.

Manville, C., Cochrane, G., Cave, J., Millard, J., Pederson, J., Thaarup, R. & Kotterink, B. (2014). *Mapping Smart Cities in the EU.* Brussels: European Parliament. Retrieved from http://www.europarl.europa.eu/RegData/etudes/etudes/join/2014/507480/IPOL-ITRE_ET(2014)507480_EN.pdf (accessed 4 May 2021).

Marsal-Llacuna, M. L., Colomer-Llinàs, J., & Meléndez-Frigola, J. (2015). Lessons in urban monitoring taken from sustainable and liveable cities to better address the Smart Cities initiative. *Technological Forecasting and Social Change,* 90, 611-622.

Meijer, A., & Bolívar, M. P. R. (2016). Governing the smart city: A review of the literature on smart urban governance. *International Review of Administrative Sciences,* 82(2), 392-408.

Meuleman, L. (2008). *Public Management and the Metagovernance of Hierarchies, Networks and Markets: The Feasibility of Designing and Managing Governance Style Combinations.* Heidelberg: Physica-Verlag.

Meuleman, L. (2019). *Metagovernance for Sustainability: A Framework for Implementing the Sustainable Development Goals.* Abingdon: Routledge.

Neuhofer, B., Buhalis, D., & Ladkin, A. (2012). Conceptualising technology enhanced destination experiences. *Journal of Destination Marketing & Management,* 1(1-2), 36-46.

Nilssen, M. (2019). To the smart city and beyond? Developing a typology of smart urban innovation. *Technological Forecasting and Social Change,* 142, 98-104.

Paskaleva, K. A. (2009). Enabling the smart city: The progress of city E-governance in Europe. *International Journal of Innovation and Regional Development,* 1(4), 405–422.

Pechlaner, H., & Volgger, M. (2013). Towards a comprehensive view of tourism governance: Relationships between the corporate governance of tourism service firms and territorial governance. *International Journal of Globalisation and Small Business*, 5(1/2), 3-19.

Pechlaner, H., Volgger, M., & Herntrei, M. (2012). Destination management organizations as interface between destination governance and corporate governance. *Anatolia*, 23(2), 151-168.

Pike, S., & Page, S. J. (2014). Destination Marketing Organizations and destination marketing: A narrative analysis of the literature. *Tourism Management*, 41, 202-227.

Praharaj, S., Han, J. H., & Hawken, S. (2017). Urban innovation through policy integration: Critical perspectives from 100 smart cities mission in India. *City, Culture and Society*, 12, 35-43.

Ruhlandt, R. (2018). The governance of smart cities: A systematic literature review. *Cities*, 81, 1-23.

Shafiee, S., Ghatari, A. R., Hasanzadeh, A., & Jahanyan, S. (2019). Developing a model for sustainable smart tourism destinations: A systematic review. *Tourism Management Perspectives*, 31, 287-300.

Sigala, M. (2018). New technologies in tourism: From multi-disciplinary to anti-disciplinary advances and trajectories. *Tourism Management Perspectives*, 25, 151-155.

Sigalat-Signes, E., Calvo-Palomares, R. Roig-Merino, B. & García-Adána, I (2020). Transition towards a tourist innovation model: The smart tourism destination. Reality or territorial marketing? *Journal of Innovation & Knowledge*, 5(2), 96-104.

Sørensen, E., & Torfing, J. (2011). Enhancing collaborative innovation in the public sector. *Administration & Society*, 43(8), 842-868.

Sørensen, E., & Torfing, J. (2017). Metagoverning collaborative innovation in governance networks. *The American Review of Public Administration*, 47(7), 826–839.

Spyriadis, T., Buhalis, D., & Fyall, A. (2011). Dynamics of destination governance: Governance and metagovernance in the composite industrial environment of destinations. In E. Laws, H. Richins, J. Argusa, & N. Scott (Eds.), *Tourist Destination Governance: Practice, Theory and Issues* (pp. 187-202). Wallingford: CABI.

Yes Milano (2020). About us – Milano & Partners. Retrieved from https://www.yesmilano.it/en/articles/about-us (accessed 15 May 2020).

# 10 Smart model of sustainable tourism development:
## Lessons from Madeira Island, Portugal

*Luiz Pinto Machado and António Manuel Martins de Almeida*

## Introduction

The tourism industry has benefited greatly from technological progress (Buhalis, 2020). Much of its progress over the years is a direct outcome of several advances made towards applying technical solutions in key areas of the tourism experience. The current social development model is based mainly on Information and Communication Technologies (ICT). Society and key players communicate, produce knowledge, and generate wealth at various levels. (Machado & Almeida, 2010). What has changed significantly is that technology has not only become an integral part of tourism but has revolutionized the way travel is planned (Buhalis, 2003; ITU, 2015, 2016). Business is conducted (Buhalis & Licata, 2002), and tourism services and experiences are created and consumed (Stamboulis & Skayannis, 2003) using technological solutions and platforms. Technology revolutionized the entire distribution channel by empowering direct communications and transactions between suppliers and consumers (disintermediation) as well as through the emergence of a plethora of new intermediaries (reintermediation) (Buhalis et al., 2019; Figueiredo et al., 2018; IEEE, 2017).

The rapid pace of development in the ICT field and the growing attention given to concepts such as smart tourism and smart destination have created several opportunities to re-think the development of the tourism sector based on substantively altered business models firmly anchored on sustainable-friendly premises. However, bringing smartness into tourism destinations requires interconnecting stakeholders dynamically through a technological platform on which information relating to tourism activities could be exchanged instantly (Zhang et al., 2018). In view of the rapid growth of technological developments, tourist destinations should improve their smartness. They should acknowledge and understand the behavior of the new generation of tourists as an opportunity to make destinations and tourism companies more competitive, based on memorable experiences and co-creation of information relating to tourism activities (Fan et al., 2019). Information supported by technology apps can be exchanged and upgraded instantly and in real time (Buhalis & Sinarta, 2019). These co-creations reinforce the motivation of those inclined to choose a destination and increase tourist satisfaction and competitiveness. Tourists affiliated with the Millennial generation are dependent on technology, as their generation has never lived without a smartphone. They will travel more and spend more than their ancestors, and influence others and their spending behavior in the process of choosing a destination (Buhalis, Parra López & Martinez-Gonzalez, 2020).

Smart tourism emerged to provide the infostructure for value cocreation (Buhalis & Amaranggana, 2015; Boes et al., 2016; Gretzel et al., 2015). All suppliers and intermediaries, the public sector and consumers, are becoming dynamically networked, which co-produces value for all operators and stakeholders interconnected within the ecosystem (Buhalis, 2019). Interoperability and ubiquitous computing ensure that everybody is interconnected. Processes are integrated towards generating value through dynamic co-creation, personalization, and adaptation to the new global context facing the tourism sector (Buhalis & Foerste, 2015; Buhalis & Sinarta, 2019).

This chapter explains the practical difficulties involved in building up the required infrastructure of a smart island/destination. These include implementation complexities as well as transformative and disruptive concepts in traditional tourism ecosystems that have been operating for years relatively smoothly. This bridges the theoretical foundations of smart tourism with empirical research focused on less studied insular geographical settings. Hence the chapter interprets operators' attitudes regarding several key factors affecting the development of smart tourism in Madeira, Portugal. This includes policy-making aspects, supply-side elements, and in-house technical competencies. Valuable insights regarding strengths, weaknesses, and challenges discuss the current state of affairs and devise a coherent and comprehensive methodology to adopt a progressive agenda focused on smart tourism on islands.

## Smart cities and smart tourism

The concept of 'Smart City' is relatively new in the scientific literature. It has emerged in the last two decades (Albino et al., 2015). It deals mainly with the economic and social aspects of transforming a city into a sustainable urban environment based on smart solutions (Winters, 2011; Manville et al., 2014). Caragliu et al. (2011) defined the smart city as concurrent with a harmonious coexistence of social investment, human capital, communications, and infrastructures with a view of promoting sustainable and efficient socio-economic development through the deployment of ICT tools. 'Smart' stands out and is a prefix in several buzzwords. Terms and concepts such as 'smart citizen', 'smart policy', 'smart networks', 'smart buses', etc., are used increasingly in city management. There is clear evidence of the wide acceptance and prominence of the Smart City concept in a wide range of policymaking related fields.

Achieving success in working in a sustainable and integrated manner is one of the main challenges of the twenty-first century, as their position as the epicenter of urban life is reinforced. The concept of a Smart City represents an environment where technology is embedded within the city management tools. This concept is well placed to synergize a city's social components to improve citizens' quality of life, while also improving city services' efficiencies, such as optimizing the use of energy and better traffic monitoring (Vicini et al. 2012; Figueiredo et al., 201). The smart city has become a common ground for the urban discourse, whose tenet has been received with enthusiasm in the media and the institutional and academic sphere. However this ideal city entails considerable challenges. Many of these hurdles are linked with the six dimensions or pillars posited by the model: population, environment, mobility, economy, quality of life, and governance (Enerlis et al., 2012; Giffinger et al., 2007; Giffinger & Gudrun, 2010). The smart city cannot succeed without the greater involvement of citizens, as smart people.

The highly complex urban structure, that has long been associated only with large cities, has changed with the new demographic. Urban settlements of this kind have slower population growth rates than other relatively smaller urban centers (Bouskela et al., 2016). Thus, intermediate cities have also grown at an accelerated pace. However, medium cities cannot be delimited exclusively based on variables such as demographic size or geographical area. The most appropriate approaches at the territorial level go beyond the classical ways of classifying and delimiting intermediate cities. They mainly focus on the intermediary functions performed by this type of cities in the territory and their vocation to articulate specific spaces with other nodes and territories in the local and regional scope (Signes et al. 2020).

The European Territorial Strategy (1999) acknowledged the importance of developing a more balanced and well-ordered European urban system. This should be able to generate a polycentric development to assure the delivery of resources, services, employment, and innovation to the majority of the population through city networks, while also seeking greater territorial cohesion (Romero & Farinós, 2004). Thus, the intermediate cities that function as regional capitals take on an essential role in these areas. They are important centers for developing industrial activities and services, research and technology, tourism, and leisure (European Commission, 1999). Many of these intermediate cities act as functional hubs for other cities and towns. They are delimited by criteria such as people's movements, urban expansion, the provision of supra-municipal services, and public transport corridors, which comprehensively articulate the territory. Therefore, these areas should be subject to territorial management and planning if the smart city approach is to be applied, especially if they are also tourist attraction poles. The territorial dimension and the applied policies can influence the dynamics of organizational innovations in the tourism sector (and related areas) and help build innovation systems (Zach & Hill, 2017).

## Smart islands and smart tourism development

The challenges facing smart cities in the interaction with the territories around them, are based on a rationale of universal and sustainable access, and environmentally friendly, shared, and democratic mobility. Although the term 'smartification', referring to techniques, results, concepts, software, data, etc., can be applied both to cities or destinations, their application may be quite complex in the context of islands. Islands, to a certain extent are isolated from the rest of the world as they are connected only via coastal/ sea and air routes and therefore function considerably differently from cities (Femenia-Serra & Neuhofer, 2018). Islands face considerable challenges and require appropriate policies and strategies (Tiago & Borges-Tiago, 2022; Spilanis et al., 2022). The *Smart Islands Initiative*, a bottom-up effort of European island authorities and communities that started in 1993, addresses the challenges of insularity. It builds on years of collaboration between European islands and seeks to communicate the significant potential of islands to function as laboratories for technological, social, environmental, economic, and political innovation (Efthymiopoulos et al., 2016). The initiative is inspired by the Smart Cities and Communities paradigm and seeks to improve lives on islands through sustainable, integrated solutions that make the most out of islands' competitive advantages.

A 'Smart Island' was defined in the project 'Smart Web services for Mediterranean Islands' (GISIG, 2014) as *an integration platform developed through the ICT PSP call. When finalized, it will provide a variety of standardized web services under a friendly 3D interface like Google Earth developed specifically for this purpose. The web services will cover various aspects of everyday life such as Civil Protection, Environment, Forest Fires Simulation and Management, Tourism, Retail Operations, Marketing, Statistics, Education, Virtual Tour, Real-Time Weather Forecasting, Transportation, Yachting Services, etc. The platform will be open-ended. The API will be made available to the developers' community, giving the ability to develop additional web services following standardized procedures.* The Smart Island concept was designed as a complex and tangled model that must be aligned to function as a perfect system, which demands time be put in place. The term was also used in the context of developing a Smart-Islands Platform for tourism support. The Smart Islands project continues the European Economic and Social Committee's (EESC) own initiative on Smart Islands. The Smart Islands Initiative underscores the role of islands in accelerating Europe's transition into low carbon, sustainable economy.

According to the website *Smart Islands Initiative*, EU ISLENET was the first network of island authorities promoting sustainable energy and environmental management, founded by the Western Isles, Shetland, Orkney, Madeira, Azores, and the Canary Islands. The Pact of Islands, the political initiative of European islands, was officially recognized by the European Parliament as an EU initiative that runs parallel to the Covenant of Mayors. This entails an expert group on islands that oversee policy and the establishment of an open platform to act as a forum for coordination and action among islands. In the 2015 EP Resolution on Special Situation of Islands, the European Parliament adopted the Resolution on the special situation of islands, calling for an Agenda for EU Islands accompanied by an EU Strategic Framework for Islands to link up financial instruments that can have a major territorial impact. The Smart Islands Forum was launched in 2016, bringing together 35 islands from 13 countries to draft the Smart Islands Declaration, currently signed locally by EU island authorities. In February 2017, Eurelectric published the *Towards the Energy Transition on Europe's Islands* report, highlighting islands' role in Europe's energy transition. On 28 March 2017, the islands made a strong comeback at the European Parliament to present the Smart Islands Initiative and communicate their potential to transform themselves into smart, inclusive, and thriving societies for an innovative and sustainable Europe. The project outlined the challenges facing islands and the potential these exhibits to usher in a low-carbon, smart, sustainable, and inclusive development paradigm. The Islands Declaration made an ambitious call for action and commits to 10 steps to become smart, inclusive, and thriving societies! From here, the islands tried to maximize their synergies and focus their efforts on seven key areas to address this challenge, namely energy, transport, water, waste, governance, ICT, and Economy as illustrated in Figure 10.1.

**Figure 10.1:** Seven key areas stated by the Smart Islands Declaration. *Source*: http://www.smartislandsinitiative.eu/

Despite the technological and societal advances recorded so far, in several cases, operators on islands are still reliant on traditional business models, management philosophies, and past successes. They often voice fears that such transformations can lead to loss of control over the production and co-creation of experiences. Others may feel concerned regarding the large amount of investment, training of labor, and capacity building needed to adopt a new management philosophy based on ICT tools, sustainable development processes, and eco, green and sustainable labels. Operators and policy-makers alike may resent the unavoidable process of integrating databases and availability of real-time data, plus the development of collaborative networks and mindsets, besides issues of transparency and accountability, all of which are closely intertwined with the concept of smart destination within the current EU programs. For that reason, any attempt to adopt the smart tourism model on an island must be preceded by careful analysis and diagnosis of the organizational structures displayed by operators and attitudes towards the adoption of new ICT tools and business models. Acknowledging the inevitability of a shift in operators' behavior is fueled by the increasing pressure to confirm the impact of the disruptive factors at work.

When tourism is addressed, the public and private sectors must think how to strengthen the industry together and develop platforms to be dynamically connected through integrated solutions. All information related to tourism and other related activities can be easily accessed understood and exchanged instantly, giving rise to quick decisions in the tourist booking process dynamically (Buhalis & Sinarta, 2019). Applying the smartness concept helps destinations to respond quickly to the needs of tourists at any time (Buhalis, 2020). This can be translated into an increase in the level of business efficiency and competitiveness, which depends on the ability of companies and tourist destinations to adapt the new practices based on cooperation and coopetition (Buhalis, 2022). Tourist destinations that do not follow this paradigm may suffer a sharp decline in both the quality of the product and the number of tourists who visit them as their competitiveness will suffer.

Destinations should adopt new models of interaction with tourists to ensure that they can deliver memorable experiences (Buhalis, 2022). The challenge for modern cities and tourist destinations is to rapidly engage with their visitors and provide accurate information regarding the different services they provide. They should also ensure access to data, facilitate mobility, and support energy efficiency. They should adopt environmental standards for cleaning and hygiene; maintain gardens and urban forests; facilitate waste collection as well as water supply and treatment, whilst controlling energy production and management. Smartness should also increase inclusiveness and accessibility for travelers by supporting tourists with mobility, visual, auditory, and cognitive impairments to deal with physical and service barriers (Michopoulou & Buhalis, 2013; Rubio-Escuderos, et al., 2021). The adoption of the smartest paradigm implies a process of re-engineering and the engagement of different stakeholders simultaneously to shape products, actions, processes, and services (Buhalis, 2020). Such a re-engineering process will optimize the collective performance and competitiveness and generate agile solutions and value for all those involved in the ecosystem in real-time (Buhalis & Sinarta, 2019).

## Case study: Madeira Island Portugal
## Smartness towards sustainable tourism development

The Autonomous Region of Madeira in Portugal is an archipelago of volcanic origin, composed of two inhabited islands and two without inhabitants as illustrated in Figure 10.2. Access was only possible by sea until the airport opened in the capital, Funchal, in 1963, which led to the development and expansion of several infrastructures and the construction of more hotels (Barros & Machado, 2010). Madeira Island's recognition as an upper-market tourism destination has been repeatedly confirmed with the awarding of the most prestigious awards in the world, both to Madeira hotels and to the island itself. For example, Madeira Island was considered by World Travel Awards (WTA) in the last years as the best island destination in the world. Visitors can choose the elegance of the island's time-honored traditional hotels or opt for one of the more recent forms of accommodation, namely smaller boutique hotels or establishments located in rural areas where they can come into closer contact with nature and the local people. The regional government of Madeira and their territorial planning departments need to ensure that the Island tourism policy and Marketing Strategy are well managed and take advantage of the opportunities that smart tourism brings. This chapter provides insights on the development path of tourism in Madeira and explores how local policymakers may be the 'missing link' needed to improve the sector prospects based on smart tourism models

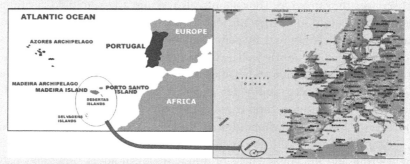

Figure 10.2: Map of Madeira Island, Portugal. Source http://reregions.blogspot.com/2010/03/madeira-archipelago.html

### The adoption of Smartness in Madeira Island

The study shows how an island destination can benefit from these developments. Qualitative research with more than 50 small and medium enterprises leaders, public administration officials, experts and others illustrates their experience, difficulties, anxieties and expectations related to implementing smart initiatives. This case study of implementing smart tourism in the Autonomous Region of Madeira emphasises the sustainability of the sector and illustrates the measures that public and private sector should practice. The study examines the level of adoption, challenges, opportunities and measures to improve the level of Smart Destination tools adoption. Several hotel units located in the Archipelago responded to the survey through their general managers and/or the environment departments. 35 units (from a total of 180) answered, corresponding to 20% of the hotel units, and 65% of the hotel beds. Some small operators with less than 50 rooms also responded to the survey.

Although the term 'smartification' is an actual application in different geographical environments, the application on an island can be different. Madeira Island as a territory of 260,000 inhabitants, seven small towns, and some villages located in 750 square km, somewhat isolated from the rest of the world, surrounded by the sea, and 1000 km away from the European continent. Despite the creativity shown by operators, through the opening of new types of accommodation and the acclaim and fame in the most market of origin, Madeira has been losing competitiveness and attractiveness as it is often viewed as old fashioned. Since 1976, Madeira has lost ground as a winter destination, partly because of competition from other Mediterranean basin destinations. Moreover, the contemporary phenomena of low-cost air travel, compounded by strong marketing strategies that attract short-break visitors to alternative tourism destinations, are also contributing factors to slowing down traditional tourism destinations. Since 2000, Madeira Tourism has profited from several initiatives aiming at adapting dozens of derelict buildings and vacant premises into modern and stylish accommodation facilities, categorized as boutique hotels, superbly positioned in the landscape, with fabulous panoramic views over the mountains, the ocean, and Funchal's city centre. In addition, the phenomenon of local accommodation has also brought new opportunities, especially to the island's interior. Many houses registered as second homes have been transformed into local accommodation units—increasing the island's accommodation capacity by 13,000 beds in just five years! Like many other regions, the development of sharing economy and AirBnB fueled this development as it injected capital for renovations and gentrification (Buhalis, Andreu & Gnoth, 2020).

Although Madeira is part of the Smart Islands Initiative, that seeks to improve life on islands through sustainable and integrated solutions that make the most out of islands' competitive advantages, there is no evidence to report an improvement in these aspects, despite the apparent potential to exploit them. Rethinking tourism as a key sector of the island, and reinforcing its importance, implies a series of changes and a reengineering in tourism management. Acknowledging that only a joint and synchronized action between the island's players will guarantee growth and sustainability is critical, especially given the current situation of a never-before-seen COVID pandemic crisis, it is estimated that it may take 6 to 8 years for tourism to reach the pre-Covid values. The lack of communication between the public and private entities is the basis of the problem.

The architecture of the 'Strategic Document Madeira 14-20' priority axes and the specific objectives associated with the selected Investment Priorities reflect the regional strategic options (Madeira 14-20, n.d.). They are aligned with the priorities of the Smart Islands Declaration and Europe 2020 Strategy of the National Reform Plan and the Partnership Agreement - Portugal 2020, within the framework of the thematic areas of competitiveness and internationalization, sustainability and efficiency in the use of resources, human capital and inclusion. Within the framework of the requirements of the budgetary consolidation process, there are plans to apply, over the next few years, a global allocation of 403 million Euros in the Island. The 'Strategic Document Madeira 14-20', regarded the four indicators for which reliable information at the regional level is available. The Island position is below the current performance of the country and far from the benchmarks established for the horizon 2020 in the objectives associated with education, innovation, employment, and energy. From the perspective of the contribution for these objectives, it is important to give priority and focus on policy interventions and instruments. These should include the domains of competitiveness and innovation and the development of human potential, stimulating a desirable balance between supply and demand for skills. In the field of energy, an emphasis was placed on efficiency of energy and the reduction of dependence on the outside to strengthen the competitiveness of the regional economic fabric. The plan also prioritised social inclusion and employment, given the density of existing problems unemployment – absolute and relative – and social exclusion. The main lines of distancing between Madeira Island and the European Union are illustrated in Table 10.2.

Portugal as a country is also looking for a sustainable growth path based on a more competitive and resilient development model. Madeira is deeply committed to the structural transformation of its development model, thus seeking to create conditions for greater cohesion and convergence in the European context. The Island's small size determines a small internal market, which condition the ability to integrate global economic chains in product segments that require scale. This includes the main primary exportable regional products such as wines, bananas, fruits subtropical, wicker and flowers. In terms of opening markets, small size and increased transport and production factors, provide the context of the incipient organization of production that makes it impossible to concentrate supply.

The strong dependence of the tourism cluster has been (when associated with the development of the real estate sector) an inhibiting factor on the diversification of the economic fabric by sustaining a relatively narrow and superficial value chain, with little integration upstream (agri-food, fishing) and downstream (culture, heritage, landscape). Tourism is one of the pillars of the regional economy, being responsible for more than 26.6% of the direct impacts in GDP and about 30% of jobs. These impacts are compounded by indirect effects in the sectors of commerce, real estate, and transport and reducing regional asymmetries, which in the period 2007-2012 registered an unfavourable evolution of economic indicators. The sector has recovered its competitiveness and presented very positive variations in the subsequent period (2012-2019), but still not enough to consider the Island as an example of sector efficiency. The COVID 19 pandemic disrupted global tourism and damaged the industry in Madeira significantly (Suk & Kim, 2021; Florido-Benítez, 2021; Rahmafitria et al., 2021),

**Table 10.1:** Smart Island indicators: Madeira Island vs the European Union

| | |
|---|---|
| Research and Development (R&D) investment | Level of investment in R&D, in 2016, below 0.3% of GDP (0.31%) Compared to 2010, the reduction is more than five times lower than the level of Portugal and well below the targets established by the PNR and the Europe 2020 Strategy (from 0.25% to 3%). In this unfavourable scenario, it is worth highlighting the delayed level of investment in R&D in the private sector, which reached 0.07% in 2016, recovering from 2010 (0.04%). |
| Education | Level of early school leaving below the national average (23.2% -14.0%). This indicator has been following a trajectory of marked recovery in recent years, even though it remains far from the objective targets of the PNR and Europe 2020 strategy [10%]. Higher education level of the population aged 30-34 years (30.5%) relatively close to the national average (33.4%), but still below the targets of the PNR and the Europe 2020 Strategy (40%) [2017 data]. |
| Employment rate | Employment rate away from the objective targets of the PNR and the Europe 2020 Strategy (75%, i.e., 69%), in a conjuncture that has revealed a gradual recovery of employment levels, even though high youth unemployment (25.2%, data at the end of 2017). |
| Climate / Energy | The objectives related to the Climate / Energy indicators are demanding for the Region, above all, the weight of renewable energy in final energy consumption, which is expected to increase from 9.9% to 20% (Europe 2020 target). |
| Poverty | Regarding poverty, data from 2009 (latest available) indicate that Madeira Island was the second Region of the country at risk of highest poverty, occupying fourth place in the ranking of Portuguese regions. |

## Smart tourism adoption on Madeira Island, Portugal

The empirical study, based on a survey (structured questionnaire) intended to elicit key actors´ opinions, attitudes, and ideas about the current stage of development of the concept of smart tourism in Madeira. Face-to-face communication resulted in much more detailed access to opinions and attitudes than would be possible via a self-administered questionnaire. Open questions offered the opportunity to get additional feedback on the topic under analysis and encouraged respondents to raise and identify worthy issues (O'Cathain & Thomas, 2004). This mixed approach offered advantages in gaining information on pre-determined issues while creating space to discuss and investigate new areas of interest. The results suggest that respondents´ degree of knowledge on smart tourism is relatively minimal, which can be explained purely on technological grounds, owing to the multiplicity of technical solutions, applications, buzzwords, and concepts. A plausible alternative explanation of the respondents' conduct may lie in the perceived need to reflect a cautious approach towards 'smart destination concepts' and the relationship with current perceived wisdom at the local level. The average respondent considers that the degree of technological development in the field of smart tourists is relatively low (mean of 2.07 based on a five-point Likert scale). Regarding what is meant by the concept of Smart Tourism Destinations, examined from the point of view of which projects should be implemented, respondents stressed four main aspects, namely:

☐ Energy efficiency and sustainability;

☐ Tourism development (the most cited example of smart destination projects to be developed), based on useful tools and applications in emerging market segments to provide better experiences;

☐ Management of data and information; and

☐ Adoption of new technological solutions.

Respondents emphasized mainly tourism and access to information-related initiatives. Only a few respondents highlighted the potential to introduce new business models, institutional arrangements, and development models based on sustainability principles, energy efficiency, and improved quality of life for residents. Implicitly, respondents also assumed a low degree of investment in R&D projects and partnerships between private and public actors, which lead to results in line with Segittur (2015) and López de Avila and Garcia (2013). When asked about readily identifiable projects and policies, 50% of the respondents justified their choices (low degree of implementation and lack of progress in smart tourism) on lack of information and practical knowledge on the subject. Others cited aspects such as: the need for further investment; lack of coordination and collaboration between private and public actors; lack of adequacy of the concept of smart destination to the fundamental realities of tourism; scepticism about the viability of these innovations; and lack of interest in adoption of smart related models. Respondents indicated a range of reasons explaining the current state of affairs but rarely felt responsible for taking smart tourism forward. In half of the cases, respondents reported a lack of knowledge in general or about examples of concrete policies and projects in the field. However, they often implied that it was simply the job of the government to do things, without disturbing much what the respondents were doing. Respondents' opinions on the degree of implementation of cluster-based smart policies initiatives are relatively low or negative (Table 10.2).

**Table 10.2:** Degree of implementation of smart initiatives

| Dimensions | Mean | St. Dev. |
|---|---|---|
| Support to entrepreneurship | 3.08 | 1.23 |
| Safety | 3.04 | 1.29 |
| Highlight the cultural and historical resource | 3.00 | 1.18 |
| Involvement of R&D and C&T entities | 2.94 | 1.16 |
| Use of ICT tools in the tourism sector | 2.87 | 1.27 |
| Tourism sector professionals' qualification | 2.83 | 1.33 |
| Green energy | 2.81 | 1.12 |
| Nature and ecosystems protection | 2.81 | 1.30 |
| Efficient transport network | 2.69 | 1.26 |
| Education of society in general | 2.68 | 1.29 |
| Transparency in public administration and government. | 2.67 | 1.16 |
| Modernisation of public administration and implementation of e-governance | 2.65 | 1.19 |
| Health | 2.65 | 1.23 |
| Achievements of the operational pilot projects in Living Lab context | 2.64 | 1.34 |
| Smart-city and smart-island led development | 2.50 | 1.28 |
| Strategic policies in the field of smart tourism | 2.48 | 1.35 |
| Tourism cluster focused approach on defining smart policies | 2.44 | 1.34 |
| Society awareness on the topic of ICT | 2.43 | 1.23 |
| Justice | 2.40 | 1.27 |
| Greater articulation between the private and public sector in policy making | 2.30 | 1.22 |
| Promotion of the destination abroad as a smart destination | 2.23 | 1.14 |

The study concludes that Madeira is in the early stages of smart tourism development, failing to take full advantage of a smart tourism destination methodology. Although several projects have succeeded in achieving technological and policy objectives, on average, respondents are only aware of one of such projects. Many respondents cited a lack of information to rank the degree of development as insufficient/fair. Moreover, the results fail to provide evidence of a holistic view of the concept of a smart destination. Respondents supported mainly tourism-related (by far) and technology-led development issues. Respondents perceive smart tourism as an opportunity to develop new market niches based on improved access to information and feedback from end-users. Their view is, perhaps, excessively focused on further developments in the tourism sector, with less attention being paid to issues of capacity building at the institutional level. Quality of life issues, governance and the adoption of business models are conspicuously absent from their priorities. It is correctly acknowledged that the concept of a smart destination is of great importance to sustaining the current levels of competitiveness and excellence. But issues of governance, residents' quality of life, and transparency and accountability are rarely emphasized by respondents, which means that smart tourism is viewed only in its narrow definition rather than as a holistic and comprehensive phenomenon impacting all aspects of societal and economic life. Respondents consider the diffusion of information as an essential step towards smart tourism and the implementation of new projects and they expect the government to take the lead.

Not surprisingly, the adoption of smart tourism tools is in its infancy as is their use in the creation of value. Therefore, the region must invest in producing a specific strategic plan for smartness to implement Smart Destination public policies. Education and training should also increase literacy on the topic, in its all components, given the disproportionate number of respondents citing lack of information on the subject. Higher levels of awareness and commitment to adopt smart tools are necessary to pursue a development agenda based on principles of a systematic and comprehensive analysis of the impact of current developments in the ICT sphere in all dimensions of economic and social life. Valuable insights in terms of strengths, weaknesses, and challenges offer ground to discuss the current state of affairs and devise a coherent and comprehensive methodology to increase the success rate in adopting a progressive agenda focused on smart tourism.

# Smart sustainable tourism development for islands

In a Smart Tourism Destination (STD), tourism service providers can benefit from a centralized information platform to make better business decisions (Buhalis & Amaranggana, 2015). Implementation of the smart city model in intermediate tourist towns or islands, on their transition to becoming smart destinations, involves an inescapable commitment to their habitat and improving the quality of civic life and the economy of cities through more sustainable and technologically advanced elements (Signes et al., 2020). While a smart tourism destination should be an innovative place, accessible to all visitors who can experience improved, more interactive, and higher-quality travel, it should also improve residents' quality of life (Garcia et al., 2018). Moreover, the key factor for the authorities, decision-makers, experts, and alike to consider when discussing the subject of a smart island is the stakeholders' willingness to participate/invest in making the necessary changes. While the tourism industry grows, we are witnessing an era of radical evolution of software environments that allow access to many tourist-related data. These data may relate to accommodation, food, beverages establishments, cultural heritage points of interest, etc., along with reviews, ratings, and tourist-generated suggestions (Figueiredo et al., 2017). Big Data (BD) provide extremely valuable insights from tourism organisations, social networks, and significant search engines and platforms, such as Twitter, Facebook, Tripadvisor and Google (Stylos et al., 2021). BD has been called the 'XXIst century oil' because they are an inexhaustible source of income and competitiveness.

The Internet of Things enables the creation of smart technological environments that connect their physical and digital infrastructures. This allows systems to be able to identify tourists' context in a pervasive but not intrusive way and attend to their needs (Kontogianni & Alepis, 2020) in real time (Buhalis & Sinarta, 2019). A range of technologies, including AI, robotics, cashless payments, AR, and VR, are already used to varying degrees, in different industries and regions, around the world, propelling a range of disruptive changes. Formatting big data to be understood by software agents is part of the progress towards Web 3.0 or the semantic web (2015 -) and to supporting computer-to-computer interoperability (Stylos et al., 2021). Self-driving autonomous vehicles, cars and drones, as well as servicing robots, will also bring major disruptions to the tourism ecosystem (Tussyadiah et al., 2017; Ivanov & Webster, 2019). Increasingly smartness and AmI (Ambient Intelligence) support real-time service, empowering the co-creation of value for all stakeholders across multiple platforms. Interactions take place in real-time, at the exact moment when consumers are willing to engage with brands (Buhalis 2020). Inevitably, smart environments transform industry structures, processes, and practices, having disruptive impacts for service innovation, strategy, management, marketing, and competitiveness for everybody involved (Buhalis et al., 2019). Future research should focus on human-computer interaction, natural language and gesture processing, AI, neuromarketing, ecosystem business management dynamics, and collective agility for competitive advantage (Buhalis, 2020).

Thus, all stakeholders should be interconnected through a web platform where information related to tourism and related activities can be exchanged instantly. All important information should be in one place, complementing each other, allowing all interested parties to access it easily and find everything they need, thus facilitating the booking process, business, and destination management, making the tourism business more efficient. Strengthening competitiveness should lead to an increase of arrivals and levels of satisfaction, and to an improvement in the destination image. The objectives of making the Island more sustainable, where its population becomes more informed and participative, are achieved intelligently, with better living conditions, fulfilling what is established in the Smart Islands Initiative to become smart, inclusive, and prosperous societies to help build an innovative and sustainable Europe.

The digital-technological revolution and the impacts of ICTs in the tourism sector highlight the importance of investing in the most appropriate and current technological applications in companies providing tourist services (Ruiz & Hernández, 2017). Smart tourist islands have acquired undeniable media, programmatic and academic validity. They should apply ICT and knowledge management to improve the quality of life of island dwellers through sustainable development. They should encourage participation, collaboration, and innovation, with a specific emphasis on adaptation of the digital economy, defined as a renewed archetype of planning and management for 21st-century cities (Signes et al., 2020).

# References

Albino, V., Berardi, U., & Dangelico, R. M. (2015). Smart Cities: Definitions, dimensions, performance, and initiatives. *Journal of Urban Technology*, 22(1), 3–21. https://doi.org/10.1080/10630732.2014.942092

Barros, C. P., & Machado, L. P. (2010). The length of stay in tourism. *Annals of Tourism Research*, 37, 692-706.

Boes, K., Buhalis, D. & Inversini, A. (2016). Smart tourism destinations: ecosystems for tourism destination competitiveness, *International Journal of Tourism Cities*, 2 (2), 108-124.

Bouskel, M., Cassalo, M., Bassi, S., Luca, C., & Facchina, M., (2016). Caminho para as Smart Cities, BID, https://publications.iadb.org/publications/portuguese/document/Caminho-para-as-smart-cities-Da-gest%C3%A3o-tradicional-para-a-cidade-inteligente.pdf

Buhalis, D., (2003) *eTourism: Information technology for strategic tourism management*, Pearson (Financial Times/Prentice Hall), London ISBN 0582357403.

Buhalis, D. (2019).Technology in tourism - from information communication technologies to eTourism and smart tourism towards ambient intelligence tourism: a perspective article, *Tourism Review*, 75 (1), 267-272. https://doi.org/10.1108/TR-06-2019-0258

Buhalis, D., (2022), Tourism management and marketing in transformation: Introduction and editor's statement, in Buhalis, D., (ed) *Encyclopedia of Tourism Management and Marketing*, Edward Elgar.

Buhalis D, Andreu L, & Gnoth J., (2020).The dark side of the sharing economy: Balancing value co-creation and value co-destruction. *Psychology and Marketing*. 37(5),689–704. https://doi.org/10.1002/mar.21344

Buhalis, D., & Amaranggana, A., (2015), Smart tourism destinations enhancing tourism experience through personalisation of services, in Tussyadiah, I., and Inversini, A., (eds), *ENTER 2015 Proceedings*, Lugano, Springer-Verlag, Wien, pp.377-390

Buhalis, D., & Foerste, M. (2015). SoCoMo marketing for travel and tourism: Empowering co-creation of value. *Journal of Destination Marketing and Management*. 4, 151–161.

Buhalis, D., & Licata, M. C. (2002). The future eTourism intermediaries. *Tourism Management*, 23(3), 207-220.

Buhalis, D., & Sinarta, Y. (2019). Real-time co-creation and nowness service: lessons from tourism and hospitality. *Journal of Travel & Tourism Marketing*, 36(5), 563-582.

Buhalis, D., Parra López, E., & Martinez-Gonzalez, J. A. (2020). Influence of young consumers' external and internal variables on their e-loyalty to tourism sites. *Journal of Destination Marketing and Management*, 15. https://doi.org/10.1016/j.jdmm.2020.100409

Buhalis, D., Harwood, T., Bogicevic, V., Viglia, G., Beldona, S. & Hofacker, C., (2019) Technological disruptions in Services: lessons from Tourism and Hospitality, *Journal of Service Management*, 30 (4), 484-506 https://doi.org/10.1108/JOSM-12-2018-0398

Caragliu, A. Del Bo, C.-Nijkamp, P. (2011): Smart cities in Europe Journal of Urban Technology 18 (2): 65-82.

Efthymiopoulos I. et al., (2016) Smart Islands Projects and Strategies. 1st European Smart Islands Forum, June 2016, Athens, Greece, Friedrich Ebert Stiftung. http://library.fes.de/pdf-files/bueros/athen/12860.pdf (30 Mar 2017)

Enerlis, E. & Young, F. & Madrid Network (2012), *Libro Blanco Smart Cities*, Imprintia, Bilbao .

## 176  Smart Cities and Tourism

EU (2017). Smart Islands Initiative - Smart Islands Event: Creating New Pathways for EU islands. 28 Mar 2017, http://www.smartislandsinitiative.eu/en/index.php (30 Mar 2017)

European Commission, (1999) *ESDP – European Spatial Development Perspective. Towards balanced and sustainable development of the territory of the European Union.*

Fan, D. X., Buhalis, D., & Lin, B. (2019). A tourist typology of online and face-to-face social contact: Destination immersion and tourism encapsulation/decapsulation. *Annals of Tourism Research*, 78, 102757.

Femenia-Serra, F.. & Neuhofer, B. (2018) Smart tourism experiences: Conceptualisation, key dimensions and research agenda, *Journal of Regional Research*, 42 (2018), 129-150

Figueiredo, M., Ribeiro, J.L., Cacho, N., Thome, A., Cacho, A., Lopes, F., & Araujo, V. (2018), From photos to travel itinerary: a tourism recommender system for smart tourism destination. In: *Fourth IEEE international conference on big data computing service and applications*. Bamberg, Germany: BigDataService, p. 85–92.

Figueiredo, A., Grande, R., & Christine, J. (2017)  As contribuições da Internet nos efeitos da sazonalidade: um estudo realizado em um hotel de pequeno porte. *Revista Brasileira de Gestão e Inovação*, 4(2), 42-63.

Florido-Benítez, L. (2021) The effects of COVID-19 on Andalusian tourism and aviation sector, *Tourism Review*, 76 (4),  829-857. https://doi.org/10.1108/TR-12-2020-0574

García, L.M., Aciar, S., Mendoza, R., & Puello, J.J. (2018) Smart tourism platform based on microservice architecture and recommender services. In: *Mobile web and intelligent information systems - 15th international conference*, MobiWIS 2018, Barcelona, Spain, August 6-8, proceedings. p. 167–80.

Giffinger, R., & Gudrun, H. (2010). Smarter cities ranking: an effective instrument for the positioning of cities? *Architecture, City and Environment*, 12, 7-25

Giffinger, R., Fertner, C., Kramar, H., Kalasek, R., Pichler-Milanović, N., & Meijers, E. (2007). Smart cities: Ranking of european medium-sized cities. Vienna, Austria: Centre of Regional Science (srf), Vienna university of technology. www. smart-cities. eu/download/smart_cities_final_report. Pdf

GISIG, (2014). Smart Webservices for Mediterranean Islands, ICT-PSP Grant 2011-14, http://www.gisig.eu/smart-islands-2/ (30 Mar 2017)

Gretzel U, Sigala M, Xiang Z, & Koo C. (2015) Smart tourism: foundations and developments. *Electronic Markets*, 25(3), 179–88. https://doi.org/10.1007/s12525-015-0196-8.

IEEE, (2017). Smart Cities "About", http://smartcities.ieee.org/about, (30 Mar 2017).

ITU, (2015) Key performance indicators definitions for smart sustainable cities, *Focus Group on Smart Sustainable Cities FG-SSC, International Telecommunication Union Telecommunication standardization sector*, Technical Report.

ITU, (2016) The ICT Development Index (IDI): Conceptual framework and methodology, http://www.itu.int/net4/ITU-D/idi/2016/ (30 Mar 2017)

Ivanov, S., & Webster, C. (2019). Conceptual framework. In Ivanov, S., & Webster, C (eds.) *Robots, Artificial Intelligence, and Service Automation in Travel, Tourism and Hospitality*. Emerald Publishing

Kontogianni, A., & Alepis, E. (2020). Smart tourism: State of the art and literature review for the last six years. *Array*, 6, 100020. DOI:https://doi.org/10.1016/j. array.2020.100020

López de Ávila, A., & García, S. (2013). Destinos Turísticos Inteligentes. *Economía Industrial*, (395), 61–69.

Machado, L.P., & A. Almeida (2010). *Turismo - Inovação e Novas Tecnologias*, Porto:Sociedade Portuguesa de Inovação / Principia Editora.

Madeira 14-20 (n.d.) Programa Operacional da Região Autónoma da Madeira, 2014-2020, Governo Regional da Região Autónoma da Madeira 18/12/14, http://www.idr.gov-madeira.pt/m1420/principal.aspx

Manville, C., Cochrane, G., Cave, J., Millard,J., Pederson, J.K., Thaarup, R. K. & Kotterink, B. (2014) Mapping smart cities in the EU, European Parliament, Brussel. http://resolver.tudelft.nl/uuid:1fac0e18-8dd3-406d-86fe-ce1e6a22e90c Retrieved from http://www.smartcities.at/assets/Publikationen/Weitere-Publikationen zum,Thema/mappingsmartcities.pdf

Michopoulou, E., & Buhalis, D. (2013). Information provision for challenging markets: The case of the accessibility requiring market in the context of tourism. *Information & Management*, 50(5), 229-239.

O'Cathain, A, & Thomas, KJ (2004) "Any other comments?" Open questions on questionnaires—A bane or a bonus to research? *BMC Medical Research Methodology* 25(4), 1–7.

Rahmafitria, F., Suryadi, K., Oktadiana, H., Putro, H.P.H. & Rosyidie, A. (2021), Applying knowledge, social concern and perceived risk in planned behavior theory for tourism in the Covid-19 pandemic, *Tourism Review*, 76 (4), 809-828. https://doi.org/10.1108/TR-11-2020-0542

Romero, J., & Farinós, J., (Eds.) (2004): *Ordenación del territorio y desarrollo territorial: el gobierno del territorio en Europa: tradiciones, contextos, culturas y nuevas visiones*. Gijón, Trea.

Rubio-Escuderos, L., García-Andreu, H., & de la Ros, J. U. (2021). Accessible tourism: origins, state of the art and future lines of research. *European Journal of Tourism Research*, 28, 2803-2803.

Ruiz, S., & Hernández, Y., (2017) Impacto de las TIC en el sector turístico y su importancia, *Universidad & Ciencia*, 6(3), 66-76s/Libro-Blanco-Destinos-Tursticos-Inteligentes-construyendo-el-futuro.pdf

Segittur. (2015) Informe destinos turísticos inteligentes: construyendo el futuro. Retrieved from http://www.segittur.es/opencms/export/sites/segitur/.content/galerias/descargas/proyecto

Signes, E.S., Palomares R.C., Merinoa B.R. , & García-Adána, I. (2020) Transition towards a tourist innovation model: The smart tourism destination Reality or territorial marketing? *Journal of Innovation & Knowledge* 5, 96-104.

Spilanis, I., Mitropoulou, A., & Buhalis, D., (2022), Insularity, small island destination. In Buhalis, D., (ed) *Encyclopedia of Tourism Management and Marketing*, Edward Elgar.

Stamboulis, Y., & Skayannis, P. (2003). Innovation strategies and technology for experience-based tourism. *Tourism Management*, 24(1), 35 – 43.

Stylos, N., Zwiegelaar, J. & Buhalis, D. (2021) Big data empowered agility for dynamic, volatile, and time-sensitive service industries: the case of tourism sector, *International Journal of Contemporary Hospitality Management*, 33(3), 1015-1036. https://doi.org/10.1108/IJCHM-07-2020-0644

Suk, M. & Kim, W. (2021) COVID-19 and the airline industry: crisis management and resilience, *Tourism Review*, 76(4), 984-998. https://doi.org/10.1108/TR-07-2020-0348

Tiago, F., & Borges-Tiago, T. (2022). Small island destination. In Buhalis, D., (ed) *Encyclopedia of Tourism Management and Marketing*, Edward Elgar.

Tussyadiah, I.P., Wang, D., & Jia, C.H. (2017). Virtual reality and attitudes toward tourism destinations. In Schegg, R., & Stangl, B. (Eds.), *Information and Communication Technologies in Tourism 2017*. Springer International.

Vicini, A. Sanna, S. Bellini, & A. Rosi, An internet of things enabled interactive totem for children in a living lab setting, *18th International ICE-Conference on Engineering, Technology and Innovation*, Munich, Germany, 2012

Winters, J., (2011), Why are smart cities growing? Who moves and who stays, *Journal of Regional Science*, 51(2), 253-270

Zach, F. J., & Hill, T.L. (2017). Network, knowledge and relationship impacts on innovation in tourism destinations. *Tourism Management*, 62, 196–207.

Zhang, H., Gordon, S., Buhalis, D., & Ding, X. (2018). Experience value cocreation on destination online platforms. *Journal of Travel Research*, 57(8), 1093-1107.

# 11 Smart City strategy as a means to improve residents' quality of life:
## The Case of Barranco, Lima, Peru

*Otto Regalado-Pezúa, Luis Felipe Galarza Cerf and Leonardo Toro*

## Introduction

A Smart City is one whose sustainable economic growth and high quality of life are due to investment in human and social capital, communication infrastructure and the intelligent management of natural resources through participatory governance (Qian et al., 2019). Smart Cities connect physical infrastructure, information and communication technology (ICT) infrastructure, social infrastructure and business infrastructure to take advantage of the collective intelligence of a city. Smart Cities often implement both advanced infrastructure and modern ICTs. Likewise, Dustdar, Nastic and Šcekic (2017) state that the Smart City strategy provides more efficient services to citizens, monitoring and optimizing existing assets, such as infrastructure, to improve their quality of life.

The concept of the Smart City is not limited to the application of ICT (Albino et al., 2015): Smart Cities can also be understood as communities in which citizens, companies, institutions and municipal agencies collaborate to integrate systems and make them more efficient, to stimulate citizen participation and to continuously improve quality of life. This allows urban performance to be improved, services to become more efficient, existing infrastructure to be monitored and optimized, and innovative business models in the public and private sectors to be encouraged (Marsal-Llacuna et al., 2015). Maldonado Amaya et al. (2020) indicate that a Smart City is composed of two concepts: urban planning and sustainable management, making use of technology to promote a more human and innovative city. Globally, an increasing number of municipalities and districts are trying to become 'smart' due to the benefits Smart Cities provide. It is necessary to understand each of the variables related to Smart Cities.

## Defining The Smart City through stakeholders and sustainability

The term 'Smart City' was coined in 1994 (Dameri & Cocchia, 2013), and, from there, it has been defined in different ways. This term can create confusion if one thinks that the only requirement for a city to be 'smart' is the use of the latest and greatest technology (Boes et al., 2016). The concept of the Smart City did not evolve from the quest for a technological utopia (Kitchin, 2015). Over the years, it has been defined in different ways, depending on the objectives of each city. For example, for Angelidou (2015), the term 'Smart City' indicates a conceptual model of urban development based on the use of human, collective and technological capital for the development of urban conglomerations. The International Standards Organization (2019) points out that Smart Cities seek to offer better services to citizens and provide a supportive living environment in which smart policies, practices and technology are put to the service of the community. Essentially Smart Cities need to:

- Achieve environmental and sustainability objectives innovatively,
- identify the need for smart infrastructure,
- incentivize innovation and growth,
- build a dynamic economy that takes advantage of resources and
- prepare for the challenges of the future.

These definitions all indicate the use of technological inputs to distinctively improve life in a given city. For a city to be considered 'smart', it must also be given a good image. The appropriate distribution of space for activities and the accessibility of various services are crucial features of a sustainable city that uses its resources efficiently (Bourdic et al., 2012). Indeed, with properly managed resources, ambitious goals can be set so that any city or district can become smart. This chapter defines a 'Smart City' as one that can optimize available resources, improve residents' quality of life and increase its economic capital in order to continue growing as a Smart City.

Many different cities are on their way to becoming Smart Cities. Indeed, approximately 26 global cities expect to become Smart Cities by 2025, of which a disproportionately large percentage – 50% – are in North America and Europe (Glasmeier & Christopherson, 2015).

Becoming a Smart City is a shared, collective task that involves local institutions, companies in the tourism sector and society in general. These stakeholders are all called upon to make new technologies their own. Likewise, Appio et al.(2019) point out that for this development to take place, it is necessary to possess high levels of both human and social capital, since the innovation process is based on knowledge and learning.

Discussing sustainability in the urban context necessitates the mention of the economic, environmental, and social dimensions of sustainable development. 'Sustainable urban development' has been defined as the way to achieve a balance between the protection of the environment and the development of urban areas: equality in terms of income, employment, housing, basic services, social infrastructure and transport (Hiremath et al., 2013). Although urban development must go hand in hand with sustainable development, the two concepts are not necessarily compatible without great effort. This continues to be one of the most difficult challenges facing urban planners and academics when it comes to decision-making and planning for sustainable cities (Bibri & Krogstie, 2017)

## Technological management of a Smart City

ICTs and advanced technological innovations provide the foundation for the development of Smart Cities; however, technology alone is not enough (Sigalat-Signes et al., 2020).The Internet of Things (IoT), according to Ahmed et al. (2017) has appeared due to technological advances and the rapid convergence of wireless ICTs, digital electronics and microelectromechanical systems (MEMS). The IoT is made up of those devices connected to the Internet (laptops, cell phones, tablets, Wi-Fi-enabled sensors, portable devices and household appliances); according to the Cisco report (Evans, 2011), the number of these devices in use has exceeded the number of human beings in the world. Most IoT applications, aside from monitoring discrete events, also extract the information collected by IoT objects. Data collection tools in the IoT environment are primarily sensor-equipped devices that require custom protocols, such as message queue telemetry transport (MQTT) and data distribution service (DDS). Because sensors are used in almost every industry, the IoT is expected to produce a large amount of data that can be used to identify potential research trends and analyze the impact of certain events or decisions. However, to generate higher profits, companies must create a platform where they can collect, administrate and analyze a massive amount of sensor data in a profitable, scalable way.

Big data tools are used to store and process large amounts of data (Stylos et al., 2021). Bibri and Krogstie (2017) point out that big data analysis enables and drives the transformation of the ecosystem at various scales. Thanks to the benefits of big data, the sustainability of the ecosystem can be understood, applied and planned. Big data tools allow companies and governments to take advantage of data collection on a massive scale to obtain competitive advantages: improved customer service because the customers are better understood or improved logistics because datasets are being monitored so forecasts can be accurate. For Joyanes Aguilar (2013), the challenges and opportunities offered by big data will offset the economic and talent expenses required for its implementation: these expenses will be compensated for by the competitive advantage that said adoption will provide. The concept of big data has fluctuated over time. It has evolved to include more and more aspects, but all definitions agree that it is a massive dataset requiring more complex information processors. The McKinsey Global Institute (cited in Joyanes Aguilar (2013)) defines "big data" as data sets whose size is beyond the capabilities of typical database software tools to capture, store, manage and analyze. For Medina et al. (2017), every citizen and device leaves a digital trail in cyberspace that represents an opportunity for companies and institutions to convert said data into useful information.

ICTs in Smart Cities manage information and share it with all stakeholders. They are also defined as systems and resources for the preparation, storage and digitized dissemination of information based on the use of computer technology (Gutiérrez et al., 2019). ICTs are a revolutionary, shocking and ever-changing phenomenon related to both technical and social aspects of life and which permeate all work, training, leisure and consumer activities. According to the International Telecommunication Union (2018), a smart and sustainable city is an innovative city that takes advantage of ICTs and other means to improve the quality of life, competitiveness and efficiency of urban operation and services while responding to the economic, social and environmental needs of present and future generations.

These tools can be applied to the creation of a Smart City, since fast data processing is needed for quicker and better decision-making so improvement projects can be carried out, which may involve traffic, the environment, social issues and tourism (Buhalis et al., 2019). This is because data processing, when it converts raw data into usable information, can aid in the implementation of these improvements, thus creating a sustainable city. A smart city can continue along a sustainable path toward future social and economic development, for example, in the tourism sector. By integrating the use of ICTs into the construction of a Smart City, it can improve the provision of services (Ruiz-Rodríguez et al., 2018).

ICTs are also a key factor in the transformation of the tourism industry, where it is important to invest in the application of more appropriate and up-to-date technology and infrastructure (Ruiz Garcia & Hernández García, 2017). An intelligent digital network can support the perfect interoperability of all interested parties, which would simplify digital interactions (Buhalis, 2020). Finally, the implementation of ICTs in cities is crucial to the collection of data related to tourism, such as the number of tourists who visit a place, which could allow tourism services to be provided in real time, optimizing strategic management that could help improve the tourist experience in the city (Sigalat-Signes et al., 2020).

## Smart City dimensions

In the scientific literature, there is a common typology of who the stakeholders in Smart Cities are in the public sector, the private sector and civil society (Sigalat-Signes et al., 2020). The transition to becoming a Smart City is linked to the six dimensions of the Smart City model, which is illustrated in Figure 11.1. This model includes the following dimensions: population, environment, mobility, economy, quality of life and governance. These dimensions relate to one another and are essential to the generation of synergy in the digital transformation process (Giffinger & Haindl, 2009; Enerlis et al., 2012; Flores Cifre et al., 2019).

The first dimension of the Smart City model, 'smart governance', deals with transparency within governance systems (Villarejo Galende, 2015; Cohen, 2014). This can be achieved through the modernization of the administration via online services that allow a simplification of processes to take place. This makes them more efficient to facilitate interaction with citizens, integrate stakeholders and develop the interoperability of digital services in order to increase citizen participation and achieve greater access to information in real time. The second dimension in the model, the 'smart economy', allows the Smart City project to define its territorial competitive advantage, resulting in the growth and development of the productive sectors and the attraction of investors (Sigalat-Signes *et al.*, 2020).

As for the third dimension, 'smart people', according to Villarejo Galende (2015) and Cohen (2014), it is related to the city's human capital score. It illustrates the extent to which the city, in cooperation with other territorial administrations, participates in the education of its citizens to improve their digital skills and creativity in order to engage in urban innovation. The fourth dimension studied, 'mobility', deals with the sustainability, efficiency and safety of transport systems and infrastructure, as well as accessibility at the local and territorial level (Sigalat-Signes et al., 2020).

The 'smart environment' dimension has to do with pollution management and the water, gas and electric grids (Flores Cifre et al., 2019). Likewise, this dimension deals with the development of projects that promote the preservation of the environment, accessibility and quality of tourism (Sigalat-Signes et al., 2020). The final dimension that is part of the model is 'smart living'. It deals with the unification, optimization and management of public and private services, focusing on the use of technology to achieve a better quality of life (Enerlis *et al.*, 2012; Sigalat-Signes *et al.*, 2020).

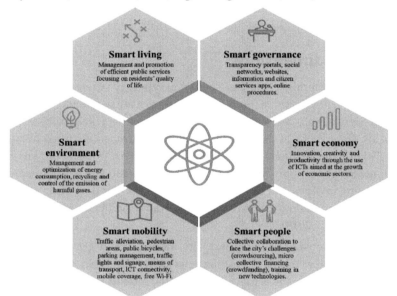

**Figure 11.1:** Model of a Smart City. Source: Adapted from Flores Cifre et al. (2019)

## The case of the district of Barranco, Lima in Peru

Smart Cities need to put in place the necessary mechanisms to become 'smart', in order to improve its residents' quality of life. Barranco, a district located on the Pacific Ocean in the city of Lima, the capital of Peru, aims to become smart to improve quality of life. Barranco is just 3.3 km² in area and possesses roughly 33,000 inhabitants. It is a National Cultural Heritage district (Municipalidad de Barranco, 2021). Barranco has also become one of the most important tourist destinations in the city of Lima. Like many other cities and districts in the world, it is experiencing a significant period of demographic growth, which is having a great impact on its residents' way of life. Barranco has been changing in terms of demographics, urban profile and zoning, which has presented new challenges for the district's government and residents. The growth of the district due to the real estate boom has generated new business opportunities. The proliferation of high-rise buildings with apartments measuring 40 m$^2$ is attracting both new inhabitants and tourists. New businesses have been converting mansions, built at the beginning of the 20th century, into shops and offices.

These two trends, the growth of the district and the arrival of new users with different customs, have been affecting Barranco in different ways. First, a greater number of cars on its streets has caused traffic congestion, noise and environmental pollution, which affect both residents and visitors. Second, the daily activities of the inhabitants have begun to change due to the opening of new businesses, such as restaurants, supermarkets, banks and pharmacies. The displacement of former residents to other parts of the district or to other districts has become more evident. This process of gentrification began around 2010 and has been perceived as a demonstration of the district government's lack of support for its residents. The implementation of a Smart City model could be the best opportunity to improve Barranco residents' quality of life, and also an alternative solution to facilitate the district government's implementation of new technologies: it would improve the urban planning process and satisfy residents' demands, thus enabling the sustainable technological development of the district.

Barranco's main indicators are presented in Table 11.1.

**Table 11.1:** Main indicators of the Barranco district

| Indicator | Value |
| --- | --- |
| Population | 34,738 inhabitants |
| Area | 3.3 km$^2$ |
| Economically active population | 84.80% |
| Residents living in houses | 42.67% |
| Residents living in apartments or condos | 35.22% |
| Apartments and condominiums | 6,461 units |
| Houses | 4832 units |
| District budget | USD 10 million per year |
| Average property value (2020) | 2,655 USD/m$^2$ |
| Home internet access | 75% of homes |
| Smartphone access | 95% of homes |
| Per capita solid waste generation | 2 kg per day |

*Sources:* INEI (2017, 2018a, 2018b, 2018c), Banco Central de Reserva del Perú (2020)

Traditional Barranco, with its narrow streets and bohemian style, is quickly becoming an attractive place for companies and investors, putting at risk its distinctive character and its ability to manage resources and services.

By analyzing current information on the district of Barranco, it is possible to understand its urban, economic, and social development and to identify the problems it is facing and their effect on residents and visitors. These problems have been organized according to the six dimensions of the Smart City model (Giffinger & Haindl, 2009) so that any problem can be dealt with by the relevant unit within Barranco's proposed Smart City model. Among the main problems facing Barranco is the low annual budget assigned to it by the department of Lima: a budget of just around USD 10 million. Moreover, it does not possess an up-to-date urban development plan, and this gap has permitted the inordinate construction of large, multi-family apartment complexes along the district's main thoroughfares and small streets, which has in turn initiated a gentrification process.

As for governance, the main problem is that the district government does not have an integrated management system (ERP) to help it identify, collect, process, and analyze information. The lack of an ERP has generated high levels of bureaucracy, making it difficult to manage both internal and external information. This has made it virtually impossible to work with measurable indicators in real time. Finally, Barranco does not possess a web platform or mobile app to offer different public services to citizens.

As for problems of mobility, unautomated traffic lights and the lack of signage on the main roads have generated intense traffic, affecting quality of life for drivers, pedestrians, and district residents in general. No efficient system to monitor public parking lots has yet been implemented, either, and although 75% of the district's population has private access to internet, cable and landline services, no public place currently offers free internet.

As for the environmental problems that afflict the district, Barranco generates around six tons of garbage daily, which is collected without a comprehensive and systematized waste collection and disposal program. It has no monitoring system for garbage trucks, nor does it track dumpsters. In terms of the economy, Barranco's main problem is that there is not much of a property-tax- and city-tax-paying culture. Although the most important economic activities in the district are commerce and tourism, neither are mentioned in the district's development plan, nor are these activities supported by technology, e.g., by an interactive tour guide app.

As for quality-of-life problems, Barranco, does not have a cadaster or an updated, digitized urban development plan. This has led to excessive growth and a rise in property values: price per square meter has increased almost sixfold in just ten years. According to data from the Central Reserve Bank of Peru, in 2007, price per square meter was USD 480, while in 2020, it was around USD 3000. As for districtwide security, although there is a command center to manage around 60 security cameras located throughout the district, crime and other problems are not being strategically mapped out. In terms of citizen problems, Barranco does not possess an ecosystem of applications for citizens to use to collaborate in the face of the problems and challenges the district faces, which include the following:

☐ The way the district's growth affects the district's historical character.

☐ The provision of adequate transportation, solid waste management, energy and security services.

☐ The loss of the district's identity caused by the influx of new inhabitants, business models and lifestyles.

Barranco citizens use the internet and are thus more informed than ever before. It is essential for the district's current government to invest in the transformation from the traditional municipal management model to models that focus on the use and adaptation of new technologies, innovation, accessibility, and sustainability in order to benefit residents. Therefore, the district of Barranco must switch over to a Smart City model to benefit from new opportunities. It must focus mainly on citizens' needs while seeking their support as it institutes public-private collaboration and technology to achieve more efficiency and sustainability. In this way, it can become a more competitive district capable of improving the quality of life of the people who live in the district and those who visit it.

# Toward the transformation of Barranco into a Smart City

Urbanization has led to long-term sustainability challenges as cities and districts seek to develop culturally, socially, and economically. Thus, Smart City initiatives have emerged as a new alternative for the efficient and effective management of urban environments, sustainable development, city competitiveness and quality of life. In this sense, many different factors are necessary to achieve Smart City success. Among them are the massive use of ICTs to improve and guarantee the quality of service and to protect the environment, thus guaranteeing sustainability over time. The main objectives of the proposed Smart City model for Barranco are its sustainable development

# 188   Smart Cities and Tourism

and the improvement of its residents' quality of life. With these goals in mind, it is essential to develop a technological ecosystem based on residents' needs. The use and promotion of ICTs will allow residents to increase their participation and help improve the district. The proposed model therefore must consider the following strategic objectives:

- The modernization of the district's public administration.
- The promotion of urban development through sustainable management supported by the use of technology.
- The development and optimization of ICT in the district.
- The development of an open data policy (based on big data governance) available to all citizens to promote citizen participation.

These strategic objectives are intended to mitigate the risks and consequences of Barranco's aforementioned problems, but first, the district must fulfill some requirements to be able to develop the solutions proposed, keeping in mind the six dimensions of the Smart City model (Giffinger & Haindl, 2009).

There are several requirements for Barranco to become a Smart City. In order to implement the Smart City model in Barranco, the district government must first institute several basic changes: it must create adequately connected digital infrastructure, set up a network of interconnected sensors and devices, institute an Integrated Operation and Command Center (IOCC) and, finally, update its communication interfaces (Bouskela, et al., 2016).

**Smart governance**: To strengthen and improve the relationship between residents and their authorities, the municipality of Barranco must implement digital management techniques. This would involve the implementation of an ERP so that the district government can integrate and administrate all of its areas, achieving in this way the ability to process information obtained in real time and improve its decision-making and distribute its resources more efficiently. The district government could be more transparent by using open data. Through the creation of a web platform and mobile application, it could facilitate citizens' ability to carry out administrative procedures and collect more information. The digital channels can also be used to help encourage citizens to participate in and help design public policies, empowering residents through digitization. Finally, social networks could be used to provide information on the history and culture of the district to show how Barranco is one of the most important districts in the Peruvian capital.

**Smart living** can improve the urban growth of the district. A participative urban plan must be developed, digitized, and provided to the public via open access. This urban plan could be designed to take into account citizens' quality of life, which would permit the redefinition of public spaces. Access for the disabled can be built into the design of public spaces in order to encourage inclusion and community. This could be reinforced through awareness-raising campaigns regarding the use of public spaces, accessibility and free movement. Moreover, a system of cameras and sensors can monitor public spaces to provide a safe environment for all residents. Barranco's digital transformation can include the creation of an electronic inventory of the properties that make up its historical patrimony, so that authorities would be aware of their location and maintenance needs. The creation of a digital platform would allow Barranco's health, education and social assistance services, as well as its recreational and cultural facilities, to be offered and promoted among its citizens.

**Smart people** are connected and networked to improve residents' social conditions and quality of life. To facilitate the process an innovation laboratory can be developed. Agreements with universities would encourage those in academia to use new technological tools to develop applications that can improve the district and the quality of life of its inhabitants. Collaboration with Barranco residents can be encouraged through the development of an online crowdsourcing platform that foments citizen participation to benefit the district, as well as the creation of a crowdfunding platform to help finance urban and culture projects.

**Smart economy** is fueled by innovation that supports competitiveness. Based on agreements between universities and educational institutions and the government of Barranco, strategic alliances can be sought to improve the local economy. Commerce and business are a fundamental part of life in the district. The development of a web platform and mobile application to access information on the businesses in the district is proposed. Through digital marketing strategies, content can be generated for social networks, to improve the relationship between the local economy and residents. As Barranco is an important tourist destination in the city, the traditional tourist office could be transformed into a virtual office, available via a smartphone application and a web platform, in order to market Barranco as a destination in real time (Buhalis & Sinarta, 2019).

**Smart mobility** is facilitated through a comprehensive transportation plan, proper road infrastructure and accessibility that would benefit the district. An automated system that uses cameras and sensors to program traffic lights and digital signage should be developed and implemented. It could be accompanied by a system that would promote the efficient use of public parking and the swift and easy location of public transport units. An intelligent electrical network could be developed to charge electric vehicles, and a public bicycle sharing program and bicycle lanes could be inaugurated. To promote inclusivity, the installation of a wireless internet network in public spaces should be prioritized.

**Smart environments** empower a balance between protecting the environment and encouraging economic activity in the district. In order to achieve this, a system to monitor and manage energy in public places should be developed. Through the installation of sensors connected to the IOCC and electricity service providers, the automated and efficient management of the level of public lighting according to weather conditions can result in monetary and energy savings. A comprehensive water management program that manages supply and infrastructure should be implemented, as well as a system to monitor the network of pipes and water purification systems. An integrated system to monitor air quality and noise pollution would also complement the development and implementation of a solid waste management plan and a network of smart dumpsters.

The Smart City model proposed for Barranco, although it includes technological solutions, focuses on the citizens and urban environment. That is why it must seek cooperation between the public sector, the private sector, academia, and civil society. Successful Smart Cities always maintain a focus on residents in order to guarantee urban development, the sustainable and responsible use of resources and the long-term preservation of the district. Achieving these criteria ensures a better quality of life for citizens and makes a city attractive for visitors and tourists. Given the particular characteristics of a district like Barranco, whose urban form, history and current economic and cultural dynamic allow it to be one of the most traditional and touristic districts of the Peruvian capital, there is a great opportunity for the transformation of its traditional management model into a Smart City model.

## Conclusions: Smart Cities toward an improvement in the quality of life

The term 'Smart City' can be analyzed from many different perspectives. This chapter has focused on the benefits that a Smart City can offer to the citizens of a district, as they are the central focus of the proposed Smart City model. A Smart City gives residents a better quality of life, making the city attractive and competitive. Indeed, this transition generates benefits for all the stakeholders that participate in it. The shift creates a cultural change in the way the district is administered, which would affect authorities in terms of resource management, and it allows residents to take a more participative role in the administration of the city they live in.

The New Urban Agenda (Ward & Smith, 2015) includes a commitment to adopt a Smart Cities approach to take advantage of the opportunities offered by digitization, clean and innovative energies and ICTs to benefit citizens, providing a greater amount of information for decision-making and the preservation of the environment, encouraging sustainable economic development and improving the quality of services offered by cities. In this sense, according to Ramón Martín Pozuelo, coordinator of the Master in Technologies for Smart Cities and Smart Grids, the purpose of a Smart City model is the sustainability of the city. This requires collaboration between the public and private sectors. The New Urban Agenda also mentions the importance of participatory practices for a city's residents and for the culture. Highlighting the role of these practices is making it possible for technology and the Smart City model to achieve a more sustainable, humane and participatory city (Boni Aristizábal et al., 2018).

Throughout this chapter, the main, transformative role that citizens can have in the installation of a Smart City model has been emphasized. The importance that technology has in the attainment of a better city for all is also highlighted. The implementation and use of big data, ICTs and the IoT allows for more and better tools to be developed to manage the city and help its residents and visitors enjoy it. However, technological development and implementation do not necessarily ensure a better quality of life for a city's inhabitants. With this in mind, this chapter has identified and classified the main problems and challenges and has related each of them to one of the six dimensions that constitute the Smart City model. Within the framework of the model, a series of actions are proposed in order to improve governance, mobility, and care for the environment through the use of new technologies. Solutions such as the implementation of an ERP for the municipal administration, innovation laboratories for citizens and an updated and digitized urban plan are identified. An integrated solid waste collection system and the development of a system to monitor and manage energy can also support the sustainability of resources. All the proposed policies have the end goal of improving the welfare of both citizens and visitors so that the district can be sustainable through time. Increasing the use of technology can transform a place into a Smart City and improve its residents' quality of life through becoming more sustainable, humane and participatory: a city of the future.

## References

Ahmed, E., Doneda, D., de Souza Abreu, J. (2017) The role of big data analytics in Internet of Things, *Computer Networks*, 129, 459–471. doi: 10.1016/j.comnet.2017.06.013.

Albino, V., Berardi, U. & Dangelico, R. M. (2015) Smart cities: Definitions, dimensions, performance, and initiatives, *Journal of Urban Technology*, 22(1), 3–21. doi: 10.1080/10630732.2014.942092.

Angelidou, M. (2015) Smart cities: A conjuncture of four forces, *Cities*, 47, 95–106. doi: 10.1016/j.cities.2015.05.004.

Appio, F. P., Lima, M. & Paroutis, S. (2019) Understanding Smart Cities: Innovation ecosystems, technological advancements, and societal challenges, *Technological Forecasting and Social Change*, 142, 1–14. doi: 10.1016/j.techfore.2018.12.018.

Banco Central de Reserva del Perú (2020) *Gerencia Central de Estudios Económicos-BCRPData*. Available at: https://estadisticas.bcrp.gob.pe/estadisticas/series/trimestrales/resultados/PD37957PQ.html (Accessed: 20 December 2020).

Bibri, S. E. & Krogstie, J. (2017) ICT of the new wave of computing for sustainable urban forms: Their big data and context-aware augmented typologies and design concepts, *Sustainable Cities and Society*, 32, 449–474. doi: 10.1016/j.scs.2017.04.012.

Boes, K., Buhalis, D. & Inversini, A., 2016, Smart tourism destinations: ecosystems for tourism destination competitiveness, *International Journal of Tourism Cities*, 2(2), 108–124 http://dx.doi.org/10.1108/IJTC-12-2015-0032

Boni Aristizábal, A. (ed) (2018) *Repensando La Ciudad Inteligente Desde La Innovacion Social Digital Ciudadana*. Madrid: Instituto Nacional de Administración Pública.

Bourdic, L., Salat, S. & Nowacki, C. (2012) Assessing cities: A new system of cross-scale spatial indicators, *Building Research and Information*, 40(5), 592–605. doi: 10.1080/09613218.2012.703488.

Bouskela, M., Casseb, M. & Bassi, S. (2016) *La ruta hacia las Smart Cities Migrando de una gestión tradicional a la ciudad inteligente*. Banco Interamericano de Desarrollo.

Buhalis, D. (2020) Technology in tourism-from information communication technologies to eTourism and smart tourism towards ambient intelligence tourism: a perspective article, *Tourism Review*, 75(1), 267–272. doi: 10.1108/TR-06-2019-0258.

Buhalis, D., Harwood, T., Bogicevic, V., Viglia, G., Beldona, S.& Hofacker, C. (2019), Technological disruptions in services: Lessons from tourism and hospitality, *Journal of Service Management*, 30(4), 484-506 https://doi.org/10.1108/JOSM-12-2018-0398

## 11: Smart City strategy as a means to improve residents' quality of life    193

Buhalis, D., & Sinarta, Y., 2019, Real-time co-creation and nowness service: Lessons from tourism and hospitality, *Journal of Travel and Tourism Marketing*, 36(5), 563-582 https://doi.org/10.1080/10548408.2019.1592059

Cohen, B. (2014) *The Smartest Cities In The World 2015: Methodology*. Available at: https://www.fastcompany.com/3038818/the-smartest-cities-in-the-world-2015- methodology (Accessed: 20 December 2020).

Dameri, R. P. & Cocchia, A. (2013) Smart City and Digital City : Twenty years of terminology evolution, *X Conference of the Italian Chapter of AIS*, pp. 1–8.

Dustdar, S., Nastic, S. & Šcekic, O. (2017) *Smart Cities: The internet of things, people and systems*. Springer. doi: 10.1007/978-3-319-60030-7.

Enerlis, Ernst & Young, Ferrovial & Madrid Network (2012) *Libro Blanco Smart Cities*. España: Imprintia.

Evans, D. (2011) *The internet of things: how the next evolution of the internet is changing everything*, CISCO white paper, pp. 1–11.

Flores Cifre, C. M., Dávila Chinchay, P. G. & Galarza Cerf, L. F. (2019) *El proceso de la gentrificación como oportunidad para el desarrollo de una Smart City en el distrito de Barranco-Lima*. Universidad ESAN. Escuela de Administración de Negocios para Graduados.

Giffinger, R. & Haindl, G. (2009) Smart Cities Ranking: an effective instrument for the positioning of cities?, *5th International Conference Virtual City and Territory*, Barcelona, pp. 703–714.

Glasmeier, A. & Christopherson, S. (2015) Thinking about smart cities, *Cambridge Journal of Regions, Economy and Society*, 8(1), 3–12. doi: 10.1093/cjres/rsu034.

Gutiérrez, C., Colmenero, R. M. J., & Sánchez Pérez, M. D. C. (2019) La competencia digital en la formación inicial de los futuros docentes: Educación Secundaria, *Formación Profesional e Idiomas*, 47, 1133–8482.

Hiremath, R. B.,Balachandra, P., Kumar,B., Bansode, S.S. & Murali, J. (2013) Indicator-based urban sustainability: A review, *Energy for Sustainable Development*, 17(6), 555–563. doi: 10.1016/j.esd.2013.08.004.

INEI (2017) *Provincia de Lima Compendio Estadístico*. Lima.

INEI (2018a) *Características de las viviendas particulares y los hogares Acceso a servicios básicos*. Lima.

INEI (2018b) *Perú: Crecimiento y distribución de la población, 2017*. Lima.

INEI (2018c) *Perú:Indicadores de Gestión Municipal 2018*. Lima.

International Standards Organization (2019) *ISO 37122:2019 Sustainable cities and communities — Indicators for smart cities*.

International Telecommunication Union (2018) *Measuring the Information Society Report*, ITU Publications.

Joyanes Aguilar, L. (2013) *Big Data: Análisis de grandes volúmenes de datos en organizaciones*. Alfaomega, México.

Kitchin, R. (2015) Making sense of smart cities: Addressing present shortcomings, *Cambridge Journal of Regions, Economy and Society*, 8(1), 131–136. doi: 10.1093/cjres/rsu027.

Maldonado Amaya, C., Mendoza Humpiri, E.F., Noriega Cortez, R.S., Piedra Nole, L.Y. & Rodríguez Quiroga, D.C. (2020) Determinación de los factores críticos para la transformación de un distrito de Lima Metropolitana en una smart city, *Esan Business*. Lima.

Marsal-Llacuna, M. L., Colomer-Llinàs, J. & Meléndez-Frigola, J. (2015) Lessons in urban monitoring taken from sustainable and livable cities to better address the Smart Cities initiative, *Technological Forecasting and Social Change*, 90(PB), 611–622. doi: 10.1016/j.techfore.2014.01.012.

Medina, A. C., Guevara, A. & Enciso, M. (2017) Big Data como fuente de conocimiento turístico. Especial referencia al Open Data y al Big Data Social, *Estudios Turísticos*, 214, 185–204.

Municipalidad de Barranco (2021) *Atractivos Turísticos*. Available at: https://munibarranco.gob.pe/atractivos-turisticos/ (Accessed: 20 December 2020).

Qian, Y., Wu, D., Bao, W. & Lorenz, P. (2019) The Internet of Things for Smart Cities: Technologies and applications, *IEEE Network*, 33(2), 4–5. doi: 10.1109/MNET.2019.8675165.

Ruiz-Rodríguez, F., Lucendo-Monedero, A. L. & González-Relaño, R. (2018) Measurement and characterisation of the Digital Divide of Spanish regions at enterprise level. A comparative analysis with the European context, *Telecommunications Policy*, 42(3), 187–211. doi: 10.1016/j.telpol.2017.11.007.

Ruiz Garcia, S. & Hernández García, Y. (2017) 'Impacto de las tic en el sector turístico y su importancia', *Universidad & Ciencia*, 6(3), 66–76.

Sigalat-Signes, E., Calvo-Palomares, R. Roig-Merino, B. & García-Adána, I (2020). Transition towards a tourist innovation model: The smart tourism destination. Reality or territorial marketing? *Journal of Innovation & Knowledge*, 5(2), 96-104. doi: 10.1016/j.jik.2019.06.002.

Stylos, N., Zwiegelaar, J., & Buhalis, D., (2021), Big data empowered agility for dynamic, volatile, and time-sensitive service industries: the case of tourism sector, *International Journal of Contemporary Hospitality Management*, 33 (3), 1015-1036. https://doi.org/10.1108/IJCHM-07-2020-0644

Villarejo Galende, H. (2015) Smart cities: Una apuesta de la Unión Europa para mejorar los servicios públicos urbanos, *Revista de Estudios Europeos*, (66), 25–51.

Ward, P. M. & Smith, C. B. (2015) Housing rehab for consolidated informal settlements: A new policy agenda for 2016 UN-Habitat III, *Habitat International*, 50, 373–384. doi: 10.1016/j.habitatint.2015.08.021.

# 12 Smart tourism destinations:
## Europe's smartest and most visited cities

*Kadir Çakar*

## Introduction

The tourism industry has enormously transformed with the rapid techno-logical developments accelerated by the internet (Buhalis, 2020). Technology is treated as the main driving factor of innovation like many other indus-tries which stem from the globalization process (Alcántara-Pilar et al., 2017). Smart tourist destinations have emerged due to the fast expansion in tourist numbers, shifts in tourist behavioural patterns, and the tourists' wide use of digital technologies (Tavitiyaman et al., 2021).

The term 'smart' stems from the philosophy of marketing, representing the use of technology-led devices and applications. 'Smart tourism destina-tions' originate from the 'smart cities' that use high levels of technology to offer better facilities, improve travellers' experiences, besides increasing the tourism firms' and destinations' competitiveness (Boes et al. 2015; Buhalis & Amaranggana, 2013; Buhalis & Leung, 2018; Gretzel, Koo, Sigala & Xiang, 2015; Shafiee et al., 2021). The development of the internet and the ICTs, along with the Internet of Things (IoT) support information exchange using big data (Stylos et al., 2021). Big data can help destinations to offer products and services to meet travellers' need at the right time in the right place to improve their tourism experiences (Buhalis & Sinarta, 2019; Bastidas-Manzano et al., 2021; Buhalis & Amaranggana, 2015; Del-Chiappa & Baggio, 2015).

Despite the increased significance of ICTs and the use of technology in several different areas for many cities (Lim et al., 2018), limited research has been conducted by scholars dealing with the issue of smart tourism concept within the context of co-creation of tourism services. Thus, this book chapter aims to examine the competitiveness of four European smart cities that are

## 196   Smart Cities and Tourism

classified as smart destinations from a comparative analysis perspective. The research aims to examine to what extent the four selected cities do offer innovative services and smart facilities based on the Smart City initiatives for both residents and visitors. Hence, the research contributes to the literature by offering valuable insights and key implications for destination managers.

# Smart tourism destinations

Smartness is considered as the converter factor of the technological advancements that have been developed with the immense use of technologic infrastructure (Boes et al. 2016; Femenia-Serra & Ivars-Baidal, 2021; Navío-Marco et al., 2018; Wang et al., 2016). From the administrators' and managers' perspectives, smartness can ensure managers make better decisions while enabling organizations to operate in a more functional and efficient way by collecting and analysing big data (Ghaderi et al., 2018). Although several authors attempted to provide a definition of the term 'smart tourism', there is no generally accepted description in the current literature (Li et al., 2016). Gretzel et al. (2015: 181) defined the smart tourism phenomenon as:

> *"tourism supported by integrated efforts at a destination to collect and aggregate/harness data derived from physical infrastructure, social connections, government/organizational sources and human bodies/minds in combination with the use of advanced technologies to transform that data into on-site experiences and business value-propositions with a clear focus on efficiency, sustainability and experience enrichment".*

Buhalis (2020) suggests that:

> *"smart tourism emerged to provide the infostructure for value cocreation ... Smartness takes advantage of interconnectivity and interoperability of integrated technologies. It works to reengineer processes and data in order to produce innovative services, products and procedures ensuring stakeholder value maximisation. All suppliers and intermediaries, the public sector as well as consumers, are becoming dynamically networked, which co-produces value for everybody interconnected within the ecosystem. Smartness increases inclusiveness and accessibility for travellers, by supporting tourists with mobility, visual, auditory, and cognitive impairments to deal with physical and service barriers..."*

These definitions of the smart tourism concept, address liveable, accessible and sustainable tourism destinations both for local residents and visitors. They depict that smart tourism possesses the potential to provide personalized, memorable and meaningful experiences through using advanced technology, while it can also ensure the use of the infostructure in the formation of value co-creation (Buhalis, 2020). The concept emerged from multi-disciplinary research (Cocchia, 2014) including: wired cities (Dutton et al., 1987); cyber cities (Graham & Marvin, 1999); intelligent cities (Komninos, 2002); knowledge cities (Carrillo, 2004); smart cities (Hollands, 2008), smarter planet (IBM 2008); digital cities (Yovanof & Hazapis, 2009); and sentient cities (Shepard, 2011).

Buhalis and Amaranggana (2013) first coined the term 'Smart tourism destinations' and it is often used interchangeably with the term 'smart city' but in the tourism context. The rapid development of ICTs paved the way in which value creation can be developed and accelerated smart technology for tourism destinations as a whole (Boes et al., 2016). 'Smart cities' precipitate the emergence of 'smart destinations' (da Costa Liberato et al., 2018; Marine-Roig & Clavé, 2015). The main difference between the two concepts is that a smart city concentrates on the citizens while a smart destination focuses on improving tourist experiences through ICTs (Boes et al., 2015).

**Table 12.1:** The evolutionary process of concept of smart tourism destination

| Author | Concept |
| --- | --- |
| Dutton et al. (1987) | Wired cities |
| Graham & Marvin (1999) | Cyber cities |
| Ishida & Isbister (2000) | Digital cities |
| Komninos (2002) | Intelligent cities |
| Carrillo (2004) | Knowledge cities |
| Hollands (2008) | Smart cities |
| IBM (2008) | Smarter planet |
| Yovanof & Hazapis (2009) | Digital cities |
| Shepard (2011) | Sentiment cities |
| Buhalis & Amaranggana (2013) | Smart tourism destinations |

The success of tourism destinations can be designed with the functions labelled as the 6As: 1) Attractions, 2) Accessibility, 3) Amenities, 4) Available Packages, 5) Activities and 6) Ancillary (Buhalis & Amaranggana, 2013) which enable tourism destinations to become more competitive (Wang et al., 2013). Smart tourism takes advantage of smart cities development (Wang et al., 2021). It is regarded as a phenomenon resulting from the integration of information technology with the tourism experience (Hunter et al., 2015). The concept of the smart city consists of 6 basic concepts, described as:

1. the smart economy (flexibility of the labour market, integration in the international market),

2. smart mobility (availability of ICTs, modern sustainable and safe transport network),

3. smart governance (participation in decision-making processes),

4. smart environment (sustainability of resource management),

5. smart living (tourist attractions, social cohesion, healthy environment) and

6. smart people (the level of qualification of human and social capital, flexibility, creativity, cosmopolitanism, etc.)

(European Smart Cities 2018; Vanolo, 2014).

The analysis of European smart cities of Amsterdam, Barcelona and Helsinki illustrated that innovation, social capital, human capital and leadership are the most important factors of smart cities (Boes et al., 2016). Park et al. (2016) described the term 'smart tourism' by classifying it into three different usages.

First *categorization*: smart tourism reflects the intelligent services in order to meet the tourists' needs that can potentially improve their satisfaction while enabling them necessary and useful information for visits to unknown destinations. The second usage of the term encapsulates a range of elements such as *tourism-related companies' marketing services and promotional campaigns*. The third usage of the smart tourism concept consists of the *synthesis of technology and tourism*. More interestingly, as in the case of organizations and firms, tourism destinations can be better positioned as learning destinations by using big data analytics (Stylos et al., 2021). This was first coined by Schianetz et al (2007), through using big data in the creation of knowledge-based on ICTs (Fuchs et al., 2014).

Based on the ICTs, smart tourism destinations cover services offering a high degree of innovation in terms of quality of life both for residents and tourists that entail open (Boes et al., 2016), multipolar, integrated and shared processes (Presenza et al., 2014). The development of the ICTs propel smart tourism cities, which leads destinations to digitally position themselves in improving the total experience of travellers and providing high quality of services to both residents and tourists to meet their needs in time (Buhalis & Amaranggana, 2015; Gretzel & Koo, 2021).

## Examining the most visited European cities

This chapter examines the degree to which Europe's four most visited cities are able to offer smart tourism products and services to visitors, by applying a multiple case study approach. According to Yin (2003) case studies can be used as a technique by a wide range of disciplines and fields in social sciences to analyse the structure of a city or a region besides investigating many other situations (e.g., individuals, groups, organizations, social, political and related phenomena etc.). Also, multiple case studies should cover two or more cases in the same research while pursuing a replication since the researcher assume the possibility of reaching identical results (Noor, 2008). After a comprehensive review of relevant literature, the case selection criteria were determined by examining inspiring and innovative cities (see Bakıcı et al., 2013; Boes et al., 2015; Buhalis & Amaranggana, 2015; Buonincontri & Micera, 2016; Gretzel et al., 2015; Liberato et al., 2018; Marine-Roig & Clavé, 2015). In addition, an analysis of the websites of European Smart Cities (2018) demonstrated the leading European smart cities. The cases were selected using purposeful sampling and the smartest cities of Europe in 2014 were identified (Cohen, 2014; Powell et al., 2018). As a result, Amsterdam, Barcelona, London, and Vienna were selected as the unit of analysis for the present multiple case study in order to better understand the differences and similarities among the selected cases (Gustafsson, 2017).

This chapter relies on qualitative material and secondary sources of data encompassing scientific articles, case studies and literature (Gustafsson, 2017). As such, data collection consists of two main stages: one is from the DMOs' websites of the selected cities and the second is based on literature, including selected peer-reviewed articles and case studies that were identified during the literature review process. Data were obtained from the DMOs' websites of the selected cities by taking into Cohen's Smart City designation which has been developed for European Smart Cities. Cases were processed through content analysis, which is often utilized by researchers to analyse the contents of literature in any field or other written texts as printed documents (Veal, 2006).

Based on qualitative content analysis of selected cities' DMO websites and key articles the data analysis process has been deductively employed. This followed the 6A's Model and Smart City dimensions of selected cities. The analysis examined the degree of smartness for the selected cities from a comparative case analysis perspective (Boes et al., 2016). The following section details results, referring to identified dimensions of smart cities/destinations relating to cities of Amsterdam, Barcelona, London and Vienna. Table 12.2 Illustrates the 6A's Model for Amsterdam, Barcelona, London and Vienna.

## Amsterdam

Amsterdam is one of the smartest tourism destinations. A key factor of smart destinations is the ability to integrate of ICTs into the city's physical infrastructure (Gretzel et al., 2015). From this perspective, with its advanced digital infrastructure of the Amsterdam Internet Exchange, which is seen as one of the world's largest data transport hub, Amsterdam as a Smart City is considered to be a developing tech and ICT hub that is home to innovative tech companies. Thus, a number of national (e.g. TomTom, Travelbird, Booking.com, WeTransfer) and international companies (i.e. Google, Facebook, Trion Worlds, Netflix, Microsoft etc.) prefer to conduct their operations and establish their headquarters in Amsterdam. Based on a high degree of innovation, driven by the use of ICTs, the Amsterdam Science Park and Urban Lab are the prominent examples of innovation. Smart Economy and Smart People constitute the main components of the Smart City initiative of Amsterdam. Particularly, the Amsterdam Science Park is considered to be an innovation district which is internationally renowned as a hub for research, education and entrepreneurship, combining innovation with collaboration. The Science Park is home to 120 companies that are regarded as of the city's most successful tech and science start-ups.

Social capital and innovation are regarded as the most important key elements of being a smart tourism destination (Boes et al., 2016). Amsterdam is dedicated to realizing its smart city initiative through the Amsterdam Economic Board. The main target is to accelerate the prosperity and wellbeing of the city while stimulating innovation and collaboration among businesses, knowledge institutes and government bodies. The city considers the five challenges: health, mobility, digital connectivity, circular economy and jobs by adopting a bottom-up management approach. They rely on smart growth, start-ups, liveability and digital social innovation that drives competition. The main components of smartness for Amsterdam city are open data, greener energy, efficient use of resources, smart mobility and sustainability. Under the Amsterdam Smart City initiative, the city reduced $CO2$ emissions thanks to the use of highly innovative technologies and partnerships between businesses, local authorities and local residents (Amsterdam Smart City, 2018; Barresi & Pultrone, 2013).

Considering management of the city, Amsterdam governance structure embraces an inclusionary management style in which the city's residents have a strong role through providing close cooperation and partnerships between businesses, local authorities, research institutions and residents deriving from dualistic cooperation. Being part of the European Union, the local government's implementation of Amsterdam is governed and maintained under the responsibility of the City Council. This reflects pluralism, social inclusion and active participation of local residents to support Smart Governance (Bakıcı et al., 2013).

## Barcelona

The popularity of Barcelona, which is the capital city of Catalonia in Spain, as a tourist city has been increasing over the last 25 years (Marine-Roig & Clavé 2015, Powell et al. 2018). With an advanced technological infrastructure including optical fibre, free WiFi and sensors to provide air quality, Barcelona is dedicated to becoming one of the smartest cities across the globe (Tieman, 2017). Smart City Initiative Smart Districts, Living Labs, Infrastructures, Services, Open Data and Management are considered major components of Barcelona (Bakıcı et al. 2013). The initiative of Living Labs was introduced by the European Union to provide collaboration and innovative markets in terms of the use of mobile applications and technologies for European citizens, companies and researchers (Komninos, 2008). Barcelona has also adopted Living Labs through which people from all spheres of life can be encouraged to create new and innovative ideas in the creation of the smarter city. The city's management and leadership style is based on a top-down approach (Boes et al. 2015). Through the initiative of Living Labs, citizen are encouraged to initiate smart ideas and co-create value, providing a bottom-up management approach (Boes et al. 2016). However, Barcelona was challenged with a high concentration of tourism in honeyspots, particularly as a result of the sharing economy (Buhalis et al., 2020).

One of the most well-known examples of the Barcelona Smart City initiative is the 22@Barcelona innovation district, which generates an integral part of urban planning project in the creation of smart city among European cities. The 22@Barcelona innovation district was designed to offer intensive knowledge-based projects situated in the industrial land of Poblenou. The primary mission of 22@Barcelona is to stimulate innovative projects based on public and private partnerships and common initiatives. Within the context of the creation of a knowledge-based society, this initiative is mainly focusing on urban innovation, economic innovation and social innovation components. Moreover, the 22@Barcelona innovation district adopts the Triple Helix model that encapsulates a high degree of collaboration and involvement of all stakeholders (e.g. government, university and industry) (Barcelona: The Innovation District, 2018). Another major component of the Barcelona Smart City initiative is the Open data initiative. Quiosc produces a series of useful maps and publications providing access to information for citizens, facilitating Smart Governance (Barcelona 2018; Bakıcı et al. 2013).

## London

London is ranked as the most visited European tourist destination (Powell et al., 2018). London with its rich historical and touristic attractions attracts visitors to museums, art galleries, musical shows and theatres. Special events organized in the city constitute the main components of touristic attractions that enhance the experiences of visitors. The Visitor Oyster Card and the London Pass have multi-functional features and provide visitors with a high level of connectivity (Gretzel et al., 2015). Innovative technological tools improve the visitor experience while increasing the co-creation of on-site experiences (Buonincontri & Micera 2016). Travellers are able to access all modes of transports with these smart cards in London. They also allow visitors to see London's most popular cultural and tourism attractions during visitors' on-site experiences stage. Given that London's smart tourism characteristics are well developed, the city mostly meets and complies with components of the 6A's model (Table 12.2).

London offers visitors inclusive facilities and activities, such as tours, museums, restaurants and hotels. Disabled people are able to enjoy visiting the city's most attractive places during their trip. Wheelchair accessible hotels are designed to provide accessible wheelchair-friendly rooms. London has recently initiated the building of London DataStore, as part of smart city initiative. Through this unit, it provides free and open data that can be accessible for any person. London ensures the open data useful platform by which stakeholders involved can discuss necessary issues.

London is trying to realize its ambition to become the smartest city across the world by paying more attention to benefit from analytics of big data along with investing in creating innovative services. This is by ensuring collaboration among several local contributors ranging from businesses, public servants, academia, civil society through practitioners. In continuation to this newly developed approach, based on intensive collaboration and cooperation, London makes an effort to know how to transform current big data into new and innovative services by empowering and encouraging people to create smart ideas to become a smart city (Smart London, 2018). The management approach of London has started to adapt and evolve a bottom-up management style through the implementation of the Unconference platform.

## Vienna

As the capital city of Austria, Vienna is considered among Europe's top ten tourist cities (Powell et al., 2018). Vienna is ranked as a smart city among other European Cities. Overall the Vienna smart city initiative is based on four major components, namely: smart infrastructure, smart mobility, smart technology and growing smart city. Vienna has a smart infrastructure that provides both residents and visitors free WiFi, mobile and responsive websites and apps for smartphones. Due to its advanced infrastructure, as in the case of Amsterdam, many international companies and organizations such UNHCR and UNIDO prefer Vienna for their headquarters. Being part of the Smart City initiative, Vienna has also adopted the start-up eco-system (City of Vienna, 2018).

The Vienna Smart City initiative is implemented through many practices such as Co-Creation Lab Vienna, Urban Living Lab, Smart Campus, Digital City Wien and Urban Innovation Vienna. These are driven by innovation based on intense cooperation encapsulating a participative approach. The Vienna Business Agency, which has been established as a part of the Co-Creation Lab, brings companies together to create innovative solutions in response to challenges.

As part of the Smart City initiative, Vienna is dedicated to providing services to its citizens and businesses through the concept of eGovernment. This is based on the virtual municipal authority website of the City Vienna. The Vienna Smart City initiative embraces a high degree of sustainability by adopting to implementation of eco-friendly and renewable energy within the context of 'Smart' renovations. For instance, the primary mission of Smart Campus is to mitigate energy and $CO2$ emissions by combining energy-saving automations. The concentration of district heating, local heating, eMobility in the plant transport and Neighbourhood and eCar sharing are regarded as other Smart City initiatives (Smart City Vienna, 2018). Following the application of Smart Economy principles, inclusive activities which are stimulated by the high degree of innovation are carried out by both stakeholders and citizens from a holistic perspective.

**Table 12.2:** 6A's Model of Amsterdam, Barcelona, London and Vienna.

| Cities/Destinations | | | |
|---|---|---|---|
| Amsterdam | Barcelona | London | Vienna |
| **Attractions** | | | |
| Rich in attractions in terms of museums, sights, galleries, exhibitions, historical monuments and buildings with fascinating architecture and famous canals. The most important are Van Gogh Museum, Rijksmuseum and Anne Frank House | There are several different Museums (53), Exhibition Centres (9) and Art Galleries (10) in Barcelona. Additionally, the city has 10 Districts and 13 Themed Routes worth to see for visitors. | Museums (e.g. British, Science, Design, National History etc.), stadium tours, art galleries (e.g. Barbican, National, Serpentine, Somerset House etc. ), buildings (e.g. Westminster Abbey, St. Paul's Cathedral) Unique attractions (Warner Bros. Studio, Buckingham Palace, Tower of London etc.), Musicals and shows The Lion King at the Lyceum Theatre, Aladdin at Prince Edward Theatre, Thriller-Live at the Lyric Theatre, Wicked at the Apollo Victoria etc.) | Rich themed exhibitions, museums (Literature Museum, Austrian Museum of Applied Arts/Contemporary Arts, Wien Museum Karlsplatz, Leopold Museum etc.) and many art galleries. |
| **Access** | | | |
| The internal mobility of the city is ensured by an advanced transport network system that is accessible to international airport with metros, buses trams, ferries and trains. | Three airports serve the city Direct railways networks with popular cities (e.g. Paris, Lyon, Maseille, Toulose, Madrid and southern and eastern Spain The city is well connected by road and has a number of car parks Barcelona Nord Bus Station has the most national and international connection 9 passenger terminals,7 for cruise liners and 4 for ferries Extensive network of roads for bikes | Accessibility is provided by variety of means: buses, underground rail network, dockland light railway, river bus services, trains, bicycle and taxi air line cable car. The city has important airports (Stansted Airport, City Airport, Luton Airport, London Southend Airport, Gatwick and Heathrow) that are accessible by different transport means to different locations and directions | The transport accessibility of the city is mostly provided by tram (with 29 tram routes, city buses (with 127 bus routes) and subways (consisting of five lines) The total passengers of public transportation of city were recorded 954 million in 2016 There is also Citybike networks for visitors |

| Amenities | | | |
|---|---|---|---|
| Amsterdam provides a wide variety of accommodation facilities to visitors (i.e. hotels, hostels, short stay apartments, bed & breakfasts, campsites, houseboats and accommodation for different target groups), different sort of bars and cafés (cocktail bars, brown cafés and grand cafés) and city also has restaurants. | Restaurants: There are many restaurants in the city that offer traditional tapas reflecting local gastronomic culture, including internationally recognized Michelin-starred ones<br><br>Hotels: The city also offers different types of accommodation facilities for different wide range of groups. | London offers a number of accommodation options from diverse range of categories (bed and breakfast, family hotels, self-catering, homestay, hostels) as well as for different groups (i.e. family friendly hotels, campus, hostels, boutique hotels, pub accommodations, budget options, cheap hotels, low-cost hotels, caravan and camping etc.) | Vienna provides a wide range of accommodation facilities for distinct target of groups with more than 400 hotels<br><br>The city also ensures traditional coffee houses those represent cultural features referring to intangible cultural heritage<br><br>There are bars, taverns, other restaurants and bistros in the city |
| **Available packages** | | | |
| There are many travel agents and tourist offices providing useful services through packages such as walking tours, conferences, incentives and special interest programmes that enable visitors to experience of magnificent Dutch history. | There are many operators/organizers that provide leisure activities through packages to visitors with several tours and walks to experience cultural assets | Some attractive packages with overnight stays through special offers are provided to visitors by institutions and/or travel related agents in the city. | There exist many organizers, companies and agencies those offer special events and venues to be held in the city. |

| Activities | | |
|---|---|---|
| There are many major activities that are annually organized (e.g. Holland Festival, Amsterdam Dance Event, TCS Amsterdam Marathon New Year's Celebration King's Day, Remembrance and Liberation Day etc.) Each year the city hosts more than 300 festivals (e.g. Het Bacchus Wijnfestival, TREK Food Truck Festival, music festivals, cultural festivals etc.) and events (culinary festivals & events, film festivals, theatre festivals, fairs & events, major sporting events etc.) | There are many useful activities and different events such as sports, concerts organized in the city particularly a wide range of sport events (e.g. golf, swimming, cycling, hockey, athletics, equestrian events, tennis, Formula 1 etc.) including water-based activities. Arcadia Anniversary Festival at Queen Elizabeth Olympic Park, RHS Chelsea Flower Show, Underbelly Festival in South Bank, Special Events: Christmas at Kew, Easter Weekend, Gipsy Kings / Boyzone / Steps at Royal Botanic Gardens Kew, The city hosts many important major events and venues: Wimbledon Lawn Tennis Championship, World Athletics Championships, NFL International Series Game and Chinese New Year Celebrations | There are major activities organized in Vienna. One of most important these activities are festivals which include several different venues (i.e. the areas of music, theatre, performance and dance), musicals, music and stage shows, operas and concerts. |
| **Ancillary services** | | |
| The city offer different rental services (coach hire, boat hire, bike, car and scooter) to visitors to improve the quality of experiences as well as support tourism. | Coaches and minibuses and car rentals are offered to visitors as additional services. There are some additional services to support tourism: bank, bureau de change, post office and tax free shopping. | Additional services offered through 19 providers ranging from furniture rental through language services, to sightseeing tours of the city etc. Online reservations and booking services are ensured by Vienna's official tourism organization to visitors including B2B services. |

**Source:** Author's compilation from DMOs' websites

## Smartness of European tourist destinations

The examination of the smartness catalysts of Europe's four most visited tourist destinations provide both theoretical and practical implications as well as offering rich insights and valuable perspectives. Both destination marketers and managers should learn from best practice, and design quality tourism products and services based on smart technology. Case studies have indicated the major constituents that pave the way in which smart city initiatives are performed. It is evident that smart tourism destinations are heavily based on primary components such as leadership, human capital, entrepreneurs, innovation and social capital (Marine-Roig & Clavé, 2015). Some commonalities as well as differences among selected cities in regard to the concept of smart tourism destinations are evident.

First, DMOs' websites of smart cities as well as social media channels are critical for communications. They are one of the most significant factors for the generation of knowledge deriving from both customer-based (traveller) and supplier-oriented Business Intelligence, as well as in the creation of big data in tourist destinations (Fuchs et al., 2014; Stylos et al., 2021). This key implication indicates that more destinations should adapt and provide social media based on ICTs. Fostered by the 2.0 Web, users can better help to provide innovative practices through which tourist destinations are able to generate and maintain competitive advantage (Heerschap et al. 2014).

Vienna, and respectively London, Amsterdam and Barcelona are leading as Smart Cities. They possess most characteristics of the 6As Model and Smart City's indicators and components. Various forms of innovative applications of smart tourism destination are evident, based on advanced ICTs infrastructure. These cities also take the lead in providing a wide variety of inclusionary activities and offer innovative and smart facilities both for their residents and visitors. Smart cities/destinations are more prone to provide opportunities for travellers, while having the potential to take more advantage from the use of Big Data (Stylos et al., 2021). This capability supports smart destinations to quickly respond to possible overtourism problems that they may face through effective use of real time big data (Buhalis, 2020; Buhalis & Sinarta, 2019).

London can be regarded as prominent among cities, as it provides inclusionary facilities and innovative services as well as smart experiences. London is fairly inclusive offering a range of products and experiences for wheelchair-users, such as accessible hotels designed to provide them wheelchair-friendly rooms. Smart City initiatives and enablers, such as partnerships, institutional and governance mechanisms to connect the smart city stakeholders (Ojo et al., 2014) appears to remain limited since relatively few

## 208   Smart Cities and Tourism

organizations are fully involved in the process. In response to this obstacle, both cities need to provide effective implementation of data governance by utilizing efficient big data analytics, through close cooperation and collaboration of involved stakeholders. In order to achieve the full gains of a smart tourism destination and gain competitiveness, London Municipality, tourism and destination management organisations need to reinvest in knowledge and technology based on ICTs. This will enable them to develop services across culture, transport and leisure activities (Buonincontri & Micera, 2016). R&D for entrepreneurship, in terms of fostering innovation, will support better achievement of smart governance, which is seen as one of the most important pillars of smart city. Hence, London should embrace a more collaborative management style which entails cooperation between all stakeholders ranging from businesses, academics, public and private organisations to citizens.

Value co-creation in Vienna as a Smart City is carried out by offering technology-oriented services that makes a difference within the context of digital government. In doing so, smart services are provided by Vienna through digital government interactions at two different types: Government to Citizens (referring to interactions among public authority and residents or citizens) and Government to Business (covers interactions between the public authority and several different business interest groups) (Kalbaska et al., 2017).

Examples and initiatives of the Living Lab in Barcelona with 22@Barcelona and Science Park in Amsterdam illustrate that both cities differ from others. They are positioned to ensure innovative services, products and high-tech infrastructures for both companies and residents in all sphere of life. Based on high tech infrastructure, Amsterdam and Barcelona are prominent smart cities in the creation of big data, while they mostly reflect the characteristics of Learning and Knowledge City as compared to other European cities.

Taking into consideration the designation of smart tourism components, Table 12.3 illustrates that the smart tourism practices of London appear to be far from the complete extensive of smart city initiative as compared to the other cases. Barcelona, Amsterdam and Vienna can potentially create innovative big data (Heerschap et al., 2014) to improve co-experiences while increasing their competitiveness. With their advanced technological infrastructure as well as their community engagement Amsterdam, Barcelona and Vienna are more able to enhance and expand their smart city services through big data analytics (Al-Nuaimi et al., 2016). While the smart city initiative of Vienna is still developing, London has a long way to move forward.

**Table 12.3:** The application of basic concepts of Smart Cities

| Concepts of Smart cities | Cities/Destinations | | | |
|---|---|---|---|---|
| | Amsterdam | Barcelona | London | Vienna |
| Smart economy | High | High | Moderate | High |
| Smart mobility | High | High | High | High |
| Smart governance | High | High | Low | Moderate |
| Smart environment | High | High | Moderate | High |
| Smart living | High | High | Moderate | Moderate |
| Smart people | High | High | Moderate | High |

**Source:** Extracted from DMOs' websites

Barcelona and Amsterdam are a prominent example of Smart Tourism Destinations as compared to other European cities described in this study. They have adopted components of smartness encapsulating a variety of dimensions, ranging from a high degree of collaboration, cooperation among stakeholders, innovation to entrepreneurship based on intense use of high tech and ICTs (Bakıcı et al., 2013). The critical success factors of smart tourism ecosystems of both cities have commonalities. First, while Barcelona's smart city initiative is immensely relying on its 22@Barcelona District, Amsterdam's smartness relies in its Science Park as an urban lab. These are excellent examples of Living Labs, whose priorities and practices are heavily fostered by the use of ICTs and innovation (Bakıcı et al., 2013; Boes et al., 2016). Relating to the start-up ecosystem, one of the most important constituents for smart tourism applications of Amsterdam is to embrace six dimensions, namely: citizens, city government, established businesses and start-ups, investors, academic institutions and community organizations (Amsterdam Report, 2015).

The smartness of all European cities examined is based on 6A's Model and Smart City components. Amsterdam and Barcelona are able to be considered as the smartest cities/destinations. Vienna reflects most of the smarter city/destination characteristics, while London can be regarded as a smart city/destination that can benefit by engaging with more communities and stakeholders. For future studies, the findings of the present study raise the question to what extent smart tourism destinations can enhance the competitiveness of regions. Moreover, smart destinations can explore how they can offer innovative and inclusive services to disabled travellers and residents in terms of accessible tourism. Future studies should also examine how smart cities or smart tourism destinations can better respond to mitigate challenges faced during global pandemic diseases such as COVID-19 and develop their resilience.

## References

Amsterdam Report. (2015), Retrieved from https://www.smartercitieschallenge. org/cities/amsterdam-netherlands, Accessed 25 May 2018.

Amsterdam Smart City. (2018) Retrieved from https://amsterdamsmartcity. com/, Accessed 25 May 2018.

Alcántara-Pilar, J. M., del Barrio-García, S., Crespo-Almendros, E. & Porcu, L. (2017) Toward an understanding of online information processing in e-tourism: Does national culture matter? *Journal of Travel & Tourism Marketing*, 34 (8), 1128-1142.

Al Nuaimi, E., Al Neyadi, H., Mohamed, N., & Al-Jaroodi, J. (2015). Applications of big data to smart cities. *Journal of Internet Services and Applications*, 6(1), 1-15.

Bakıcı, T., Almirall, E. & Wareham, J. (2013) A smart city initiative: the case of Barcelona. *Journal of the Knowledge Economy*, 4 (2), 135-148.

Barcelona: The Innovation District. (2018), Retrieved from http:// www.22barcelona.com/documentacio/22bcn_1T2010_eng.pdf, 28 May 2018

Barcelona. (2018), Retrieved from http://www.barcelonaturisme.com/wv3/en/, Accessed 8 April 2018.

Barresi, A. & Pultrone, G. (2013) European strategies for smarter cities. *Tema. Journal of Land Use, Mobility and Environment*, 6 (1), 61-72.

Bastidas-Manzano, A. B., Sánchez-Fernández, J. & Casado-Aranda, L. A. (2021) The past, present, and future of smart tourism destinations: a bibliometric analysis, *Journal of Hospitality & Tourism Research*, 45(3), 529-552.

Boes, K., Buhalis, D. & Inversini, A. (2015) Conceptualising smart tourism destination dimensions, in *Information and Communication Technologies in Tourism 2015*, Springer, Cham, pp. 391-403.

Boes, K., Buhalis, D. & Inversini, A., (2016), Smart tourism destinations: ecosystems for tourism destination competitiveness, *International Journal of Tourism Cities*, 2(2), 108 – 124

Buhalis, D. (2020), Technology in tourism - from information communication technologies to eTourism and smart tourism towards ambient intelligence tourism: a perspective article, *Tourism Review* 75(1), 267-272 .https://doi. org/10.1108/TR-06-2019-0258

Buhalis, D. & Amaranggana, A. (2013) Smart tourism destinations. In *Information and Communication Technologies in Tourism 2014*, Springer, Cham, pp. 553-564.

Buhalis, D. & Amaranggana, A. (2015) Smart tourism destinations enhancing tourism experience through personalisation of services. In *Information and Communication Technologies in Tourism 2015*, Springer, Cham, pp. 377-389.

Buhalis, D., Andreu, L. & Gnoth, J., (2020), The dark side of the sharing economy: Balancing value co-creation and value co-destruction. *Psychology and Marketing*. 37(5), 689–704. https://doi.org/10.1002/mar.21344

Buhalis, D. & Leung, R. (2018) Smart hospitality—Interconnectivity and interoperability towards an ecosystem. *International Journal of Hospitality Management*, 71, 41-50.

Buhalis, D. & Sinarta, Y., (2019), Real-time co-creation and nowness service: lessons from tourism and hospitality, *Journal of Travel and Tourism Marketing*, 36(5), pp.563-582 https://doi.org/10.1080/10548408.2019.1592059

Buonincontri, P. & Micera, R. (2016) The experience co-creation in smart tourism destinations: a multiple case analysis of European destinations. *Information Technology & Tourism*, 16 (3), 285-315.

City of Vienna. (2018), Retrieved from https://www.wien.gv.at/english/administration/statistics/, Accessed 15 March 2022.

Cocchia, A. (2014) Smart and Digital City: A systematic literature review', in Dameri R., Rosenthal-Sabroux C. (eds.), *Smart City. Progress in IS*. Springer, Cham, pp. 13-43.

da Costa Liberato, P. M., Alén-González, E. & de Azevedo Liberato, D. F. V. (2018). Digital technology in a smart tourist destination: the case of Porto. *Journal of Urban Technology*, 25(1), 75-97.

Del Chiappa, G. & Baggio, R. (2015) Knowledge transfer in smart tourism destinations: Analyzing the effects of a network structure. *Journal of Destination Marketing & Management*, 4 (3), 145-150.

Dutton, W.H., Blumler, J.G. & Kraemer, K.L. (1987) *Wired Cities: Shaping Future Communication*. Macmillan, New York.

European Smart Cities, (2018) Retrieved from http://www.smart-cities.eu/, Accessed 2 April 2018.

Femenia-Serra, F. & Ivars-Baidal, J. A. (2021) Do smart tourism destinations really work? The case of Benidorm, *Asia Pacific Journal of Tourism Research*, 26(4), 365-384.

Fuchs, M., Höpken, W. & Lexhagen, M. (2014) Big data analytics for knowledge generation in tourism destinations – A case from Sweden. *Journal of Destination Marketing & Management*, 3 (4), 198-209.

Ghaderi, Z., Hatamifar, P. & Henderson, J. C. (2018) Destination selection by smart tourists: the case of Isfahan, Iran. *Asia Pacific Journal of Tourism Research*, 23 (4), 385-394.

Graham, S. & Marvin, S. (1999) Planning cybercities: Integrating telecommunications into urban planning. *Town Planning Review*, 70 (1), 89-114.

Gretzel, U., and Koo, C. (2021) 'Smart tourism cities: a duality of place where technology supports the convergence of touristic and residential experiences', *Asia Pacific Journal of Tourism Research*, 26(4), 352-364.

Gretzel, U., Sigala, M., Xiang, Z. & Koo, C. (2015) Smart tourism: foundations and developments *Electronic Markets*, 25 (3), 179-188.

Gretzel, U., Koo, C., Sigala, M. & Xiang, Z. (2015) Special issue on smart tourism: convergence of information technologies, experiences, and theories. *Electronic Markets*, 25 (3), 175-177.

Gretzel, U., Werthner, H., Koo, C. & Lamsfus, C. (2015) Conceptual foundations for understanding smart tourism ecosystems. *Computers in Human Behavior*, 50, 558-563.

Gustafsson, J., (2017), Single case studies vs. multiple case studies: A comparative study. Retrieved from https://www.diva-portal.org/smash/get/diva2%3a1064378/FULLTEXT01.pdf. Accessed 23 November 2018.

Heerschap, N., Ortega, S., Priem, A. & Offermans, M. (2014) Innovation of tourism statistics through the use of new big data sources. In *12th Global Forum on Tourism Statistics*, Prague, CZ.

Hollands, R. G. (2008) Will the real smart city please stand up? Intelligent, progressive or entrepreneurial?. *City*, 12 (3), 303-320.

Hunter, W. C., Chung, N., Gretzel, U. & Koo, C. (2015) Constructivist research in smart tourism. *Asia Pacific Journal of Information Systems*, 25 (1), 105-120.

IBM. (2008) Smarter Planet, Retrieved from https://www.ibm.com/smarter-planet/us/en/, Accessed 9 April 2018.

Ishida, T. & Isbister, K. (Eds.). (2000) *Digital Cities: Technologies, experiences, and future perspectives*. Springer Science & Business Media, Heidelberg, Berlin.

Kalbaska, N., Janowski, T., Estevez, E. & Cantoni, L. (2017) When digital government matters for tourism: a stakeholder analysis. *Information Technology & Tourism*, 17 (3), 315-333.

Komninos, N. (2002) *Intelligent Cities: Innovation*, Routledge, Knowledge Systems and Digital Spaces.

Komninos, N. (2008) *Intelligent Cities and Globalisation of Innovation Networks*, Routledge, Abingdon.

Li, Y., Hu, C., Huang, C.& Duan, L. (2017) The concept of smart tourism in the context of tourism information services. *Tourism Management*, 58, 293-300.

Lim, C., Kim, K. J.& Maglio, P. P. (2018). Smart cities with big data: Reference models, challenges, and considerations. *Cities*, 82, 86-99.

Marine-Roig, E. & Clavé, S. A. (2015) Tourism analytics with massive user-generated content: A case study of Barcelona. *Journal of Destination Marketing & Management*, 4 (3), 162-172.

Noor, K. B. M. (2008) Case study: A strategic research methodology. *American Journal of Applied Sciences*, 5 (11),1602-1604.

Navío-Marco, J., Ruiz-Gómez, L. M. & Sevilla-Sevilla, C. (2018) Progress in information technology and tourism management: 30 years on and 20 years after the internet- Revisiting Buhalis & Law's landmark study about eTourism. *Tourism Management*, 69, 460-470.

Ojo, A., Curry, E. & Janowski, T. (2014) Designing next generation smart city initiatives- harnessing findings and lessons from a study of ten smart city programs, *Proceedings of the European Conference on Information Systems (ECIS)*, June 9-11, Tel Aviv, Israel.

Park, J. H., Lee, C., Yoo, C.& Nam, Y. (2016) An analysis of the utilization of Facebook by local Korean governments for tourism development and the network of smart tourism ecosystem. *International Journal of Information Management*, 36 (6), 1320-1327.

Powell, R., Kennell, J.& Barton, C. (2018) Dark Cities: A dark tourism index for Europe's tourism cities, based on the analysis of DMO websites. *International Journal of Tourism Cities*, 4 (1), 4-21.

Presenza, A., Micera, R., Splendiani, S. & Del Chiappa, G. (2014) Stakeholder e-involvement and participatory tourism planning: analysis of an Italian case study. *International Journal of Knowledge-Based Development*, 5 (3), 311-328.

Schianetz, K., Kavanagh, L. & Lockington, D. (2007) The learning tourism destination: The potential of a learning organisation approach for improving the sustainability of tourism destinations. *Tourism Management*, 28 (6), 1485-1496.

Shafiee, S., Ghatari, A. R., Hasanzadeh, A. & Jahanyan, S. (2021) Smart tourism destinations: a systematic review, *Tourism Review*, 76 (3). https://doi. org/10.1108/TR-06-2019-0235

Shepard, M. (2011) *Sentient City: Ubiquitous computing, architecture, and the future of urban space*, Cambridge, MIT Press.

Smart London. (2018) Retrieved from https://www.london.gov.uk/, Accessed 27 May 2018.

Stylos, N., Zwiegelaar, J. & Buhalis, D., (2021), Big data empowered agility for dynamic, volatile, and time-sensitive service industries: the case of tourism sector, *International Journal of Contemporary Hospitality Management*, 33 (3), 1015-1036. https://doi.org/10.1108/IJCHM-07-2020-0644

Tavitiyaman, P., Qu, H., Tsang, W. S. L.& Lam, C. W. R. (2021) The influence of smart tourism applications on perceived destination image and behavioral intention: The moderating role of information search behavior, *Journal of Hospitality and Tourism Management*, 46, 476-487.

Tieman, R. (2017) Barcelona: Smart City Revolution in progress, Retrieved from https://www.ft.com/content/6d2fe2a8-722c-11e7-93ff-99f383b09ff9, Accessed 28 May 2018.

Vanolo, A. (2014) Smartmentality: The smart city as disciplinary strategy. *Urban Studies*, 51 (5), 883-898.

Wang, D., Li, X. R. & Li, Y. (2013) China's 'smart tourism destination' initiative: A taste of the service-dominant logic. *Journal of Destination Marketing & Management*, 2 (2), 59-61.

Wang, X., Li, X. R., Zhen, F. & Zhang, J. (2016), How smart is your tourist attraction?: Measuring tourist preferences of smart tourism attractions via a FCEM-AHP and IPA approach. *Tourism Management*, 54, 309-320.

Wang, X., Zhen, F., Tang, J., Shen, L. & Liu, D. (2021), Applications, experiences, and challenges of smart tourism development in China, *Journal of Urban Technology*, 1- 26.

Veal, A. J. (2006) *Research Methods for Leisure and Tourism: A Practical Guide.* London, Pearson Education Limited.

Yovanof, G. S. & Hazapis, G. N. (2009) An architectural framework and enabling wireless technologies for digital cities & intelligent urban environments. *Wireless Personal Communications*, 49 (3) 445-463.

Yin, R.K. (2003) *Case Study Research: Design and Methods*, 3rd Ed., USA, Sage.

# Conclusion

The concept of the smart city emerged during the last decade as a combination of ideas about how information and communications technologies might improve the functioning of cities, enhancing their efficiency, improving their competitiveness, and providing new ways in which problems of poverty, social deprivation, and poor environment might be addressed. Most smart cities definitions highlight common characteristics, features, and components that may specify the perspectives of smart cities. Ultimately smart cities aim for the enhancement of the quality of life for a particular segment – city citizens – through utilizing information technology hardware, software, networks, and data on different city areas and services. The concept has attracted worldwide interest, including from governments, companies, universities and institutes.

Smart cities are dynamically responsive urban areas that use various ICTs such as the IoT, cloud computing, big data and space geographical information integration, to sustainably improve the quality of life for businesses, residents and tourists through collaborative leadership and engaged citizens. Smart cities invest in human and social capital as well as communication infrastructure to fuel sustainable economic growth. Ultimately smart cities aim to improve the quality of life through participatory governance and sustainable management of natural resources. Similarly smart tourism addresses the ecosystem that serves the tourism industry and explores how interoperability and interconnectivity can enhance the entire ecosystem and develop value for all stakeholders.

Looking at the previous literature, most of the books in this area are written by practitioners. This is one of the first books by academics on smart cities that focus primarily on tourism marketing and management, services marketing and urban studies. It aims to serves as a key reference point for smart cities researchers, scholars, students and practitioners. With its three parts and 12 chapters, the book not only provides a better understanding of city services but also of enhancing and evaluating locals' (and visitors') experience and city decision making process by creating liveable environments and business solutions. Examples from multiple cities from around the world illustrate the successful implementation of smart cities and smart tourism.

The book is designed based on social science background. It addresses a rapidly developing innovation and by instigating a comprehensive source, it provides a strong platform for students, scholars, and practitioners in the field of business and management to develop their sharing economy knowledge further. Its practical approach is also a valuable source for students and practitioners in the field of business and management. The book offers new insights and stimulates potential future research opportunities and areas of interest in different aspects of smart cities and smart tourism.